Ethnic Relations
in the USSR

Ethnic Relations in the USSR

The Perspective from Below

Rasma Karklins
University of Illinois at Chicago

Boston
UNWIN HYMAN
London   Sydney   Wellington

Unwin Hyman Inc.
8 Winchester Place, Winchester, Mass. 01890, USA

Published by the Academic Division of
Unwin Hyman Ltd
15/17 Broadwick Street, London W1V 1FP, UK

Allen & Unwin (Australia) Ltd,
8 Napier Street, North Sydney, NSW 2060, Australia

Allen & Unwin (New Zealand) Ltd in association with the
Port Nicholson Press Ltd,
60 Cambridge Terrace, Wellington, New Zealand

First published in 1986
Second impression 1989

Library of Congress Cataloging in Publication Data

Karklins, Rasma
  Ethnic relations in the USSR.
  Bibliography: p.
  Includes index.
  1. Soviet Union—Ethnic relations. I. Title.
  DK33.K37   1985   305.8'00947   85-11149
  ISBN 0-04-323028-8 (alk. paper)

British Library Cataloguing in Publication Data

Karklins, Rasma
  Ethnic relations in the USSR: the perspective from below.
  1. Ethnology—Soviet Union
  I. Title
  947'.004   DK33
  ISBN 0-04-323028-8

Set in 10 on 11½ point Palatino by Paston Press, Norwich
and printed in Great Britain by Billing and Sons Ltd, London and
Worcester

For my parents

Contents

List of Tables

Note

In those instances where no specific source is listed for data presented in a table, the source consists of this author's survey research with a sample of 200 Soviet Germans who emigrated to the Federal Republic of Germany in 1979. In Russian transliterations the system of the Library of Congress is used.

Acknowledgements

In the long course of research on a topic one accumulates many debts, and it is a pleasure to be able to thank the people who made this book possible.

I am grateful to Professor Jeremy R. Azrael, my graduate adviser at the University of Chicago, who encouraged me to pursue my interest in comparative and Soviet ethnic studies. I wish to thank especially him for urging me to submit a grant proposal to the National Council for Soviet and Eastern European Research leading to the start of this work; I appreciate the financial support granted to me by the National Council during 1979 and 1980. I am also grateful to the Slavic Area Committee of the University of Chicago for seed money provided from a grant from the Ford Foundation as well as office space. In later stages of research the Office of Social Science Research of the University of Illinois at Chicago provided funds for typing and for preparing the data for computerized analysis. The political science department of the University of Illinois at Chicago generously provided me with release time from teaching in the final phases of manuscript preparation.

This project was greatly improved as a result of the insightful comments received from Professors Teresa Rakowska-Harmstone and Walker Connor, as well as from the anonymous reviewers. I also wish to thank Professor Alexandre Bennigsen for sharing his profound understanding of Islam in the USSR.

For their excellent research assistance my thanks are due to Rita Bruvers, Elvira Schulz, and Vida Kuprys. Helen Hicks was a most reliable and helpful typist. But above all, I am indebted to my husband, Jānis, for his unwavering belief in me and for his intellectual and emotional support in getting this book finished.

Some segments of this study have been previously published and I am grateful to the editors of *Soviet Studies*, *Studies in Comparative Communism*, and *Cahiers du Monde Russe et Sovietique* for permission to reuse the material.

The question of the political implications of multiethnicity in the USSR and elsewhere has attracted the attention of many distinguished scholars. My work builds upon their thought and research. Where I am aware of such intellectual debts, I have acknowledged them in the notes. Inevitably some indirect influences have not been acknowledged. I have attempted to repay these scholarly debts by writing the best book I can at this time.

Introduction

This is a study of the dynamics of Soviet ethnic relations and politics primarily from the point of view of the participating "common man" in the non-Russian borderlands. It intends to show that ethnicity in the USSR is not just a cultural or historical given, or a political identity to be manipulated from above, but has concrete meaning for its people and a concrete impact on their everyday lives. Nationality affects friendships and marriages, has a major impact on the organization of communal life, influences relationships at the place of work and within institutions, affects cultural and political perceptions and activities, and is a source of economic and social competition.

While nationality issues have increasingly come to be perceived as one of the potentially most significant sources of change in the Soviet Union, the approach taken in their study usually has been one focusing on governmental policies and programs and on social trends as evident in statistics and other general data. It is the contention of this study that this is insufficient and that we have to add an investigation of the content and implications of the behavior and beliefs of the citizenry. In the case of a closed society such as the Soviet one this is difficult to do and is easily challenged by the contention that the citizenry's outlook is irrelevant to the Soviet regime, but we shall nevertheless venture forth in the belief that enough material is available to justify an investigation of this sort and that *a priori* conclusions are a barrier not only to the perception of change, but to change itself.

Focus of Study

This study intends to raise a great number of questions, some of which are simpler to state and answer than others. What does it mean to belong to one or the other nationality, to live in one or the other region, to speak one or the other language? How do members of different ethnic groups identify and perceive each

1

other. Do they group themselves in personal and social relationships? And if so, why? Do ethnic communal values and ties persist, and in what forms? Does the average non-Russian care in what language his children are educated, whom they marry, or how they interact with their native society? What are the main factors influencing ethnic relations? Does governmental policy help to overcome strains and conflicts, or does it enhance them, or even create new ones? What are popular perceptions of official ethnic politics in the USSR, what are reactions to changes in governmental policies and are there attempts to influence them?

Thus applying the "perspective from below," first of all, means focusing on the values and the outlook of the mass of people who make up the population of the USSR. It means analyzing ethnic attitudes in various contexts and asking about the quality of ethnic encounters in the streets, in shops, at places of work or in schools, and within circles of friends and families. We want to examine ethnic relations both at the microlevel of interactions between individuals and small groups and at the macrolevel of relations between whole nations and populations. We also want to ask about links between the two levels. Moreover, we want to investigate the sources of differing perceptions and behavior in order to round our understanding of ethnic relations in the USSR as observed today and as they are likely to develop in the future.

The choice of this focus departs from the tradition in Soviet studies which has emphasized elite politics and the macro-analysis of social, economic, and political trends. In the case of nationality studies this has meant that most research has focused on programmatic pronouncements, the official policies of central and republic authorities, leadership changes, the assessment of regional or ethnic socioeconomic disparities, and the analysis of demographic and linguistic trends and their implications.[1] While this previous research has contributed to our understanding of nationality policy and problems in the USSR, it has remained inconclusive in regard to the core question whether the multi-ethnic Soviet system is becoming increasingly integrated or disintegrated. While some analysts imply that ethnic consciousness and differentiation is increasing, others contend that the gap between the various peoples is narrowing. This difference in assessments has been due mostly to gaps in our empirical knowledge as well as inadequacies of conceptual clarifications. This study hopes to ameliorate both problems.

Empirically the primary missing link in Soviet nationality studies has lain in the area of popular perceptions, values, and

2

goals. The type of data used for their study in other societies, namely, records of public debates, election results, or mass surveys, has been unavailable. This problem is well known, and from its inception the entire field of Soviet studies has suffered from it. Students of Soviet society make do with limited sources, or alternatively generalize or do not attend to the problem at all. The latter has largely been the fate of the study of the subjective aspects of Soviet ethnic developments. Recently, however, two new data sources have emerged which alleviate existing constraints. During the past fifteen years the Soviets have published results of many ethnosociological surveys and Western scholars have, at the same time, undertaken surveys among recent emigrants from the USSR now living in the West. Although both sources are imperfect if used on their own, their complementary use and evaluation within the context of comparative Western research on ethnic relations can go a long way in bridging the gaps in our knowledge. This is intended to be the empirical contribution of this study.

Conceptually we intend to do a variety of things. For one, we shall emphasize definitional clarity by differentiating between various types of ethnic groups in the USSR and by drawing lines of differentiation between social environments. Secondly, we shall enumerate our main hypotheses. Last but by no means least, we shall use the concepts and theories developed in the general literature on comparative ethnic relations as the basic framework of evaluation and analysis. This literature has been growing dramatically during the past two decades, and while we shall rely on its main findings to date, we also hope to contribute to this field. With its many and varied nations and nationalities, differential cultures and historical backgrounds as well as variance in degrees of economic modernization and social mobilization, the USSR clearly represents a most important case for the comparative study of ethnicity and ethnic politics.

Concepts and Hypotheses

It is the primary hypothesis of this study that the quality of interethnic relations in the USSR varies according to the nationalities involved, the ethnic composition of environment, and the level of interactions and the social context. While most analysts of Soviet nationality developments and problems note distinctions between nationalities, few outline the patterns and contexts of differentiation systematically or present an explicit framework for analysis as we intend to do here.

(1) The first and most important part of this framework is the contention that ethnic relations differ according to social sphere and context, and that findings about one cannot automatically be extrapolated for another, since different factors tend to play a role in each case. While factual observations suggested this proposition early in the research process, it can also be found in the comparative and theoretical literature on ethnic relations, which has referred to it with terms such as "structural determinants" or "situational patterning."

The latter relates to the argument that ethnic boundaries and identities are situationally defined. Thus studies of racial attitudes in the USA have shown that the same white individuals may have favorable orientations toward blacks at a workplace which has long been successfully integrated, yet are hostile in a neighborhood where presence of the blacks is seen as a threat to the value of their homes. Studies of interethnic contact and collective behavior in race riots and similar situations have also shown that the feelings aroused may change rapidly on the basis of subtle cues and circular reactions.[2] The point is that each individual has a variety of social roles through which he relates to events. Alternative social roles are typically defined by occupation, social standing, class, ethnicity, sex, family relationships, and associational links, each of which will tend to be more dominant in some situations than in others.[3] Although it is simpler and analytically more tempting to think that way, it is extremely rare that one of the roles is the sole determinant of action in any one context. What we are referring to here is the well-known problem of crosscutting loyalties and social cleavages.

Looking at the same phenomenon from another point of view, it also suggests that it is a mistake to think of any of these roles as being influential in only one sphere of life, for example, occupation being important only in the context of work and not in family or associational relationships. Similarly, it is a misconception to think of ethnicity as applying to the "purely ethnic" sphere, whatever that might be—presumably certain cultural activities, traditions, or emotional proclivities. Ethnicity plays a larger or smaller role in a large number of social and institutional contexts; it has a structural dimension as well as an attitudinal one.[4]

4

The study intends to use the Soviet case to show the specificity of ethnic attitudes and interactions and how it is defined by given contexts, types of groups involved, institutional structures and policies, complexities of task fulfillment, stratification and conflicts of interest, as well as character and strength of communal identity. This intent forms the basis for the organizational subdivision of the five middle chapters of this book. Thus after an initial chapter on ethnic identification, we shall first discuss unstructured group relationships, and then turn to interactions within institutions (schools and the military), the workplace, and the family and community.

(2) It is furthermore contended that it is important to draw an analytical distinction between three levels of nationality interactions in the USSR. Ethnic relations and politics have to be discussed both at the individual and at the group level, with the latter being further subdivided between a republic and an all-union level in the case of the larger nations.

At the highest level the entire USSR is taken as the unit of analysis and the focus is on evaluating the position of various nationalities in a unionwide context. Thus one might inquire about the proportion of individual national groups in the CPSU or about unionwide rates of intermarriage. Alternatively, one could discuss ethnic group relations within centralized institutions such as the armed forces; or analyze the central government's policy toward individual nationalities as they are dispersed all over the Soviet Union, for example, the denial of the Crimean Tatar request to return to the Crimea. One could also assess central policy toward republic-based nations such as the Lithuanians or Georgians, although here care has to be taken to distinguish whether one is talking about the nationality or about the entire republic population which includes members of other ethnic groups.

The intermediate level of analysis of ethnic relations in the USSR concerns the relations between various ethnic groups within individual territorial subunits of the USSR, and most important, within union republics. The Union of Soviet Socialist Republics is a federal state constituted from fifteen nation-based republics; within each of these one finds a titular nationality giving its name to the respective republic as well as other nationalities. Of these the local Russians are the most important politically and usually also numerically. For people in the Soviet Union a large part of their life and perceptions—maybe even most of it—is focused on the republic they live in, and we shall therefore define ethnic relations on the group level primarily as those between the major nationalities within republics.

The lowest level on which ethnic relations take place is that of individual interactions and perceptions, for example, as they pertain to intermarriage. It is analytically helpful to think of the personal level as a separate type of relationship, yet it is also related to group identity, standing, and perceptions. To clarify some of these links this study will begin with macrolevel interactions and will then proceed to the microlevel. More specifically we shall begin with two chapters discussing intrarepublic ethnic relations, then move to educational and military institutions which touch on all three levels of interactions, and conclude with a survey of individual relations at work and in marriage.

(3) It is our third major hypothesis that ethnic relations and processes in the USSR differ according to the nationalities involved, and that the major differences are those between territorially based nationalities and extraterritorial and dispersed groups. This is in part linked to the next point, in the sense that the territorially based groups—especially the union republic nations—are the ones most likely to constitute a majority in certain areas or contexts, but there are other factors playing an even more important role. Thus territoriality provides a people with a much more distinct historical and cultural identity as well as more clearly identifiable cultural, economic, and political interests. This is true not only for the USSR, but worldwide. In his wide-ranging comparative analysis of ethnic relations E. K. Francis has used the terms primary and secondary ethnic groups to differentiate between minority nationalities which became such in the course of territorial annexation and those resulting from large-scale migration. He also notes that social consequences of this basic difference in origin are crucial since territorially based nationalities typically continue to represent comprehensive subsocieties able to satisfy all social needs of their members, whereas secondary ethnic groups are able to do so only in a limited way, opening the way for a more substantial influence of the closest majority nation.[5]

In his societal theory of race and ethnic relations Stanley Lieberson has drawn similar distinctions between migrant and indigenous groups, arguing that the politics of their interactions differs greatly depending on which is subordinate to the other.[6] Although we want to postpone lengthier references to his political argument, it is important to recognize at this stage that

6

a number of theorists of ethnic relations see different patterns of relations pertaining to primary and secondary ethnic groups.

Thus it is a basic proposition of this study that a clear distinction between primary and secondary ethnic groups in the USSR is imperative if conceptual and analytical confusion is to be avoided. In the Soviet Union most nationalities are primary ethnic groups and not secondary ethnic groups as in the USA and other immigrant societies. The bulk of the non-Russian population is constituted by fourteen nations residing in their traditional homelands which today form the fourteen union republics named after the respective indigenous people such as the Ukrainians, Latvians, Armenians, and Uzbeks. These nations differ substantially from each other (for details see Chapter 1), and the USSR is thus not only a multiethnic and federal state, it is also a multilingual and multicultural society. Heterogeneity is further enhanced by differences in religious and historical backgrounds, and regional and ethnic differentials in socioeconomic development. This extensive heterogeneity complicates the clear and incisive presentation of the "nationality problem," but makes it even more imperative to draw clear lines of distinction and categorization.

The spectrum of variation is also broad among secondary ethnic groups, which are defined as dispersed migrant nationalities. Some of them are extraterritorial in their entirety, such as Soviet Jews,[7] Soviet Germans, and Crimean Tatars, but in other cases the migrant group is a segment of a territorially based nation. If one disregards the Russians which are a special case, the Ukrainians and Belorussians constitute the largest migrant segment in the USSR. This is partly related to their size, but it is also a consequence of official migration policy which has favored Slavic outmigration to the periphery of the USSR.

It is important to differentiate between primary and secondary ethnic groups because ethnic relations and perceptions differ from one to the other. As a rule, primary groups are more concerned about retaining their ethnic identity. The frequency of interactions differs as well; primary groups interact only in so far as they live in close proximity or are intermixed in regional or unionwide get-togethers or institutions. Among the latter the Soviet armed forces are most significant since they mix young men from all nationalities for the duration of two to three years. Other than that, the primary ethnic groups mostly interact with secondary groups who have moved to their respective territories. The second most prevalent form of ethnic interaction is that

7

between members of two secondary groups, for example, Ukrainians and Belorussians living in Kazakhstan.

In the Soviet case the distinction between primary and secondary ethnic groups is reinforced by governmental policy. Since the mid-1930s secondary ethnic groups have had practically no administrative or cultural rights. In contrast, primary ethnic groups have limited administrative prerogatives within their own territories, they enjoy more or less extensive native language educational systems and other cultural provisions as well as a degree of proportionality in cadre selection and advancement. We shall elaborate on these provisions and their consequences later on, at this time it is most important to point out the differential status of various types of ethnic groups. And here we also have to mention the exceptional position of the Russians. Their case is unique, in that they not only constitute the primary nationality of their titular republic, the Russian Soviet Federative Socialist Republic (RSFSR), but also make special claims in those republics where they basically constitute a secondary ethnic group. Stanley Lieberson's distinction between subordinate and superordinate migrant groups is helpful in clarifying the nature of this special status and claim. While all other secondary nationalities are subordinate to the primary ethnic groups, the Russians are not. They are officially treated as the dominant state nation throughout the entire USSR. We shall show that this is a source of conflict with the titular nations of the non-Russian union republics who feel that within "their" republics they should be the decisive group.

The Russians, too, are an ethnic group. While this seems a self-evident truism, it has to be stated because there is a tendency in nationality studies to focus only on minorities, in our case the non-Russians. This study wants to emphasize the two-sidedness of ethnic relations; because of their number and dispersion, the Russians constitute the major partner in ethnic relations union-wide. This relationship is most apparent within the fourteen non-Russian republics, and since the republic nations also constitute the great bulk of the non-Russian population of the USSR, our geographic focus will be on them.

(4) It is a further hypothesis of this study that ethnic relations and processes differ substantially according to the ethnic environment in which they take place. One must differentiate between a minimum of three distinct types of ethnic environments in the USSR: the one in which Russians form a majority: the one in which an indigenous non-Russian nationality such as the

8

Uzbeks or Estonians form a majority: and the one in which no one ethnic group forms a numerical majority, so that we find a mixed, or "international" environment. In the jargon of social science we hypothesize that the ethnic composition of environments, which can be measured numerically, constitutes an "independent" variable which has a major impact on other factors.

This point is more important than immediately meets the eye. The differences involved are not just a matter of degree, but concern in part opposite processes and divergent trends. This is particularly true for the two types of environments where one nationality predominates, namely, the Russian or the indigenous non-Russian one. To state a simple formula one can say that if a nationality dominates an environment numerically, it will also more than likely dominate it culturally, linguistically, socially, and in some ways even politically. While this is easily understood if the dominant nationality is Russian, especially by a Western audience which is used to hearing about the USSR referred to as "Russia," the case of a non-Russian predominance has to be elaborated upon. In the Soviet Union there are whole regions as well as a multitude of social contexts in which Russians form a minority—and sometimes are absent altogether—and in these contexts "ethnic relations" mean something different than in the mixed and Russian-dominated environment. To provide just one example, there are many areas in the non-Russian republics where children from mixed local–Russian marriages take on the nationality of the local parent rather than the Russian one. This happens because in contexts like these Russians constitute the *de facto* ethnic minority, and while the notion of Russians being a minority nationality may sound paradoxical to some,[8] it is an important one for the full appreciation of the complexities of ethnic relationships in the USSR.

Environments in which a non-Russian nationality forms the majority are mostly found in the borderland republics, but another major line of differentiation exists between urban and rural areas. Within the republics, smaller towns and rural areas generally include a larger proportion of local nationals than do cities and large industrial centers. This means that the "internationalist" and Russian-dominated environments are usually urban, while the native environments predominate in the countryside. As aggregate census statistics show, the indigenous nationality in 1970 (cf. Table A.1, p. 230) constituted a majority of the rural population in *all* union republics except Kazakhstan, while among the urban population this was true for only about one-half of the republics, and in the case of the capital cities for only six of the republics. Changing trends will be analyzed later, but one might note that with the exception of Latvia and Estonia the percentage of the indigenous population in the urban areas has been on the rise.

While the following chapters will elaborate on the ways in which the patterns of interethnic relations and ethnic processes differ according to ethnic environment, the difference itself has to be emphasized here because often it has been ignored. Thus the preoccupation of Soviet works with processes that promote ethnic integration has resulted in them being primarily focused on mixed internationalist as well as Russian-dominated environments. Soviet research has tended to focus on urban and industrial centers and has underemphasized the significance of divergent rural–urban ethnic settlement patterns. In the words of Iurii Arutiunian, the doyen of Soviet ethnosociologists,[9]

> The nationality aspects of Soviet rural life have been virtually ignored up to now, on both the scholarly and the practical level. Yet they are of great significance. In contrast to the urban population, which is predominantly a mixture of nationalities, the rural population of almost every Union republic is dominated by a single nationality. As a rule, the members of non-indigenous nationalities live in single-nationality villages "of their own."

Arutiunian's reference to the monoethnic composition of many villages illustrates another point, namely, that while it is useful to look at data about the aggregate spatial distribution of nationalities, these statistics are insufficient in so far as they ignore possible subdivisions and substructures. Thus the statistics showing the predominance of one major nationality in the countryside of each republic do not inform us about villages or whole collective farms where the majority is formed by another nationality, nor do the population statistics of capital cities indicate the presence or absence of ethnic neighborhoods. Ideally the analyst should have a detailed ethnodemographic map of the entire Soviet Union, clearly identifying areas with differential patterns of ethnic mixing.[10] But even then one would want to know about the ethnic composition of other microenvironments affecting the lives of people such as individual places of work, schools and other institutions, clubs or circles of friends and acquaintances, and, of course, families.

(5) It is a further contention of this study that the quality of ethnic relations is affected by the perception of nationalities as to how well their basic interests are safeguarded. This, as well as the questions of who decides the distribution of values, constitutes the political core of ethnic relations. It matters what policy is chosen, by whom, and whether decisions are made on the basis of consensus or subordination. Among the many substantive issues and decision-making points nationalities are concerned about, this study will emphasize three. The first of these concerns the physical intermingling of nationalities as affected by migration patterns, institutional structures, job selection, and military service assignments. The second issue focused upon is language. The USSR is not only a multiethnic and federal state, it is also a multilingual society and the question of linguistic facility and behavior is of economic and political cultural consequence. The third political issue to be highlighted concerns socioeconomic interests as represented by access to higher education.

Sources and Methodology

This study relies both on general and specific Soviet and Western sources. The most specific source consists of survey research to be introduced below. The general literature on nationality relations in the USSR as well as Soviet statistics require no special introduction and will be referred to in the text as appropriate. A few comments should be made, however, about the content and usefulness of the mass of Soviet policy-oriented writings.

If one reads official Soviet pronouncements and resolutions about nationality relations and developments in the USSR, the picture presented is one of ethnic harmony and a progressive convergence of the many nations into a single internationalist whole. Over time a variety of terms and propositions have been used to outline the social process involved, but a new concept has been in force since the early 1970s, namely, that of the "new historical community of people—the Soviet people." Since this formulation was used at the Twenty-fourth Party Congress, it has reappeared in practically every speech and written exposition on nationality policy and developments, including the new Soviet Constitution of 1977.[11] While there is some controversy over the extent of the merging and the exact definition of the new community,[12] the use of the term *narod* (a people or nation, very similar to the German term *Volk*) suggests that it is close to being a new ethnic identity rather than just a civic one.

11

This new unified community is said to have already come into existence, and it is projected that it will be progressively strengthened during the coming decades. Among the general causes the most important are seen to be "the very nature of the socialist society which bases itself on communal property; the establishment of a legislative framework for the equality of nations; and ever-increasing social equality in society." The list of more specific factors is headed by the escalating and "all-enhancing role of the Russian language as the language of interethnic relations,"[13] followed by the intensification of various economic, cultural, and social ties between the peoples of the Soviet Union. The mixing of populations through migration and the exchange of cadre is seen as another crucial process, and so is the mixing of nationalities at places of work and in various institutions. Ethnic intermarriage and the proliferation of "new traditions" are pinpointed as additional unifying forces, submerging ethnic and religious boundaries in the familial and communal spheres.[14] All of this is supposed to create a new all-Soviet consciousness: "it leads the thinking of Soviet people out of the framework of the concepts 'my,' 'national,' and 'republic,' it educates them in a broader civic approach, and requires them to proceed in all questions from the priority of interests common to all the people."[15]

Since statements like these are so frequently encountered in Soviet publications, they leave an impression on the reader, including the Western analyst trying to evaluate Soviet ethnic policy and developments. But while one has to be aware of the official perception of the status and future of ethnic integration, its usefulness for concrete analysis is limited. Material published in *Pravda* and similar sources primarily serves as a normative guide for party workers and the populace and as such tends to idealize relationships and to exhort continuous efforts toward achieving the next step in the development of socialism. If this type of material mentions complexities and problems at all, then it is only in order to urge a concerted effort in their liquidation. It reveals little about empirical relationships or even concrete policy approaches, two aspects to be emphasized in this study. As we shall demonstrate, empirical materials as well as the analysis of day to day policy frequently contradict the propositions found in the normative and exhortative sources and paint a much more complex picture of contrasting social trends and numerous policy dilemmas.

12

Compared to other societies, the empirical study of ethnic relations in the USSR is severely hampered by the shortage of primary data, especially in the area of policy evaluations and attitudes. Nevertheless, the diligent and careful search of Soviet materials, as well as the use of unorthodox sources such as emigrant surveys, provide a sufficient basis for analysis. As already indicated, this is a study of the significance of ethnicity from the average citizen's point of view, and while this view can partly be obtained from reports of journalists and other observers, it is methodologically more convincing to use survey data. Since it is not possible for Western scholars to conduct surveys in the USSR, the next best approach is to combine the secondary analysis of surveys undertaken by Soviet scholars with that of primary survey research conducted with recent Soviet emigrants now living in the West. If used alone, each of these sources exhibits major problems; but if used together, most of these problems can be overcome, or at least identified. Nevertheless, even the complementary use of these two sources leaves many lacunae, which we hope will not be so large as to impede the view of the overall picture.

As to the advantages and problems of ethnosociological surveys conducted in the USSR, the advantage obviously is that it is conducted in the society under study, and often consists of large-scale efforts directed by scholarly institutes. Since the mid-1960s research about ethnic processes and relations has greatly intensified and many articles and books have been published as the result. Throughout this study we shall make frequent individual references to this body of research and we, therefore, abstain from specific references and comments at this time.[16] One should, however, note some general problems that Western scholars encounter when using these materials in secondary analysis.

Thus there are indications that not all results of the research have been published, and most data are presented in a manner which precludes additional computations or reanalysis. Methodological information is scarce, which again hinders a comprehensive use. Thus the formulation of survey questions is rarely reported, although it matters a great deal. Usually information about the conditions under which surveys were conducted is lacking as well, making it difficult to estimate the extent to which respondents felt that the confidentiality of their replies was guaranteed. While this can be a problem in any society, it is

13

much more so in the Soviet Union where citizens are aware from their childhood on that they have to be careful in what they say. In Soviet surveys, frankness constitutes a special problem, even more so if local agitators and party personnel are used as interviewers, as has been the case in at least one widely cited study.[17]

The quality of Soviet ethnosociological research varies according to its scholarly leadership and according to the period when it was conducted. The methodologically most rigorous, empirical, and ideologically unhampered work was conducted between 1969 and 1972, whereafter a clampdown occurred and political influences increased.[18] But even before, and even if conducted by the most reputable scholars, survey research in the USSR has not existed in a political vacuum. It has been formally charged with providing practical recommendations to policy-makers, so that "optimal solutions may be found in the management of socioethnic development."[19] Thus researchers have to avoid contradicting the official rhetoric and contention that internationalism and the "coming closer" of the various nationalities is progressing exponentially. Soviet ethnosociologists are circumspect in their statements and interpretations, especially in the introductory and concluding segments of their writings.[20] Nevertheless, they also present data which are helpful in perceiving the complexity of Soviet multiethnic reality, and it is for this reason that this study will make extensive references to Soviet research.

Our second primary data source consists of surveys undertaken with emigrants who have recently come to the West, and especially a survey the author herself conducted with 200 Soviet Germans who came to West Germany in 1979. The interviews were conducted orally in Russian or in German, depending on which language the respondent knew best. A structured questionnaire was developed after pretests and replies were recorded in writing.

Interview research with emigrants poses many special problems, one of the primary ones being the question of representativeness of results. There are, however, two sides to the problem, one methodological and the other conceptual in nature. Methodologically the main problem is that no matter what care one takes in securing a good sample from the population pool available, emigration as such sets definite constraints in sample selection. In our case these are that compared to the overall population of the USSR, the Soviet Germans include few highly educated persons, their regional origin is lopsided (the emphasis is on residents of Kazakhstan and Central Asia), and they represent only one Soviet nationality.

To interject an introduction to this group one may note that the Soviet census of 1979 listed a total of nearly 2 million Soviet Germans. They are descendants of peasant colonists invited by Russian tsars to settle in the Volga and Black Sea areas as well as in the Ukraine during the eighteenth and nineteenth centuries. Until 1941 the majority of Soviet Germans lived in self-contained villages in these same areas, although German settlements also existed in Siberia, the Altai, and in Central Asia. There were German schools and other cultural provisions in nearly all German settlements until the late 1930s, most extensively in the Volga German ASSR.

After Hitler's attack on the Soviet Union in June 1941, the Volga Germans and many Germans from the Caucasus and the Ukraine were deported to camps and forced settlement areas in Siberia, the Altai region, and Northern Kazakhstan. A segment of the Soviet German population escaped this fate in 1941 because they lived in regions quickly overrun by the invading forces, but most of these people were repatriated to the USSR and also taken to the Siberian settlements when the tide of war changed in 1944–5.

The "special settlement" restrictions against the Soviet Germans were lifted in 1955 and political rehabilitation followed in 1964. In the following decades many migrated southward to Kazakhstan and Central Asia, with smaller groups migrating westward to the Baltic republics and Moldavia. This migratory movement reinforced the German minority's identity as a secondary ethnic group with only minimal cultural recognition in the form of a few German-language newspapers. Although today the Soviet Germans live scattered all over the USSR, half of them, that is, nearly 1 million, live in Kazakhstan. In some cases German villages and kolkhozes persist.[21]

Individual Germans began leaving the USSR after 1955 in order to join relatives in the West, but a major emigration movement started in 1972, reaching annual rates of 7,000–9,000 in 1976 to 1979. A subgroup of individuals who reached West Germany between February and September 1979 form the population from which a sample was drawn for our survey;[22] in order to limit the impact of secondary impressions received in the West all interviews were conducted within the first four weeks after arrival. As a result, memories about experiences in the Soviet

Union were fresh and many respondents still used the present tense when talking about life there; the term "we" was also used very much.

Conceptually emigration as such is often perceived as biasing the attitudes and perceptions of the respondents. Past emigrant research has shown that this by no means has to be the case,[23] and a large part of the problem can be overcome if one is careful in the type of conclusions drawn. In this study we recognize that conclusions must remain tentative, especially also in light of our relatively small sample. More important, however, we do not argue that the "marginals," that is, the percentage rate in which findings are reported are significant, but rather that this is so in case of observed internal variance in the data, even more so if the same pattern of variance occurs in parallel surveys undertaken in the USSR or in other societies. To illustrate, Chapter 6 mentions that both the Soviet German emigrant survey and Soviet surveys show a pattern according to which considerably more people reject ethnic intermarriage than interethnic contacts at work. Such a congruence of findings strengthens confidence in the value of both types of data.

We also want to argue that depending on approach and conceptualization, the liabilities of sample selection can be turned into an asset. This is the case, for example, in regard to the circumstance that our sample represents only one Soviet nationality. Having been dispersed all over the USSR since World War II, the Soviet Germans have the advantage of being able—as a group—to relate experiences made in a broad variety of locations and are, therefore, especially suited for an inquiry focusing on comparisons between various Soviet regions. Since the respondent group basically is "the same" in all regions, differences found tend to reflect the ethnic environment in which it has lived rather than respondent idiosyncrasies.

What's more, many questions[24] were addressed to the sample as informants and observers, rather than as respondents. We asked what they observed in the relations between the indigenous nations and Russians among whom they lived, and one can argue that an observer role tends to be more neutral than that of a direct participant. There is a further special advantage in the low occupational level of our sample. Since the majority of respondents worked as truckdrivers, nurses, factory or construction workers, farmhands, and similar, their observations are based on everyday experiences and closely embody the perspective "from below" we aim to depict. Such data can communicate

16

a sense of the grassroots political contexts and implications of issues that go unacknowledged officially.

Our interview schedule consisted of a mixture of systematic closed and open-ended questions, and the findings are reported both by quotation and in statistical summaries, providing a synthesis of qualitative and quantitative data. Replies to open-ended questions were recorded verbatim, and although some are summarized in table form, direct quotations will be used as well. Many respondent statements are not only intriguing and informative in content, but also highly suggestive in form. Such evocative material communicates a sense of the problems referred to and a kind of understanding which quantitative illustrations have difficulty in providing.

In sum, our approach is one which tries to make the best of a data base which is flawed in strict methodological terms both in the case of the emigrant surveys as well as the research published in the USSR. In both instances we shall rarely suggest that the percentage rates given for a certain reply are meaningful, but rather that it is useful to examine variance—for example, by region or the issue to be attended to—as well as to analyze what other factors are associated with replies. In a larger perspective this focus on internal variance fits well with our concern to highlight the heterogeneity and variance found in ethnic relations in the USSR both as it applies to the many Soviet nationalities as well as to social and political contexts.

Organization of Study

Our inquiry will start at the "macrolevel" of ethnic relationships between groups and whole nations and will then switch to the individual level. As already suggested, this approach relates to the contention that only a combination of the two levels of analysis, as well as of both qualitative and quantitative data, can lead to a comprehensive understanding of ethnicity in the USSR.

In order to understand the basis of ethnic relations and politics in the Soviet Union one, furthermore, has to be aware of the ways in which its citizens are identified by nationality. People are officially categorized according to nationality both in their personal documents and in governmental rosters. Parallel to this official identification—which entails varied consequences both for individuals and groups—ethnic identification occurs unofficially in everyday relations between people. The perceptions of the identity of others as well as of oneself determine differentiated patterns of interaction. While the middle chapters focus on the consequences of formal and informal ethnic identification, Chapter 1 discusses how it occurs.

Chapters 2–6 examine the particulars of ethnic relationships in specific contexts. We first turn to an analysis of unstructured group relationships at the union republic level, focusing on the two basic population groups found in every non-Russian republic, namely, the titular nationality and the Russians. While ethnic boundaries at this macrolevel are also defined by communal and religious particularism discussed in Chapter 7, this chapter highlights basic ethnic gaps in historical and political perceptions as well as the role of social and linguistic competition. These are the determinants of the overall ethnic climate in non-Russian republics and their explication at the outset of the study draws attention to the political dimension of ethnic relations in the USSR.

Chapter 3 enlarges on this discussion by analyzing the current political dynamics as well as future trends in the development of nationality power. Regional comparisons and contrasts help in pinpointing the major relevant factors which include differing demographic trends and stages in socioeconomic and cultural development. Chapter 4 focuses on two highly structured and governmentally organized and planned institutions, namely, schools and the armed forces. Comparisons between these two institutions are especially intriguing in so far as each is organized according to the opposite pattern, that is, while education is basically (with many important exceptions) segregated according to language of instruction (until 1959 by nationality), recruits from all nationalities serve in ethnically mixed units, in which Russian is the only official language. The latter approach to multiethnicity in institutional contexts appears to be more integrative functionally, but what does it do to attitudinal integration? This question is discussed by analysis of some of our interview data, by comparisons with the pattern of ethnic interrelationships in the educational sphere, by references to other approaches used in the USSR in the past, and to insights found in the general literature of comparative ethnic relations.

The workplace constitutes another type of social institution, and Chapter 5 examines ethnic interactions in this sphere. The focus is on survey results about ethnic preferences in regard to coworkers and supervisors. While we are in part talking about interactions between small groups, individual perceptions

18

dominate. This is even more true in the case of personal ethnic relationships examined in Chapter 6, although the question of ethnic intermarriage is also of communal concern. Here we present findings on both intermarriage attitudes and behavior, one of the main conclusions being that they are greatly affected by cultural and religious affinities. While past writing on Soviet nationality relations have similarly pointed to the importance of such affinities between the respective Slavic, Baltic, or Muslim nations, our study has the advantage of presenting empirical measures such as social distance scales and statistics on intermarriage patterns.

Ethnicity is closely related to cultural, communal, and religious life, and Chapter 7 discusses the degree to which particularism in these areas is maintained and what its implications are both for ethnic relations and Soviet politics.

The study concludes with a summary of the ways in which ethnicity affects both individual and collective relationships in the Soviet Union.

Notes: Introduction

1 For some recent examples compare Jeremy R. Azrael (ed.), *Soviet Nationality Policies and Practices* (New York: Praeger, 1978); Teresa Rakowska-Harmstone. "The nationalities question," in Robert Wesson (ed.), *The Soviet Union: Looking to the 1980s* (Stanford, Calif.: Hoover Institution, 1980), pp. 129–53; Grey Hodnett, *Leadership in the Soviet National Republics* (Oakville: Mosaic Press, 1978); Donna Bahry and Carol Nechemias, "Half full or half empty?: the debate over Soviet regional equality," *Slavic Review*, vol. 40, no. 3 (Fall 1981), pp. 366–83; Brian D. Silver, "Soviet nationality problems: analytic approaches," *Problems of Communism*, vol. 28, no. 4 (1979), pp. 71–6; and George W. Simmonds (ed.), *Nationalism in the USSR and Eastern Europe in the Era of Brezhnev and Kosygin* (Detroit, Mich.: University of Detroit Press, 1977).

2 cf. M. L. Kohn and R. M. Williams, "Situational patterning in intergroup relations," *American Sociological Review*, vol. 21 (April 1956), pp. 164–74; and J. D. Lohman and D. C. Reitzes, "Deliberately organized groups and racial behavior," *American Sociological Review*, vol. 19 (June 1954), pp. 342–4, as cited in Daniel Glaser, "Dynamics of ethnic identification," *American Sociological Review*, vol. 23 (February 1958), p. 36.

3 See also Crawford Young, *The Politics of Cultural Pluralism* (Madison, Wis.: University of Wisconsin Press, 1976), p. 38.

4 This has been well argued by Ira Katznelson, "Comparative studies of race and ethnicity," *Comparative Politics*, vol. 5, no. 1 (October 1972), esp. pp. 137–43; cf. also Joan Vincent, "The structuring of ethnicity," *Human Organization*, vol. 33, no. 4 (Winter 1974), pp. 375–9, and Jonathan Y. Okamura, "Situational ethnicity," *Ethnic and Racial Studies*, vol. 4, no. 4 (October 1981), pp. 452–65.

5 E. K. Francis, *Interethnic Relations: An Essay in Sociological Theory* (New York: Elsevier, 1976), p. 207.

6   Stanley Lieberson, "A societal theory of race and ethnic relations," *American Sociological Review*, vol. 26, no. 6 (December 1961), pp. 902–10.

7   During the past few decades the Soviet Jewish minority has been a special focus of interest for Soviet policy-makers as well as Western analysts. Our references to it will be limited, since the emphasis here is on primary ethnic groups and since this complex topic deserves a detailed discussion that is beyond the scope of this study. For the most authoritative existing research compare the numerous publications by Zvi Gitelman, as well as Victor Zaslavsky and Robert J. Brym, *Soviet–Jewish Emigration and Soviet Nationality Policy* (New York: St. Martin's Press, 1983), *passim*.

8   It would not sound unusual to Soviet ethnosociologists like Susokolov, who specifically states that "Russians in the urban environment of some other Soviet republic are regarded as an ethnic group": A. A. Susokolov, "Vliianie razlichii v urovne obrazovaniia i chislennosti kontaktiruiushchikh etnicheskikh grupp na mezhetnicheskie otnosheniia (po materialam perepisei naseleniia SSSR 1959 i 1970 gg.)," *Sovetskaia etnografiia*, 1976, no. 1, p. 101.

9   Iu. V. Arutiunian, "Natsional'no-regional'noe mnogoobrazie sovetskoi derevni," *Sotsiologicheskie issledovaniia*, 1980, no. 3, p. 73.

10 While such a detailed map or data base does not exist at this time, some Soviet and Western scholars have tried to piece it together for individual republics. On Moldavia see M. N. Guboglo, *Razvitie dvuiazychiia v Moldavskoi SSR* (Kishinev: Shtiintsa Press, 1979), esp. pp. 72–7; and for a recent study of Estonia see Rein Taagepera, "Size and ethnicity of Estonian towns and rural districts, 1922–1979," *Journal of Baltic Studies*, vol. 13, no. 2 (Summer 1982), pp. 105–27. B. M. Ekkel' has tried to provide a statistical index of ethnic mixing: see Ekkel', "Opredelenie indeksa mozaichnosti natsional'nogo sostava respublik, kraev i oblastei SSSR," *Sovetskaia etnografiia*, 1976, no. 2, pp. 33–42.

11 *Konstitutsiia (Osnovnoi Zakon) Soiuza Sovetskikh Sotsialisticheskikh Respublik* (Moscow: Politizdat, 1977), p. 4.

12 For good summaries of divergent interpretations see M. I. Kulichenko, "Obrazovanie i razvitie sovetskogo naroda kak novoi istoricheskoi obshchnosti," *Voprosy Istorii*, 1979, no. 4, pp. 3–23; and Walker Connor, *The National Question in Marxist–Leninist Theory and Strategy* (Princeton, N.J.: Princeton University Press, 1984), pp. 404–7.

13 The citations are taken from A. P. Egurnev, "Mezhnatsional'nye braki i ikh rol' v sblizhenii natsii i narodnostei SSSR," *Nauchnyi kommunizm*, 1973, no. 4, p. 32. Nearly identical formulations can be found in a large number of Soviet sources, for example, G. T. Tavadov, "Osobennosti sovremenogo etapa razvitiia natsional'nykh otnoshenii v SSSR," *Nauchnyi kommunizm*, 1980, no. 3, pp. 25–35.

14 On the integrative role ascribed to migration see especially V. A. Shpiliuk, *Mezhrespublikanskaia migratsiia i sblizhenie natsii v SSSR* (L'vov: Vishcha Shkola, 1975), p. 7, and *passim*. On intermarriage see Egurnev, "Mezhnatsional'nye braki," pp. 28–36; and Iu. V. Bromlei, *Sovremennye problemy etnografii* (Moscow: Nauka, 1981), p. 333.

15 M. I. Kulichenko (ed.), *Osnovnye napravleniia izucheniia natsional'nykh otnoshenii v SSSR* (Moscow: Nauka, 1979), p. 94.

16 For good surveys of the main studies and publications see ibid., pp. 26–8, 190–231, as well as Bromlei, *Problemy etnografii*, *passim*.

17 A. I. Kholmogorov, *Internatsional'nye cherty sovetskikh natsii. (Na materialakh konkretno-sotsiologicheskikh issledovanii v Pribaltike)* (Moscow: Mysl', 1970), pp. 50–1.

18 For an excellent discussion of developments in Soviet sociological research see Dmitri N. Shalin, "The development of Soviet sociology," *Annual Review of Sociology*, 1978, no. 4, pp. 171–91. See also V. Zaslavsky, "Sociology in the contemporary Soviet Union," *Social Research*, 1977, no. 2, pp. 330–53; and William A. Welsh (ed.), *Survey Research and Public Attitudes in Eastern Europe and the Soviet Union* (Des Moines, Iowa: University of Iowa, 1980).

19 Iurii V. Arutiunian, "Konkretno-sotsiologicheskoe issledovanie natsional'nykh otnoshenii," *Voprosy filosofii*, 1969, no. 12, p. 129.

20 For a lament about the contradiction between general introductions and the empirical point of religious studies see *Pravda*, 15 May 1983, p. 3.

21 cf. Ann Sheehy, *The Crimean Tatars, Volga Germans and Meskhetians: Soviet Treatment of Some National Minorities*, Report No. 6, new ed. (London: Minority Rights Group, 1973); Rasma Karklins, "The interrelationship of Soviet foreign and nationality policies: the case of the foreign minorities of the USSR," Ph.D. dissertation, University of Chicago, 1975; and Sidney Heitman, *The Soviet Germans in the USSR Today* (Cologne: Berichte des Bundesinstituts für ostwissenschaftliche und internationale Studien, 35, 1980).

22 The sample of people surveyed was drawn randomly with some stratifying adjustments made for age, geographic origin, gender, and religion. As for age, persons younger than 44 were deliberately oversampled to make up two-thirds of our total sample in order to secure a respondent population which has in most cases grown up in the post-Stalin Soviet Union and is, therefore, bound to relate experiences formed in this most recent era. Groups of emigrants were also over- or undersampled depending on their last republic of residence in the USSR since we wanted to interview people from various regions. In light of the unequal dispersion of the German population of the USSR as well as the vicissitudes of Soviet emigration policy, considerable regional imbalances remain, especially an overrepresentation of respondents who had lived in Kazakhstan (cf. Table A.7, p. 236). Slight adjustments in sample selection were also made to avoid a predominantly female sample in the older age group as well as an overrepresentation of Baptists and Mennonites. Our sample included seven cases of non-interviews (3.5 percent), which represent instances where people could not be contacted, as well as several instances where prospective respondents turned out to be handicapped and, therefore, not available for interviewing. The latter includes one deaf and three retarded persons. There were sixteen individuals (8 percent) who refused to be interviewed. This refusal rate is very similar to the one encountered in general survey research in the West and is not regarded as a methodological problem.

23 Thus the findings of the Harvard Project conducted in the early 1950s have constituted a cornerstone of postwar Sovietology. See especially Alex Inkeles and Raymond A. Bauer, *The Soviet Citizen, Daily Life in a Totalitarian Society* (Cambridge, Mass.: Harvard University Press, 1959).

24 The questions are cited in the text as well as in individual tables.

1

Ethnic Identity and Identification

People living in the Soviet Union have a dual identity. One of these identities is common to them all, since they are all "Soviets," but the other identity varies in more than a hundred ways as there are more than a hundred officially recognized nationalities. Although the largest, the Russians are just one of these groups, and although foreigners frequently equate "Russian" with "Soviet," no Soviet citizen would make that mistake, being acutely aware of the difference between nationality and citizenship. Citizenship is a civic identity referring to membership in a state, whereas nationality is an ethnic identity referring to membership in a people.[1] In those—rather few—states made up of only one people, citizenship and nationality overlap, but they do not overlap in multiethnic states of which the USSR is one.

Awareness of the ways in which its citizens are identified by nationality is the first crucial step in understanding the ethnic relations and ethnic politics of the Soviet Union. Formal and informal ethnic cognition and categorization are the precondition for differentiated treatment and patterns of interaction,[2] and we thus have to inquire how it takes place. How do people in the USSR know who belongs to which nationality?

There are several ways in which ethnicity is identified. The traditional way has been to enumerate tangible ascriptive characteristics by which one group of people differs from another. The aspects typically focused on have been historical and cultural origin, race, and religion. The description of such identifying traits has been the prerogative of scholarly specialists; "the man in the street" only becomes aware of these differentiations in so far as he is exposed to the respective literature. How does he

22

himself identify people he meets in everyday encounters? This is the second aspect of ethnic identification to be dealt with in this chapter, that is, the informal social reality of ethnic perception. This informal appraisal not always overlaps with the scholarly one, some distinctions are obfuscated and others are highlighted. Among the latter the racial identification of some people as "blacks" is especially striking. It is unlikely that any anthropologist studying the peoples of the Soviet Union would use this category.

The informal ethnic identification of others is highly subjective, and so is self-identification. This perception not only relies on tangible characteristics, psychology is involved as well. Although ethnic consciousness is widely seen as the most decisive dimension of ethnic identity, it is also recognized to be a sorely elusive phenomenon. In this study we shall try to assess its meaning and strength through a score of survey results as well as behavioral indicators. We shall begin by examining the patterns of ethnic self-identification as evident in the census-taking process and in the formal choices of nationality made by children from mixed marriages.

The last sentence already alludes to a further form of ethnic identification found in the Soviet Union and this is the administrative practice of officially identifying each Soviet citizen by his or her nationality (natsional'nost') at birth, and throughout their whole life. People are bureaucratically categorized according to nationality in all personal documents and in governmental rosters, and everybody has an official ethnic identity, be it Uzbek, Russian, Georgian, Jew, Latvian, or other. While this administrative ethnic identification has a life of its own, it also reinforces the strength of the traditionally "inherited" ethnic identity as well as personal identification.

Subsequent chapters will explore the role of ethnicity in personal life as well as in communal, institutional, and sociopolitical contexts, but this chapter intends to show the basis for ethnic identification. It will outline the sources and patterns of traditional, personal, and administrative ethnic identification. It will also show that ethnic identity is not constant and includes a significant subjective element. Thus one finds that in the USSR personal ethnic identification can diverge from "passport nationality," which for its part can diverge from the nationality registered by the official census-taker. As concerns informal identification, the categories applied vary, in that people use both the official designations as well as transcending categories such as

Slavs or Balts, or Europeans and Central Asians. As the following discussion will show, the criteria for identification are many.

Traditional Ethnic Identity

The traditional way of looking at ethnic identity is nominal and ascriptive, by an enumeration of historical background, cultural and linguistic origin, and religious tradition. Usually there is also a mention of the size of group and the primary region of settlement. In this section we will follow this precedent by shortly summarizing these characteristics for the major Soviet nationalities.[3] Other characteristics such as political–administrative status, levels of socioeconomic development, and demographic trends are discussed in other parts of this study.

With a total of 137 million, the Russians constitute the largest ethnic group of the Soviet Union; proportionately they come to 52 percent of the Soviet population (1979 census). The large majority of the Russians live in their titular republic, the RSFSR, settlement being most compact in the western and central regions. Russian is a Slavic language, and the Russian Orthodox Church has historically dominated religious life. As fellow Slavs, the Ukrainians and Belorussians are most closely related to the Russians, but they constitute distinct national groups with separate cultural identities. The 42 million Ukrainians are the second largest nationality, and the Belorussians took fourth place in 1979, after the 12 million Uzbeks.

Although the majority of Ukrainians have traditionally belonged to the Eastern Orthodox Church, most Western Ukrainians were Uniate Catholics before the forced union of this church with the former at the end of World War II. The war was also instrumental in the incorporation of the western Ukraine— or eastern Poland, if you will—into the Soviet Union. It is in this area that national cultural autonomy and separatism have the most supporters. Except for a brief interlude in 1918, the bulk of the Ukraine has been linked to Russia for decades. Although 86 percent of the Ukrainians reside in their titular republic (cf. Table A.3, p. 232), the remaining 14 percent represent 5 million Ukrainians scattered over the rest of the USSR where they form a major secondary ethnic group.

The Belorussians are another significant migratory group, although the majority again resides in its own northwestern union republic. Some Belorussians are Catholics, but most have

24

traditionally belonged to the Eastern Orthodox Church. Due to this, and their linguistic closeness to the Great Russians and geographic and historical proximity to Russia proper, the Belorussians are the one union republic nation most vulnerable to assimilation.

The situation is much different in regard to the non-Slavic nationalities, especially the Iranic and Turkic Muslims. This subgroup of nations includes the Azerbaijanis in the south, the Tadjiks, Uzbeks, Turkmen and Kirghiz in Central Asia, and the more centrally located Kazakhs and Tatars. Together they numbered 36 million at the time of the 1979 Census. Except for the Tadjiks who speak an Iranian language, these peoples use mutually intelligible Turko-Tatar languages. They are also close in their Islamic religious tradition, and for this reason we shall in this study summarily refer to them as the "Muslim peoples." This categorization is widespread among Western scholars and was also quite acceptable in the early Soviet state which even witnessed the existence of a Muslim Communist Party.[4]

The Armenians and Georgians represent two ancient Christian nations living in the southern part of the Caucasus. Each maintains its own highly distinctive old alphabet, national traditions, and autonomous churches. Numbering about 4 million people each, the Armenians stand out among non-Russian territorial peoples, in that just 66 percent live in the Armenian SSR, with the rest residing in the adjacent republics and elsewhere in the USSR (cf. Table A.3, p. 232).

There are other non-Slavic Christian nations, the most important four of which reside in the western regions of the USSR. They are the Moldavians, the Lithuanians, Latvians, and Estonians. The Moldavians live in the historical province of Bessarabia, most of which belonged to Romania until World War II. Their language is indistinguishable from Romanian, except that it is now written in the Cyrillic alphabet. In contrast, the three Baltic peoples continue to use the Latin alphabets in writing their distinctive languages. While Estonian is a Finno-Ugric language, Latvian and Lithuanian form the Baltic branch of the Indo-European language family. By religion most of the Estonians and Latvians are Lutheran, whereas Lithuanians are predominantly Roman Catholic. Estonia, Latvia, and Lithuania were independent republics between 1918 and 1940, when they were taken over by Soviet forces and incorporated into the USSR. This forcible incorporation has not been recognized by the USA and other western states. Numerically the three Baltic nations come to some 6 million people, more than 90 percent of which live in their traditional homelands.

There are, in addition, Karelians, Udmurts, Mordvinians, and dozens of other smaller ethnic groups living in various parts of the Soviet Union. It is beyond the scope of this study to refer to these at any length. There can be no doubt that in whatever way it is measured, ethnic heterogeneity is considerable. For each of the ethnic groups one or the other facet of its traditional identity is more significant. For the Muslims it is their religious tradition and way of life; for the Balts, language and the memory of political independence. These points will be considered further in later chapters.

Informal Ethnic Identification of Others

Individual and group contacts attain an ethnic dimension only if the people involved are able to and do identify each other by nationality. Subsequent chapters will discuss the consequences of ethnic categorization: here we shall focus on the sources of ethnic cognition in anonymous daily encounters such as in shops or on the bus, as well as in more structured situations such as at work or in a club. What specifically is it that informs people whether others are of their own or of another nationality?

Soviet surveys as well as our own survey with Soviet German emigrants provide some answers. Thus we asked "how does one know that somebody belongs to a certain national group?"— leaving the question open-ended, so that replies could be categorized from verbatim statements. A comparable question used in a Soviet survey—"what, in your opinion, primarily differentiates members of various nationalities?"—provided preformulated multiple-choice responses;[5] but in spite of these slight differences in methodology as well as in question formulation, the findings are strikingly similar. Thus language is cited most frequently in both surveys, followed by physical appearance, dress, and distinctive forms of behavior.

Although both surveys pinpoint the same factors, there is some difference in emphasis. The Soviet survey ranks "language, features of character . . . and distinctive forms of behavior"[6] first, and mentions physical appearance less than our own survey. More detailed comparisons are curtailed by the Soviet authors not citing their exact data, but it is likely that the divergent emphasis on physical features is related to the different regional focus of the studies. The Soviet survey was conducted in the Tatar ASSR, whereas the majority of German emigrant respondents lived in Kazakhstan and Central Asia where ethnic distinctions in the appearance of people play the largest role (see Table 1.1). When talking about these distinctions, many respondents mentioned traits of the native populations such as slanted eyes, dark hair or eyes, facial structure (mostly high cheekbones), or dark skin. The wearing of distinctive dress was also most often mentioned in regard to Central Asia, and many described specifics such as Uzbeks and Tadjiks wearing different types of round caps. One description of Kirghiz was: "They look very different, they are burned by the sun and wear their national dress" (173),[7] and another respondent from Kirghizia said that "one can distinguish the nationals according to their dress, their faces, the way they speak—they talk to each other in their native language" (151).

It is an advantage of the Soviet German emigrant survey that it allows comparisons between regions; thus one finds that physical distinctions are least often cited by those persons who resided in the Baltic republics (see Table 1.1). The relatively high ranking of physical appearance by respondents from the RSFSR is not as surprising as it might appear since our survey included people who had lived in outlying areas with distinctive native populations such as the Komi, the Baskhirs, or the Kazakhs of the Altai.

Some further elaborations and clarifications should be made about the summary data provided in Table 1.1. There are three subcategories for the language variable. The categories "use of native language" and "do not speak Russian" are not identical since the latter includes both people who noticeably do not know Russian as well as those who know it but make a point of not using it (mostly in Estonia). Overall the ethnic identification of others by language is cited most frequently for the Baltic republics, and "have accent when speaking Russian" most often appears in regard to non-Russians living in the RSFSR.

The category "behavior" includes remarks about distinctive temperament—for example, the friendliness and hospitality of Georgians—as well as politically accented behavior. Thus a respondent who had lived in Lithuania stated that nationalities are distinguishable "according to their character and views; the Lithuanians are for their independence, freedom" (73).

While language use, an accent, physical appearance, or behavior serve to identify the nationality of other persons, individuals apparently also volunteer this information or give it

Table 1.1 "How Does One Know that Somebody Belongs to a Certain National Group?"

| Trait specified | Total, N = 208* (%) | Kazakhstan, N = 76 (%) | By region | | | |
			Central Asia, N = 40 (%)	Baltic, N = 36 (%)	Moldavia and other, N = 23 (%)	RSFSR, N = 33 (%)
Language:						
Use of native language	22	20	15	39	35	9
Do not speak Russian	10	8	7	14	13	12
Have accent	6	3	—	8	9	19
Physical appearance:						
Face/eyes/hair	24	30	25	8	17	30
Color of skin	9	13	13	7	4	3
Dress	14	14	30	8	5	9
Behavior	8	5	7	8	4	15
Other	7	7	3	8	13	3
Totals	100	100	100	100	100	100

* Some respondents mentioned several traits, causing larger N.
Source: Survey of Soviet German emigrants, 1979.

when asked. Thus the American guides for a 1978 agricultural exhibition of the USA noted to their considerable surprise that during the exhibit's stay in Kazakhstan:[8]

> One of the most common questions posed to guides was "What is your nationality?" and when the answer came back "American," visitors would persist until they got a more satisfactory answer—the guide's ethnic background.

This is just one illustration that the determination of other people's ethnic identity is important to many.

While informal ethnic identification is a pervasive social reality in the USSR, its intensity varies both geographically and situationally. In geographic terms the previously cited Soviet survey of the Tatar ASSR points out that people in larger urban centers pay less attention to the nationality of the people they meet in the streets than is the case in smaller urban centers or rural regions.[9] The question is also less relevant the more monoethnic is the population of an area. Thus ethnic identification plays a comparatively small role in the large Russian metropolises, such as Moscow and Leningrad, which are the cities most frequently visited by Westerners and where many of the more prominent Soviet dissidents or official representatives have spent their lives. The contrast between these cities and outlying non-Russian regions was noted by a dissident Soviet writer who was in exile during 1978–80 in the city of Yermak in the Pavlodar oblast of Kazakhstan:[10]

> The tenseness of relations between the various national groups in the city and the region is obvious. Yermak's ethnic composition was totally unprecedented for me, relative to what I had seen in Leningrad and Moscow. As a rule, the question of nationality doesn't arise among people in those two cities. To inquire about a recent acquaintance's ethnic background is considered an impolite gesture in Leningrad, even among common people. Kazakhstan (at any rate, Yermakov region) is riddled with ethnic barriers, although the authorities fail to acknowledge it: they try to appear neutral. Any acquaintance begins with a question about one's nationality, unless this is clear from the color of one's skin or the shape of one's eyes. The support of one's "clan" is considered the ethical basis of life, and to violate this is a moral transgression even in the eyes of the passive members of an ethnic community.

Ideally one would like to draw an ethnic map identifying with varying degrees of shading areas where ethnic identification is more or less salient. In such a map Kazakhstan certainly would emerge as being highly affected, whereas nearly monoethnic locales such as Moscow and Leningrad would be shown to be much less so.

Besides geographic variance in the pertinency of ethnic identification, there are contexts in which lines of ethnic differentiation are obfuscated. Thus Ukrainians and Belorussians living outside of their native republics frequently are not perceived as separate ethnic groupings, but are counted as Russians,[11] especially by the indigenous populations of the non-Slavic republics. This recategorization is mostly due to language use. Both our respondents and Soviet census data show that linguistically the Ukrainians and Belorussians living outside of their own republics tend to become Russified. Thus no matter what their official or personal ethnic identification, these people have "assimilated" into Russians in the eyes of their social partners. This means that subjectively the Russian ethnic group living in the non-Slavic union republics is larger than is the case objectively.

The same lack of ethnic differentiation occurs in institutional settings such as within the armed forces, and especially the officer corps. Even though individual officers may officially be non-Russian, the great majority of officers are perceived to be Russian by the enlisted men (cf. Chapter 4). The same phenomenon applies to other contexts in which centralized control is most pervasive (who can easily identify the non-Russians in the Politburo?) Although the tendency of ethnic obfuscation is strongest toward Ukrainians and Belorussians, it also occurs in regard to other nationalities, mostly dispersed groups and individually dispersed members of territorial groups. This is the more true the less distinctive the individual persons are in their physical appearance and the more Russified they become linguistically. Or to return to a point made earlier, the same factors determining ethnic recognition cause nonrecognition if they are absent.

In the non-Russian regions the lines of ethnic differentiation tend to become simplified, typically into "Russians" and "locals."[12] As will be shown at more length later, this division takes on a racial overtone in Central Asia and Kazakhstan where the basic subdivision tends to be one between "whites" and "blacks," or "Europeans" and "Asians." While the latter draws attention to racial and regional differences between population groups, language use is the one distinguishing trait that plays a role all over the Soviet Union. This conclusion apparently is also at the basis of the new Soviet linguistic policy which has increasingly emphasized the integrating role of the Russian language.

"Nationality" as a Category in Personal Documents

The identification of nationality is standard practice in virtually all official papers in the USSR, be they personal identity cards, application forms, job records, or else. Conversationally this is referred to as the fifth point since the item *natsional'nost'* typically appears fifth in row after other standard items of personal identification such as name, gender, and year and place of birth. While "nationality" on the one hand represents a simple piece of biographical information, it also is a regulatory device used by Soviet bureaucracy. The purpose may be rather innocent—one recent emigrant said that nationality was recorded on library cards in order to know in what languages books should be acquired—or it may be more consequential if it is used for determining whether an individual will receive a residence permit,[13] or when it affects educational or occupational mobility.

The main document certifying personal identity is the internal passport. Soviet press accounts have given the following examples of situations in which the presentation of one's passport is required:[14]

for registering for a course of study, taking a job, claiming mail or pensions, buying an automobile or other means of transportation, buying plane tickets or goods on credit, witnessing wills and other documents at a notary's office, or doing other things.

And:[15]

The passport is needed when registering for a residence permit and when applying for permission to change one's residence, when applying for admission to an educational institution or for a job, and when registering a marriage. Unless a passport is presented, post offices will not give people money orders, letters or telegrams arriving by general delivery.

Thus the passport accompanies the Soviet citizen not only at major life events such as marriage, but also on numerous daily errands. In some of these the official nationality of the person involved may make no difference at all, but there are others when it does. In addition, the registration of nationality on the papers as such enhances its pervasive presence in the minds of people engaged in these transactions.

The system of internal passports was introduced in 1932 and the most recent statute implementing some changes was adopted on 28 August 1974. One of the major reforms was the omission of social class as a major identification category, and in the years preceding the new statute there were suggestions that nationality should be omitted as well. Besides rumors to this effect which upset at least some of the non-Russians,[16] the Soviet authorities let out trial balloons in the form of letters to the editors of newspapers stating that nationality often was an unclear category and that with the advance of socialism only citizenship should be recorded in the passport.[17] Nevertheless, nothing was changed, and although there have been no explanations for retaining nationality as an official passport category, one may assume that it was due to its usefulness as a regulatory device.

In the Soviet Union nationality is officially determined by the nationality of one's parents. There is no individual choice, except if the parents belong to different ethnic groups. In this instance the youngster getting his or her first internal passport at the age of 16 may choose between the two alternatives; the motives for particular choices are a fascinating subject and will be discussed in the last section of this chapter. Once an official nationality has been entered in the passport, "no subsequent change in nationality entry is permissible."[18] Thus, legally, nationality is an immutable ascriptive characteristic of every Soviet citizen.

"Nationality" as a Census Category

The official identification of their personal nationality in the internal passport and the census is quite straightforward for most people in the Soviet Union, but there are subgroups such as persons of mixed parentage, migrants, and small extraterritorial ethnic groups, for whom complexities arise. It is worthwhile to discuss these instances in some detail because they provide insights about ethnic relations, and also because nationality is used as a major category in Soviet statistical accounts which on their part constitute the basis for assessing macrolevel ethnic trends. Even though Soviet and Western scholars make frequent use of ethnic statistics, few have discussed their quality and meaning.

For one, it is important to recognize that the widely used Soviet census statistics are based on ethnic self-identification, whereas other statistics, such as those relating to the nationality of party members or university students, are derived from recordings of the legal nationality. Since their origin differs, the two types of data cannot be assumed to overlap (this assumption has been made in most aggregate analyses of Soviet ethnic trends).[19] Moreover, the two official ethnic identities are somewhat fluid, even though passport nationality is much less so than census nationality. This, as well as some of the factors affecting ethnic self-identification, can be illustrated by material derived from the experiences of those of our Soviet German respondents who participated in the last Soviet census taken in January 1979.

We first asked about the way in which nationality had been established by the census-taker. Although one of the respondents thought that "in Russia, only the passport matters," passports were examined only in a few cases (10 percent of our sample). The overwhelming majority said that the census-taker had registered their nationality on the basis of their verbal statement. A few guessed that they had not been asked to show their papers because a local administration—that of a *sovkhoz*, for example—already knew their nationality. However, this guess appears mistaken and one may wonder why anyone at all had to show a passport since officially Soviet census-takers were not supposed to ask for it. The verbal self-identification of census subjects was supposed to be decisive[20] and apparently was indeed in at least 90 percent of the cases.

This procedure itself is suggestive as a tacit acknowledgement by the Soviet census authorities that "nationality" is a category open to subjective interpretation. Individuals were given the opportunity to claim a nationality other than that inscribed in their internal passport and, as our interview data suggest, quite a few may have done so. In spite of the statute cited above, there appear to be ways of changing one's official passport nationality as well.[21] The same motives and problems underlie both cases— either changing one's passport or claiming a new nationality in a census. Some people have a genuine difficulty in identifying their nationality—particularly those of mixed parentage—and others feel it to be advantageous to change their nationality, or are impelled to do so.

Turning first to the latter cases, it is notable that 80 percent of our respondents were able to provide illustrative examples. The following causes of nationality change were mentioned: growing up without parents, acquiring a spouse of different nationality, consequences of war and border disputes, negative image of own ethnic group, and considerations of career and better living conditions. Some typical remarks are given below.

Orphans "Yes, it is possible to change one's nationality to Russian, but that is done mostly by children without parents who have been raised in orphanages" (85). "My husband did not know what to consider himself; once, in the 1970 Census, he stated himself to be a German, but at other times a Russian . . . He had grown up in an orphanage after his parents died of hunger in Siberia in 1947 and the orphanage registered him as a Russian" (147).

Mixed marriages "An acquaintance married a Russian woman, he took her last name and had his nationality changed to Russian in his passport" (177). "In mixed marriages, where one partner is German, they usually claim Russian nationality" (145).

Consequences of war and border disputes "There were cases just after the war when people did not want it to be known that they were Germans" (141).[22] "When we were released from the camps, a KGB man asked us whether we did not want to change our nationality" (91). "In those parts of Lithuania which previously belonged to Germany there are Germans who have registered themselves as Lithuanians . . . now some claim their German nationality because they want to emigrate" (172).

Negative image of particular ethnic group "Germans and Jews do that frequently, [they] change their last names too . . . [they] do not want to be looked at askance" (91). "Germans are somehow set apart, they are treated differently. When I was in school, in the eighth-grade class, I was such a fool then, I wished only to be a Russian, then I would be like all the others" (96). "Yes, there are quite a few Germans who want to be thought of as Russians . . . because of the television programs, they always show the Germans to be so much more stupid than the Russians" (98).

Career and better living conditions "Yes, in order to live better some change passports, some even change their last names" (168). "[It is done by] those who want to get ahead and are hindered by their nationality—specialists, artists, or scholars" (166).

When asked about groups other than the Soviet Germans, quite

34

a few respondents also knew cases of nationality change. The examples cited most frequently were those of Ukrainians and Belorussians living outside of their own republics, as well as Jews and Poles; some mention was also made of Mordvinians and Udmurts. One respondent had lived in a border area of Georgia where many Azeri Turks had claimed Georgian nationality in order to get ahead better. For Kazakhs and Kirghiz the reply was negative, while in the case of Estonians one respondent thought that some might claim Russian nationality, and another denied it saying, "the Estonians do not turn themselves into Russians, they stick firmly to their own [nationality]" (171). There was an intriguing remark about gypsies: "wherever they are born, that is the nationality they claim: Moldavian in Moldavia, Ukrainian in the Ukraine, and Kazakh in Kazakhstan" (84). Generally one notes that the persons most likely to change their nationality have an extraterritorial status or belong to the smaller ethnic groups and peoples. Since the official nationality is most frequently changed to Russian, the tendency is also stronger among those with stronger cultural affinities with the Russians.

The difficulty of determining the nationality of children from ethnically mixed families is another example that the "nationality" category in the Soviet census is by no means unproblematic. Interethnic marriages amount to approximately 15 percent of all marriages in the USSR (see Chapter 6). Accordingly the number of children of mixed parentage is considerable, and since children constitute a substantial part of the persons accounted for in the census, one should discuss how their nationality is determined.

As noted above, procedures matter. Officially parents were to state the nationality of their children, and "only in families where father and mother belong to different nationalities and the parents themselves have difficulty in determining the nationality of the children is preference to be given to the nationality of the mother."[23] This sounds clear enough, but it ignores the role of coincidence and subjectivity since, in practice, the decision on what to say about the nationality of children may be made by just one parent, whichever happens to be present at the time of the census-taker's visit. The parent has a variety of choices: he may claim all the children to be of his—or the spouse's—nationality, or the children may be "divided up" between the parents (such as in one case where all the girls had been registered with the mother's last name and nationality, and all boys with the father's

35

last name and nationality), or the children may be ascribed a nationality different from that of either parent. As our interviews suggest, all these variations occur, although the first appears to be the most frequent.

If all children are registered with the nationality of one of the parents, what is it that determines a particular choice? It is curious that the Soviet census authorities have given preference to the mother in the case of undecided nationality since one frequently encounters a tradition of the father being decisive. This is most true for Muslim peoples, but an ethnological survey conducted in the Baltic republics also found that "often, in accordance with local tradition, children from mixed families are regarded as being of the same nationality as the father, even when the family does not speak his native tongue and the children do not know it."[24] Soviet studies of choices made by youngsters acquiring their first personal passport at the age of 16 show a pattern which probably also applies to the census. If one of the parents belongs to the nationality of the republic in which the youngster lives, he or she will most frequently choose that nationality. Otherwise, if one of the parents is Russian, the youngster usually chooses the Russian nationality.[25] Thus the groups most likely to lose nationality members through the process of intermarriage are those living outside their own republics, the small peoples without republic status, and the extraterritorial groups such as Germans, Jews, Poles, and Koreans; or in the terminology outlined in the Introduction, the secondary ethnic groups.

Having raised the problem of the complexity of the nationality category in the Soviet census and in passport regulations, one may well ask about the scope of the problem. A rough numerical measure is provided by the data on intermarriage which suggest that approximately 15 percent of Soviet families face a specific problem, but this number increases if one adds members of monoethnic families from groups who for one reason or other do not want to identify with a particular national group. Why?

Ethnic Self-Identification

One way of studying the determinants of ethnic self-identification is to analyze data on the choice of nationality by children from mixed families. The nationality of children under the age of

16 is registered according to a statement of the parents,[26] but at the moment of receiving their first personal passport the young-sters can choose between either parent's nationality. The data on these choices as registered by ZAGS (Registry Office) are unavail-able to Western scholars directly, but reports of a number of Soviet ethnosociologists who have used them clarify some major points.[27] These data also provide a poignant illustration for one of the main themes of our study, namely, that where ethnic relations and processes are concerned, one finds considerable regional and group-related differences in the USSR.

In light of numerous Soviet statements according to which "the consolidation of nations and changes in ethnic self-consciousness taking place in our country are parts of a new demographic process, that forming a new historical commu-nity—the Soviet people,"[28] it is ironic that the rules for filling out the passport form specify that the choice of nationality is limited to the nationalities of the parents—choosing a third ethnic designation or simply a "Soviet" nationality is not allowed. There are indications that in spite of the rules, some juveniles choose a nationality other than that of either parent. Apparently this most frequently occurs in the case of children of two non-local and non-Russian parents, and typically Russian is the nationality chosen.[29]

Such exceptional cases aside, the choice of official nationality by teenagers from ethnically mixed families occurs in several patterns, which can be subsumed under: (1) instances when the choice of Russian nationality predominates, and (2) instances when a territorially based non-Russian nationality tends to dominate; although there may be exceptions, the available data suggest that there is no third case of a non-Russian extraterri-torial nationality "gaining" through intermarriage:

(1)   The instances where the Russian nationality is predomin-antly chosen by the second generation in ethnically mixed families are, in order of intensity of dominance:

   (a)   when a family consists of one Russian parent and a non-Russian parent who is not of the indigenous nationality. As a comparison of the last four rows of Table 1.2 indicates, the Russian nationality will be chosen somewhat less frequently if the non-Russian parent is Ukrainian, but even then the range of choice is between 64 and 90 percent pro-Russian;[30]

Table 1.2 Choice of Passport Nationality by Teenagers from Ethnically Mixed Families

Nationality of parents, 1,2	Percentage of 16 year-olds choosing nationality of one or other parent, by location										
	Kiev (Ukraine)	Minsk (Belo-russia)	Kishinev (Moldavia)	Vilnius (Lithu-ania)	Riga (Latvia)	Tallinn (Estonia)	Ashk-habad (Turk-menia)	Kazan (Tatar ASSR)	Chebok-sary (Chuvash ASSR)	Saransk (Mordvin ASSR)	
1 Local	43.7	24.2	40.3	52.2	57.0	62.0	94.0	33.4	2.2	18.7	100%
2 Russian	56.3	65.8	59.7	47.8	43.0	38.0	6.0	66.6	97.8	81.3	
1 Local	89.0	85.0	65.6	80.0	75.0	n.a.	87.5	74.0	36.0	56.0	100%
2 Other	11.0	15.0	34.4	20.0	25.0	—	12.5	26.0	64.0	44.0	
1 Russian	—	77.0	75.6	64.0	74.7	66.0	66.5	81.0	86.4	89.8	100%
2 Ukrai-nian	—	23.0	24.4	36.0	25.3	34.0	33.5	19.0	13.6	10.2	
1 Russian	91.7	93.0	74.5	81.0	83.0	90.0	62.2	90.0	93.3	90.0	100%
2 Other	8.3	7.0	25.5	19.0	17.0	10.0	37.8	10.0	6.7	10.0	

Note: The data cover the period 1960–9; for data listing the incidence of each variant of interethnic marriage see Table 6.3.
Source: L. N. Terent'eva, "Forming of ethnic self-consciousness in nationally mixed families in the USSR," in Sociological Studies: Ethnic Aspects, Papers presented at the Eighth World Congress of Sociology, Toronto, Canada (Moscow 1974), p. 45.

    (b)   when a family consists of one Russian parent and one indigenous parent of an ASSR nationality located within the RSFSR. The data in Table 1.2 again suggest that the tendency for this choice is relatively strong; this is also supported by other Soviet surveys;[31]

    (c)   when a family consists of one Russian parent and one indigenous Ukrainian, Belorussian, or Moldavian parent, at least if they reside in the capital cities (cf. Table 1.2).

(2)   There are two main contexts in which a territorially based indigenous nationality gains through intermarriage:

    (a)   when one of the parents is of the local nationality and the other is of a nationality other than Russian. Except for the Chuvash, who seem to rank at the bottom of ethnic prestige scales, the local nationality gains in these situations, especially so within union republics (Table 1.2);

    (b)   the other context for local gains concerns marriages between locals and Russians in the Muslim, Trans-caucasian, and Baltic union republics. This is most obvious in the case of Turkmenistan (Table 1.2), and other Soviet data suggest that this pattern is typical for marriages between Russians and Muslims.[32] A similar, although less decisive dominance can be observed for the Baltic nations. As Table 1.2 indicates, more than one-half of the offspring choose the indigenous nationality. It is likely that the local nationalities dominate even more intensively than is evident from this table since it refers only to capital cities which tend to have the strongest Russian presence.

What influences the decision to choose the nationality of one or the other parent? The ethnic composition of the environment plays a role, and so apparently does the character of the non-Russian nation and its degree of differentiation from the Russians. Commenting on more than one-half of the affected teenagers in Kiev and Minsk choosing the nationality of their Russian parent rather than the Ukrainian or Belorussian one, L. N. Terent'eva, who has studied these questions closely, states:[33]

The ratios in the choice of nationality in the capitals of the Ukrainian and Belorussian SSR are evidently influenced by ethnic kinship of the three Slav peoples together with the predominant role of the Russian language as the basic language of communication.

In contrast, the Central Asians and Kazakhs are more distinctive in their language, religion, history, and physical appearance as well as by retaining a strong communal identity. Exogamy is rare, and if it occurs, the non-local spouse and the children tend to be "nativized" (see Chapter 7).

Another motive in nationality choice is the social and economic advantage to be gained. It can be advantageous to be Russian, but so can belonging to the indigenous nationality, especially in Central Asia and Kazakhstan (see Chapter 3). This was also pointed out by a Soviet sociologist trying to explain why youngsters from mixed Kazakh/Russian and Kazakh/Tatar families living in Northern Kazakhstan preferred the Kazakh nationality by 67 to 90 percent. He notes:[34]

> Probably this phenomenon can be explained by the influence of "their own" national environment and the nationality politics which are conducted in the USSR. It is quite understandable that the equalization of different cultural and economic levels is inevitably linked to certain aid and advantages for the members of the indigenous nationality.

The Soviet Union is not the only place where the choice of official ethnic identity has been affected by calculations of socioeconomic advantage, the same has been observed in other multiethnic states.[35] Comparative studies have also shown that children of mixed parentage almost invariably identify with the dominant group in a society,[36] which makes such choices a good measure of dominance.

In sum, one finds that while there are regions in the Soviet Union—mostly the entire RSFSR, some areas of the Ukraine, Belorussia, and Moldavia—in which the Russian nationality predominates in forming the ethnic self-consciousness of children from mixed families, territorially based nationalities are dominant in other instances. This is most true for Central Asia and Kazakhstan, presumably for the Caucasus, and to a lesser extent the Baltic republics. Thus statements of Soviet ideologues claiming that the influence of the Russian nationality is progressing all over the USSR are misleading. Not only are there regional differences of major proportions, there are contexts in which the reverse pattern holds true, that is, there are whole regions and subregions where the local nationalities assert their ethnic dominance.

The range of differential ethnic attractiveness—or dominance, however one wants to call it—covers just about the entire spectrum of theoretical possibility. There is Ashkhabad where 94 percent of children with one Russian and one local parent chose the local nationality, and there are cases at the other extreme such as Saransk where 98 percent of the children of mixed parentage chose Russian as their official nationality (Table 1.2). It is much more desirable to be a Russian in the Chuvash ASSR (a subunit of the RSFSR) than to be a Russian in Turkmenia. Conversely, being of the local nationality is much more highly prized in the Turkmen SSR than it is in the Chuvash ASSR. The differential "value" of national identities is related to the overall prestige of nations, cultural and religious affinity, and socioeconomic and political advantage.

Conclusions

Ethnic identification is the precondition for ethnic differentiation in personal and social relations, by bureaucracies, or in statistical accounts. Knowing how it takes place thus is the first crucial step toward understanding ethnic relations in a society. This is not easy. There is a tradition of tortuous academic debates about what constitutes a nation or an ethnic group, resulting in alternative listings of objective and subjective traits. Our approach is to avoid this theoretical discussion and concentrate on presenting empirical data about the society under study.

Our first conclusion is that there are several dimensions to ethnic identity and identification. The most basic one is the traditional categorization of ethnic groups according to language, religion, historical background, settlement area, and similar descriptive factors. Another approach is to focus on the informal perceptions people have of others. This cognitive and subjective identification is similar to ethnic self-identification, but the latter is more elusive to empirical study. We used two sets of data to obtain a preliminary sense of the process and patterns of self-identification, namely, self-identification of nationality in the Soviet census and the self-identification of children from mixed families. The choices made also provide a first indication of the political value assigned to having one or the other official ethnic identity. The official registration of nationality in passports and other documents and its consequences constitutes one of the more interesting and, at the same time, underexplored facets of Soviet ethnic processes and politics.

In the past most studies of Soviet nationalities have relied on the traditional approach of identifying ethnic groups according to objective differences in language, religion, and history. We add a discussion of administrative ethnic identification and subjective perceptions of self and others.

As to the perception of others, the most direct outward characteristics playing a role are language, physical appearance, and behavior. Other criteria become evident in the terms used to refer to various groupings; thus regional origin is suggested by the use of terms such as "Central Asian," "Caucasian," or "European," and traditional religious background plays an obvious role in designations such as "Muslims." The latter also implies a certain cultural commonality, as do terms such as "Slavs" and "Balts." As is evident from our respondents, racially based categorizations such as "blacks" and "whites," also are used. This list of terms as well as the general literature on ethnic identification indicate that ethnic categories denote overlapping and sometimes alternative ascriptions for one individual such as European, Christian, Moldavian. Furthermore, "a person may have a different identification pattern for each ethnic identity which he may ascribe to himself or to others, and each ascription alternative may have a different salience at different moments."[37] This brings us back to the point that ethnic identity embraces multiple levels and is heavily contextual.[38] This differential significance of ethnicity is one of the themes of the next chapters.

Another major theme to be pursued concerns the implications of the official administrative registration of ethnic identity in personal documents. Politically it is the most interesting form of ethnic identification. It is a formal recognition of the dual identity of Soviet subjects as citizens and nationality group members. Official practice prevents legal "assimilation" into another ethnic group; the ethnic identity of parents is inherited by their children. Even children with mixed parentage can only opt for one of the parents' ethnic identities. What is the political rationale of this policy which appears to be in conflict with the official Soviet pronouncements about the gradual emergence of "a new historical community—the Soviet people" and thus imply that sooner or later all subjects will be solely "Soviets"?

In seeking an answer we are breaking new ground, since with the exception of Victor Zaslavsky, no Western or Soviet analyst has discussed this question. It is one of those issues that is greatly underreported in Soviet publications and for the understanding of which the contributions made by former Soviet subjects has been crucial. The official registration of passport nationality represents a cornerstone of the political management of ethnic processes.[39] It is both the precondition and the means for the differential treatment of individuals and groups. In practice, this can mean many things, including "affirmative action" for formerly disadvantaged groups. As has been amply demonstrated in other societies, the debate about the justice or political wisdom of such policies is complex, and we shall therefore return to it in the course of the next chapters which will provide more context for assessing this complexity.

At this time it should, however, be pointed out that the perspective taken by participants in Soviet politics depends on their identity as either primary or secondary ethnic group members. Primary ethnic group members tend to favor or be neutral about official ethnic categorization and its consequences. In contrast, the members of dispersed and extraterritorial groups tend to reject it. This is indirectly illustrated by the choices made by children with mixed parentage; whenever a parent belonged to a primary nationality, his or her ethnic identity is favored by the youngster making his choice for life. It is more attractive and valuable to be a member of a primary rather than a secondary nationality in the USSR.

This is also partly illustrated by our discussion of the way in which nationality is identified in the Soviet census-taking process. It relies on self-identification which according to all indications is quite straightforward for the primary nationalities. Certain ambiguities arise, however, in the case of members of secondary ethnic groups who more easily re-identify and typically choose the identity of Russians or another primary nationality. One may add that in the perception of informal observers the ethnic identity of these people will be obfuscated as well. Thus both the census results and informal ethnic categorization tend to favor the larger primary ethnic groups, while the formal passport identification perpetuates the official identification of all groups, including the smaller secondary ones.

In spite of these exceptional cases when ethnic re-identification or obfuscation occurs, and in spite of some geographic and situational variance, the primary conclusion of this chapter is that ethnic identification is a pervasive reality in the Soviet Union. It occurs informally in everyday life, people are asked about it both by social partners and by bureaucrats, and it is formally fixed in their documents. Ethnic identification is ubiquitous and as such provides the basis for the formal and informal ethnic structuring of personal, social, and political relations in the USSR.

Notes: Chapter 1

1 Linguistic ambiguity adds to the confusion in English-speaking countries, since "nationality" in English refers to both "a legal relationship involving allegiance on the part of an individual and protection on the part of a state" as well as "a people having a common origin, tradition, and language and capable of forming or actually constituting a nation state": *Webster's New Collegiate Dictionary*, 1977.

2 See also Tamotsu Shibutani and Kian M. Kwan, *Ethnic Stratification: A Comparative Approach* (New York: Macmillan, 1965), p. 48.

3 The literature describing the historical and cultural identity of the various minority nations is broad. For a good overview see Zev Katz, Rosemarie Rogers, and Frederic Harned (eds.), *Handbook of Major Soviet Nationalities* (New York: The Free Press, 1975); Viktor Ivanovich Kozlov, *Natsional'nosti SSSR* (Moscow: Statistika, 1975); and S. A. Kovalev and N. Ia. Koval'skaia, *Geografiia naseleniia SSSR* (Moscow: Izdatel'stvo Moskovskogo universiteta, 1980), pp. 135–147; cf. also Tables A.1 and A.2, pp. 230, 231.

4 Alexandre A. Bennigsen and S. Enders Wimbush, *Muslim National Communism in the Soviet Union* (Chicago: University of Chicago Press, 1979). Contemporary Soviet sources also occasionally refer to the "Muslim peoples" of the USSR: T. S. Saidbaev, *Islam i obshchestvo* (Moscow: Nauka, 1978), p. 194.

5 G. V. Starovoitova, "K issledovaniiu etnopsikhologii gorodskikh zhitelei," *Sovetskaia etnografiia*, 1976, no. 3, p. 47. The author also cites a number of other Soviet surveys which have asked the same question; it was not possible to check these, since they include rarely accessible sources such as doctoral dissertations: cf. ibid., no. 7.

6 ibid., p. 47. Another Soviet survey conducted with Tatars of Western Siberia posed a slightly different question, with slightly different results. The question used was "in what way do you see yourself distinctive from people of another nationality?" Language was again mentioned most frequently, followed by traditions and customs, and religion. The author implies that Russians were interpreted to be the "other nationality" by most respondents: N. A. Tomilov, *Sovremennye etnicheskie protsessy sredi sibirskikh tatar* (Tomsk: University of Tomsk Press, 1978), pp. 118–19.

7 The number in parentheses identifies each respondent in the research files; quotes indicate verbatim replies translated from German or Russian.

8 International Communication Agency, Office of Research and Evaluation, *Agriculture: USA Exhibit*, Research Report R-26-78, p. 6. This report deserves additional quoting, "The question of personal documents in America, or the lack thereof, fascinated the visitors. Most did not know that Americans have no standardized internal passport or any other universal identification document, but rely instead on drivers' licenses, work I.D. cards, student cards, credit cards, and other forms of identification. Visitors reacted variously to this information. People often had the notion that the guides were all American citizens as they were all Soviets, but American 'nationality' had

to be something different. They imagined that in the U.S., as in the Soviet Union, one's nationality was officially determined and written down somewhere. They were often surprised to find out that this is not the case." ibid., p. 28.

This example illustrates how people project their own experience to others—that is, the Soviets assume that "nationality" is as relevant to Americans as it is to them—and they also assume that it is a category in official personal documents in the USA; and vice versa, many Americans project their experience of ethnicity to the USSR.

9   In large urban centers of the Tatar ASSR about one-fifth of the respondents said that they paid no attention to nationality; this was true for one-sixth of the overall sample: Starovoitova, "Etnopsikhologii," pp. 47–9.

10 Mikhail Cheifets, "National antagonism in Kazakhstan," Radio Liberty Background Report 12/80, p. 2.

11 See also A. A. Susokolov, and A. P. Novitskaia, "Etnicheskaia i sotsial'no-professional'naia gomogennost' brakov (po materialam otdela ZAGS Kishineva v poslevoennyi period)," *Sovetskaia etnografiia*, 1981, no. 6, p. 18.

12 The "locals" frequently also include subgroups which are ethnically distinctive but are rarely identified as such by "the man in the street."

13 Some locations, such as the capital cities, are much more desirable places to live in than others, but people need official permits to move away from a former place of residence and for taking up a new domicile. This mechanism of bureaucratic control of the population by the Soviet state is greatly underexplored; in the case of the Soviet Germans our interviews indicate that a change of residence became increasingly difficult in the 1970s. Thus, beginning with 1972–3, officials refused to register them in the Baltic republics, sometimes alluding to an unpublished decree. The respondents also stated that it is very difficult to get around the official registration hurdles, although some people manage through bribes or by evasion. For a few stipulations of the registration system see "On adoption of the statute on the passport system in the USSR," *Soviet Law and Government*, vol. 14, no. 3, (Winter 1975–6), p. 71.

14 *Izvestiia*, 30 September 1982; trans. in *Current Digest of the Soviet Press* (*CDSP*), vol. 33, no. 39, p. 20.

15 *Pravda*, 25 December 1974, p. 1.

16 Information volunteered by a number of Soviet German respondents who suggested that the non-Russian republic nationalities regard the current practice as a safeguard of their rights.

17 L. I. Maksimov, "Kak byt' s natsional'nostiu Andreiki?" *Literaturnaia gazeta*, 15 August 1973. See also *Turkmenskaia iskra*, 3 September 1977 and Victor Zaslavsky and Yuri Luryi, "The passport system in the USSR and changes in Soviet society," *Soviet Union/Union Sovietique*, vol. 6, pt. 2 (1979), p. 149.

18 "On adoption of the statute . . .," p. 70.

19 The inaccuracies introduced probably are minor in most cases, but analysts should at least be aware of them. See Chapter 3 for references to studies of ethnic trends which are based on the two types of statistics.

20 Tsentral'noe Statisticheskoe Upravlenie pri Sovete Ministrov SSR, *Vsesoiuznaia perepis' naseleniia—vsenarodnoe delo* (Moscow, 1978), pp. 45–51.

21 Several respondents stated that it was possible to do so by merely filing an application with ZAGS (Registry Office). Others emphasized that either a husband or wife could change their nationality at the time of a marriage ceremony. Still others thought that it was only possible illegally, through bribes. Two mentions were made of Germans who had at some time assumed Russian nationality and later fought prolonged court battles to regain their German nationality.

22 Fear of negative consequences was also cited by a Soviet ethnographic team which found that nearly one-half of the Germans in Transcarpathia had not admitted to being German in the census of 1959: I. N. Grozdova, and T. D. Filimonova, "Vengry i nemtsy sovetskogo Zakarpat'ia (po materialiam polevykh issledovanii)," *Sovetskaia etnografiia*, 1970, no. 1, pp. 138–9.

23 *Perepis' naseleniia*, p. 51.

24 O. A. Gantskaya and L. N. Terent'eva, "Etnograficheskie issledovaniia natsional'nykh protsessov v Pribaltike," *Sovetskaia etnografiia*, 1965, no. 5, p. 18.

25 For a more detailed discussion and sources see following pages.

26 L. N. Terent'eva, "Forming of ethnic self-consciousness in nationally mixed families in the USSR," in *Sociological Studies: Ethnic Aspects* (Moscow: Papers presented at the Eighth World Congress of Sociology, Toronto, Canada, 1974), p. 35, states that, in cases of disagreement between the parents, the baby is registered after the nationality of its mother, but this practice may differ regionally since another Soviet source mentions that there are cases where within the same family some children are identified by their father's nationality and others by their mother's. See E. P. Busygin and N. V. Zorin, "Interethnic families in the national republics in the middle reaches of the Volga," in Regina E. Holloman and Sergei A. Arutiunov (eds.), *Perspectives on Ethnicity* (Paris: Mouton, 1978), p. 170.

27 For the first, and pathbreaking, study see L. N. Terent'eva, "Opredelenie svoei natsional'noi prinadlezhnosti podrostkami v natsional'no-smeshannykh sem'iakh," *Sovetskaia etnografiia*, 1969, no. 3, pp. 20–30.

28 Terent'eva, "Forming of ethnic self-consciousness," p. 34.

29 Busygin and Zorin, "Interethnic families," p. 170; and Yu. A. Evstigneev, "Interethnic marriages in some cities of Northern Kazakhstan," *Soviet Sociology*, vol. 13, no. 3 (1974–5), pp. 11–13.

30 A. P. Egurnev, "Mezhnatsional'nye braki i ikh rol' v sblizhenii natsii i narodnostei SSSR," *Nauchnyi kommunizm*, 1973, no. 4, p. 33, cites a sample of children from Russo-Ukrainian marriages in Northern Kazakhstan (Tselinograd and Petropavlosk) where the Russian nationality was chosen in 91 percent of the cases. The percentage was higher (93–100 percent) in the case of Russo-Belorussian families, and lower (29 percent in Petropavlosk and 42 percent in Tselinograd) in Russo-Tatar families.

31 See, for example, N. A. Tomilov, "Sovremennye etnicheskie protsessy u tatar gorodov Zapadnoi Sibiri," *Sovetskaia etnografiia*, 1972, no. 6; trans. in *Soviet Sociology*, vol. 18, no. 2 (1979), p. 32.

32 Surveys conducted in Northern Kazakhstan show that children from mixed Kazakh–Russian families predominantly chose the Kazakh nationality: 96 percent in Balianaulsk raion, 87 percent in Erinakovsk raion, 67 percent in Petropavlovsk, and 90 percent in Tselinograd. See A. B. Kalyshev, "K voprosu ob opredelenii natsional'noi prinadlezhnosti molodezhi v mezhnatsional'nykh sem'iakh," *Izvestiia Akademii nauk Kazakhskoi SSR, Seriia obshchestvennykh nauk*, 1982, no. 3, p. 81; and Egurnev, "Mezhnatsional'nye braki," p. 34. On Estonia see also Jaan Pennar, "The nationality of the children of mixed marriages in Tallin," *Radio Liberty Research Bulletin*, RL 120/83, 16 March 1983.

33 Terent'eva, "Forming of ethnic self-consciousness," p. 39.

34 Egurnev, "Mezhnatsional'nye braki," p. 34.

35 Joseph Bram, "Change and choice in ethnic identification," *Transactions of the New York Academy of Sciences*, 2d ser. vol. 28, no. 2 (December 1965), p. 247.

36 Shibutani and Kwan, *Ethnic Stratification*, p. 204.

37 Daniel Glaser, "Dynamics of ethnic identification," *American Sociological Review*, vol. 23 (February 1958), p. 31.
38 See Introduction; and Donald L. Horowitz, "Ethnic identity," in Nathan Glazer and Daniel P. Moynihan (eds.), *Ethnicity: Theory and Experience* (Cambridge, Mass.: Harvard University Press, 1975), p. 118.
39 cf. Victor Zaslavsky, *The Neo-Stalinist State: Class, Ethnicity and Consensus in Soviet Society* (Armonk, NY: Sharpe, 1982), p. 93.

2

The Ethnic Climate in Non-Russian Republics

The goal of this chapter is to characterize the general ethnic climate in the non-Russian union republics of the USSR. Later we shall examine ethnic interrelationships by separate spheres of life since they constitute the building-blocks for understanding the whole structure of ethnic relations. But there are a number of more general and all-encompassing dimensions to the issues which permeate all spheres of life and, at the same time, constitute a topic on their own since we are dealing with a separate level of analysis. This is the union republic level of relationships between the two basic population groups found in every non-Russian republic, namely, the indigenous population and the Russians.

Intrarepublic ethnic relations are here defined as the relations between the respective titular nationality of each non-Russian union republic and the local Russians. Although members of other ethnic groups also live in the non-Russian union republics, they will be disregarded in the ensuing discussion since the titular nationalities and the Russians represent the numerically and politically most important populations. If one wants to understand the core problems of ethnic politics in the Soviet Union, it is necessary to investigate the quality of overall relationships between the republic nationals and the Russians. One also has to study the perceptions they hold of each other in a macrocontext.

In this and the following chapter the theoretical points of departure are the conflict model of society as outlined by macro-sociologists such as Dahrendorf, Coser, and others. It conceptualizes relations between subgroups in society as being polarized both in the sense of a clash of interests over scarce values as well as "zero-sum" competitive situations. Another facet of this model is that it highlights the contrasting evaluations and perceptions of the conflicting groups, rejecting the notion that there is only one point of view unaffected by contrasting interest or values. For us this means that ethnic relations are perceived as revolving around conflicting claims about the dominance of cultural, economic, and political values.[1]

The first part of this chapter will clarify the content of the conflict of interests between the two basic population groups in the non-Russian union republics. It is three-dimensional and relates to politics, socioeconomic distribution, and culture. We shall choose one major issue to illustrate each of these dimensions. The issue of colonization by settlers from other republics is taken as the example for political territorial controversy and power in the decision-making process. Access to higher education for its part is a good focus for the discussion of socioeconomic competition, while the issue of language use and dominance in the republics will be taken as the proxy for the entire cluster of cultural rivalry and conflict over decision-making in this area.

Our interviews as well as other sources indicate that stereotypes and sociopsychological barriers influence the way nationalities are named and perceived. What is more, the relations between the two primary populations in non-Russian republics revolve around a clash of identities, perspectives, and interests. The ethnic, cultural, and historical identity of the titular republic nations culminates in a political–territorial quest for dominance in their "own country." They have a strong notion of being the proprietors of their respective republics and of being naturally entitled to a dominant cultural, economic, social, and political role within their native environment. To the degree that the Russians living in the republics represent challenges to this claim they are resented and verbally attacked, especially in anonymous group contacts. This is most typically the case during daily chance encounters in the streets, in shops, or on the bus, as well as at mass events such as sports contests, cultural spectacles, and even May Day demonstrations. While these expressions of popular attitudes are significant in themselves as indicators of very basic and usually latent relationships, they also have an indirect effect on all other subdimensions of ethnic interactions, and it is this all-encompassing influence that the term "ethnic climate" hopes to denote.[2]

While later chapters discuss ethnic relations between individuals or groups within circumscribed social or institutional settings, the focus of this and the next chapter will be on the macrolevel relationships between the two basic population groups found in every non-Russian republic—the indigenous people and the Russians—as well as on the complementary issue of center–periphery relations. One could also say that while later our approach to ethnicity will be more sociological—discussing family and communal relationships, work, and social institutions—here we deal with more directly political topics such as the territorial and federal–political content of ethnic identity and claims, the continuing impact of history, issues in linguistic and cultural politics, and the distribution of both prestige and political and economic power.

The issues discussed in this and the following chapter are closely linked. Here we first outline the precept of territorial and settlement rights, then provide two short case studies of ethnic competition as it applies to language use and access to higher education. We conclude by discussing the problems of accurately measuring the quality of macrolevel ethnic relations and, at the same time, venture our own synopsis. Chapter 3 will follow up by discussing contemporary trends in nationality power in the republics and what they suggest for the future development of nationality relations.

The Territorial–Political Factor

Among the conflicting interests between the two dominant population groups in the non-Russian republics the first aspect to be dealt with is the political impact of the territorial and historical identity of the indigenous nations. The fourteen major non-Russian nations which lend their names to their respective union republics live in their traditional homelands with which they have strong bonds. One expression of this attachment is their reluctance to migrate. The great majority of individuals belonging to a republic nationality continue to live in their titular republics (for exact data see Table A.3, p. 232). This territorial–demographic rooting of the major nationalities is the primary determinant of ethnic relations in the USSR since it causes the major type of ethnic interaction to take place within the individual union republics and between the indigenous population and the local Russian population, most of which has migrated to the borderlands in the relatively recent past.[3] The contemporary multinationalism of the Soviet Union reflects the colonial expansion of Russia into geographically contiguous regions during the past few centuries.

The territorial rooting also has major consequences for the quality of ethnic relations since it sets a baseline for perceptions and evaluations. Thus the republic nations perceive their respective republics as their very own homeland with which they identify emotionally, in which they have certain proprietory rights, and within which other population groups basically are foreigners. For the Baltic nations this perception is intensified by the recent political history of having experienced independent and internationally recognized states which were forcibly occupied by the Red Army in 1940. In their case the Russian presence is not only ethnically and culturally alien, but politically oppressive as well. A similar political connotation permeates ethnic relations in other areas such as the western Ukraine. The comparative literature on ethnic integration pinpoints historical memories of a non-voluntary union as a major impediment to long-term integrative success,[4] and even though Soviet historiography and children's school history lessons tell a different story, at least part of this historical memory is bound to be passed on from generation to generation.

While historical memories of the process of union with the tsarist empire and the USSR play a role in the integration of the periphery with the center, they also have an impact on intra-republic ethnic relations in the sense that the Russians living in the republics are perceived as representatives of the center and as the personification of the center's attempt to establish unbreakable cultural, economic, and political ties with the republics. Consequently the physical presence of a significant number of Russians in the non-Russian republics becomes both the concrete and symbolic focus of nationality relations. Conflict over the settlement of Russians—as well as other non-locals, who generally are less significant numerically and politically—has thus been a recurring phenomenon from the beginning of Russian and Soviet rule.[5] It is especially significant that the issue has come up every time that a "national communist" group has emerged in any of the non-Russian republics. As early as the 1920s Muslim communists opposed the colonization of their lands by Russian and Ukrainian settlers. Thus the first Kazakh party leaders threatened to stop Russian colonization by sending the colonists back to Russia. In 1927 they further tried to carry out

51

a land reform at the expense of the European settlers and had to be stopped by intervention from the center. The same problem of colonization emerged as an issue in the Caucasus. There were two purges of "national communists" in Azerbaijan between 1923 and 1925 after local leaders had demanded an end to Russian colonization and the replacement of non-Turks by Turkic workers.[6]

In the postwar period concern about the effects of mass in-migration of Russians and other Slavs has been openly voiced by local communist party (CP) leaders in Kazakhstan and Latvia, the two republics whose ethnic identity has been most endangered by migration. Thus the First Secretary of the CP of Kazakhstan took an "obstructionist" attitude toward Khrushchev's Virgin Lands program developed in 1954 since "he was afraid the expansion of cultivation would necessarily mean the influx of [non-Kazakh farmers] into his Republic."[7] The central authorities reacted by replacing him and his second in command, also a Kazakh, by two Russians, one of them Leonid Brezhnev. In 1959 Berklāvs, the Deputy Minister of the Latvian SSR, and other Latvian officials and party members were similarly purged for having advocated local interests too strongly. One of the accusations against them was that:[8]

out of false fear that the Latvian Republic could lose her national character, some comrades tried to artificially hinder the objectively determined process of population resettlement. In their speeches, they repeatedly asserted that one could, for example, not allow the mechanical growth of the population of Riga even by one person.

More recently a samizdat protest letter by seventeen Latvian communists smuggled to the West in 1972 denounced various pressures of Russification in Latvia, pinpointing the large-scale influx of Russians as one of the main problems.[9]

On a popular level our interviews with Soviet Germans—especially those who have lived in Kazakhstan or Central Asia—indicate that "why don't you go back to your Russia?" is one of the most frequently heard verbal attacks natives use in conflict situations with local Russians. Slogans such as "Russians out of Kazakhstan" are also said to appear on ballots cast in local elections (74). A mathematics student related how easily ethnic tensions erupted at Karaganda University which she attended in the late 1970s. Her most vivid experience of this occurred during the general student meeting officials had called to denounce her for wanting to emigrate. After several ritualized speeches, one Russian student ill-advisedly posed the rhetorical question "Where would we end up if everyone could get permission to emigrate? What would happen if I, for example, wanted to emigrate to America?" The Kazakh students in the audience spontaneously started shouting, "That would be great, just leave as early as possible." A general melee started up and the meeting ended in disarray with Kazakh students shouting at Russian students, and vice versa.

Respondents who have encountered such incidents emphasize that the locals frequently add the justification "this is our land" or "we are the masters of this land" to their demands. The Russians for their part react with consternation. There is a huge gap between the perception of the indigenous population who views the Russians as foreign inmigrants and colonizers and the perception of Russians who see their presence as fully justified and beneficial to the locals. Thus a respondent from Kazakhstan noted that "if a Kazakh says something, the Russians reply 'we have educated you, therefore be quiet'" (187). While the Russian perception of the Russians as *Kulturträger* and economic benefactors is most pronounced in the case of Kazakhstan and Central Asia, the role of "liberators" is emphasized in the case of the western republics, primarily the Baltic and the Ukraine. The comment of a respondent who had lived in Lithuania that "the Russians feel like liberators, feel rather proud" (123) is typical of this.

There is also an obvious gap in perceptions about proprietorship of the non-Russian borderlands. While even those nationals who accept the basic union with the USSR perceive their titular republic as being uniquely "theirs," the Russian population appears to hold a notion of historically given entitlement to these areas as a "natural" extension of their own homeland.[10] If they have any doubts at all, then it is only as a result of coming into contact with native claims. This is illustrated by replies to one of the questions posed to our Soviet German emigrant respondents, that is, whether they thought that the Russians feel at home in the respective non-Russian republic of residence. The great majority of respondents (70 percent) replied affirmatively, although there is some regional variation suggesting that this feeling is significantly less pronounced in Kazakhstan than, for example, in the Ukraine, Moldavia, or Belorussia (see Table 2.1). In those instances where it was thought that Russians did not feel at home

Table 2.1 *Perceptions of Russians "Feeling at Home" in Non-Russian Republics*

	Kazakhstan, N = 62 (%)	By region Central Asia N = 34 (%)	Baltic, N = 34 (%)	Other,* N = 21 (%)
Yes	60	76	71	90
No	34	21	21	5
Don't know	6	3	8	5
Totals	100	100	100	100

* Includes Moldavia (N = 14), Ukraine (N = 5), Belorussia (N = 1), and Georgia (N = 1).

in a certain republic the typical elaboration provided was that it was due to the unfriendly behavior of the locals. Thus: "The Kazakhs don't want the Russians to live there and as a result the Russians feel as strangers" (45); "They remain immigrants . . . the Latvians make jokes and the Russians realize that they aren't the local population, frequently one has to know Latvian to get along" (119); "No they don't feel at home there, because the Kazakhs are black people and they don't fit together, the characters don't fit. The Kazakhs don't like the Russians" (188); "No, the Russians are under pressure . . . in the universities . . . and [the Kazakhs] won't let you pass when you're on a bus, and if one says something, there is a fight" (4).

Some respondents also indicated that this hostile behavior is increasing in Kazakhstan and Central Asia and that some Russians leave as a result (170, 69, 121). One Soviet German family had itself moved away from Kirghizia due to the increasing aggressiveness of the Kirghiz. The women in the family had become afraid to go out at night, fights including the use of knives had become commonplace among the men, and the Kirghiz were reported as saying "this is our land, we'll get you to move away yet" (87).

Those Russians who were born in the respective non-Russian republic or have lived there for a long time are considerably more likely to feel at home, especially if they know the local language. The republic nationals also tend to more easily accept this subgroup of Russians. Thus in the Baltic republics those Russians who have lived there since the period of independence or who know the local language are regarded as a special group of "local Russians" with whom relations are much better. To quote one respondent: "Those who know the language do feel at home, but the attitude toward immigrants is one of rejection" (60, from Latvia). This illustrates the multidimensionality of ethnicity and that differentiations are made not only according to ascriptive identity, but also by language, length of residence in a specific location, and so on.

As local Russians lose their foreign image by an extended period of residence as well as a degree of linguistic and cultural integration into the republic environment, their relations with republic nationals improve. L. M. Drobizheva, in her 1981 study summarizing the work of Soviet ethnosociologists, refers to the same finding when she says that Russians and others who have lived in a republic for a long time and know the language of the indigenous nationality feel more "comfortably" there.[11] Or in the words of another Soviet source, "the adaptation of the migrants is a major sociopsychological problem. In the course of ethnosociological studies it was found those migrants who master the language and norms of interaction of the indigenous nationalities acclimatize best of all."[12]

Findings like these suggest that it is possible to use the extent of local language knowledge by Russians and their length of residence in particular republics as partial quantitative indicators of the quality of ethnic relations in various regions. More will be said about the language aspect below. As concerns length of residence, more systematic research is needed to arrive at a precise measure of it for all regions of the USSR. To date analysts have paid little attention to this point, typically just citing the number and percentage of Russians present in a specific region, without any indication of possible turnover rates due to in- and outmigration. That this rate may be high is suggested by Rein Taagepera's research on the Baltic republics, in which he estimates that there are at least fifty departures for every 100 new arrivals.[13] Such a high turnover rate among the Russian population of non-Russian republics enhances the image of Russians as foreigners and is not conducive to community building.

Language Competition and Conflict

In societies such as the Soviet Union where multiethnicity largely overlaps with multilinguality, the quality of ethnic relations is closely linked to the congruence of language attitudes, the extent of reciprocal language knowledge, and the consequences of language policy for cultural and political interests as well as socioeconomic mobility. Again our discussion will focus on macrorelations within the non-Russian republics, although one should remember that language affects all contexts within which members of different Soviet nationalities meet.

Turning first to the issue of language attitudes, one finds that they are not only influenced by sociopsychological factors such as language loyalty and the prestige of certain languages, but most important, by the reality of language competition. In every non-Russian republic two languages compete with each other in a multitude of social contexts, and while the republic nationals typically prefer to use their native language, the Russian population as well as central representatives press for the use of Russian. In his analysis of language competition in a variety of multilingual states Stanley Lieberson argues that:[14]

Competition is inherent between languages in contact because the optimal conditions for their native speakers are normally incompatible. In the simplest setting in which there are two mother tongues in a population each speaker would like to use his tongue as widely and as frequently as possible. For those whose native tongue is A, this would occur if the entire population had A as its mother tongue or if native speakers of B all become bilingual. The same set of optimal conditions, however, hold for those with B as their mother tongue, except that the languages are reversed.

Nevertheless, although competition always carries the seed of conflict, it does not automatically lead to it, since much depends on the particulars of a situation.

As it stands, language conflict is most intense in the Transcaucasus and the Baltic region. One of our respondents suggested some of the reasons when saying that "the Caucasians, especially the Georgians, are proud nations, they have an old culture, their own alphabet, they are nationalists and proud of what's theirs" (144). Other sources similarly indicate that in the case of the Caucasian and the Baltic nations ethnic identity is inextricably linked to language and culture, whereas in the case of the Central Asians, identity is more affected by the Islamic way of life. Nevertheless, language may take on a more prominent role at a later stage of development in Central Asia. It has been noted that in this region modernization has meant both the spreading of the

Russian language among the indigenous populations as well as advancement and modernization of the native languages.[15] This implies that language competition is likely to increase with time.

Contemporary language conflict in the Caucasus, the Baltic region, and elsewhere, is due to a major gap in the perceptions of the two principal population groups about the extent to which one or the other language should be used in various contexts. The republic nationals feel that they have a right to have their native languages dominate all spheres of communication within "their republic" and that everybody living there should learn and use them. There are numerous reports of locals refusing to reply to strangers in the street or to customers in a shop or restaurant, if addressed in Russian. Typically the native will state that he does not understand Russian, or will say something to the effect that "in Georgia you have to speak Georgian" or "in Estonia you should speak Estonian."[16] Russians for their part feel insulted by such behavior and often respond with a hostile remark of their own since, in their perception, Russian should be accepted as the dominant means of communication unionwide.

With the exception of Switzerland, which has developed an elaborate system for the protection of language rights, this type of conflict occurs in other federal systems as well, and it is important to recall that much of ethnic strife is closely linked to language conflicts. This has been shown in cases such as that of the Habsburg Empire, but there is no lack of contemporary examples either, be they India or Belgium or Canada.[17] In the latter case there are striking similarities with the situation in the USSR, although the conflict over ethnic rights in Quebec is much more open than in any of the Soviet union republics. Since we have insufficient data on the USSR, considering the Quebec case is suggestive.

The gap between the perceptions of the Quebecois and those of the English-speaking population is very similar to the one found between the Russians and various republic nations. When the Quebec legislature in 1974 passed Bill 22 making French the official language of Quebec, this was welcomed by French-speakers, but the English-speaking population of Canada reacted with a storm of protest.[18] Opinion surveys further illustrate the wide gap of views on the language issue. Thus when asked whether English Canadians should speak French when in Quebec, English monolinguals agreed only to 26 percent, while bilinguals agreed in 46 percent of the cases, and French speakers in 88 percent of the cases. An even wider gap emerged on the question

Table 2.2   *Evaluation of the Need to Know a Second Language*

Purpose for which knowledge of the other nationality's language is important	Russians intelligentsia (%)	workers (%)	Estonians intelligentsia (%)	workers (%)
For the fulfillment of official duties	69	33	n.d.	n.d.
For the improvement of qualifications	34	20	n.d.	n.d.
For communal work	48	30	n.d.	n.d.
For interaction and contact with coworkers	70	64	90	76

Source: Iu. Arutiunian, and Iu. Kakhk, *Sotsiologicheskie ocherki o Sovetskoi Estonii*, Tallinn, Periodika, 1979, pp. 83–4.

of whether French Canadians are right in wanting to be served in French in public accommodations. While 97 percent of French Canadians said yes, only 50 percent of Canadian bilinguals and only 16 percent of the monolingual English-speakers thought so.[19] If a comparable survey were to be conducted in the USSR, results most likely would be similar.

Soviet surveys avoid politically sensitive questions such as the desirability of the preferential usage of one or the other language in non-Russian republics, but more neutral ethnolinguistic questions help in evaluating the role of language facility for the quality of ethnic relations. Thus a survey conducted in Estonia in the mid-1970s found that both Estonians and Russians thought that mastering the language of the other nationality was most important for better and closer interaction with coworkers. While there is some gap in the perceptions of the two nationalities, it is not major in this case, that is, while 76–90 percent of the Estonians stated that the knowledge of Russian was important for better association with coworkers, 64–70 percent of the Russians thought so in regard to facility in the Estonian language (see Table 2.2). This survey also indicates that Russian intellectuals in Estonia see knowing Estonian as more important than Russian workers, especially as it concerns their fulfillment of official functions. There also is a correlation between the respondents' own facility in the other language and their evaluation of its need, that is, those knowing the other language were most likely to see the need for it, while those not knowing it were least likely to say so.[20]

As later chapters will show, other Soviet ethnosociological surveys have found that language knowledge is associated with a more positive attitude toward other ethnic supervisors, co-workers, and marriage partners. Our interviews with Soviet German emigrants suggest the same. Since studies undertaken in Canada also indicate that knowledge of another nationality's language enhances the development of feelings of community with this other group,[21] measures of language facility can be used as partial indicators of ethnic attitudes, although caution is advisable since other factors such as numerical relationships, settlement patterns, and linguistic closeness also play a major role.

Nevertheless, if one takes the aggregate data on language knowledge as reported in the Soviet census statistics as an indicator of ethnic attitudes and interaction, one finds that the extent of integration is limited. This is especially true for the Russian population of the non-Russian republics most of which does not know the local languages. Lack of local language knowledge is most pronounced in the Central Asian republics, Kazakhstan, and Azerbaijan, where only 1–9 percent of Russians are fluent in the respective local language. The highest percentage is reported for Lithuania (37 percent), followed by the Ukraine and Belorussia (31 percent); while the latter rates might be explained by the closeness of the three Slavic languages, it is harder to explain the Lithuanian case. It may be related to length of residence. Overall there has been a slight increase in the extent of local language knowledge among Russians since the census of 1970 (cf. Table A.4, p. 233).

Soviet census statistics also show that a large segment of the non-Russian republic populations does not know Russian fluently. In the case of Estonia and the three Caucasian republics, as well as Tadjikistan, Turkmenistan and Kirghizia, the respective percentage rates are a low 24 to 35 percent. Among the nationals of Moldavia, Lithuania, Kazakhstan and Uzbekistan Russian language knowledge is in a median range of 50–53 percent and it is highest in the cases of Belorussia (79 percent), the Ukraine (63 percent), and Latvia (61 percent). As might be expected, a comparison to the data from the 1970 Census shows a gradual increase in the aggregate knowledge of Russian, with two interesting exceptions. In Uzbekistan knowledge of Russian is reported to have jumped from 13 percent in 1970 to 53 percent in 1979, and in Estonia official reports note a drop from 28 percent in 1970 to 24 percent in 1979 (see Table A.4, p. 233). While the extraordinariness of the Uzbek data is such that there is reason to doubt their accuracy, the Estonian case could be explained by mass resistance to the learning and use of Russian by Estonians as well as their deliberate underreporting of their facility of Russian to the census-takers. In both instances the basis for the phenomenon is attitudinal and reflects an ethnopolitical rejection of the Russian presence in Estonia. These data also provide a poignant illustration of the two-sidedness of the linkage between language knowledge and ethnic attitudes: the increased knowledge of another nationality's language not only enhances feelings of community, but the lack of the latter can also inhibit the learning of the language of the other nationality. This is supported by sociolinguistic studies which show that—given the same learning conditions—people with a positive attitude toward a language and its speakers learn it better than those without it.[22]

While the extent of bilingualism, language attitudes, and ethnic relations are closely linked to one another, so is language policy. An educational and state policy encouraging reciprocal bilingualism could go a long way in defusing language competition and conflict—as is demonstrated, for example, in Switzerland—but such an approach has surfaced only sporadically in the Soviet Union, most decidedly so in the 1920s. After some reversals in policy brought about in the 1930s, the most decisive changes occurred after the educational reform of 1958/9 and again since the mid-1970s. As is also analyzed in Chapter 4, the educational reform of 1958/9 involved the granting of parental choice in the type of school children would attend, which in practice implied an increase of non-Russian children enrolling in Russian-language schools. While this was interpreted as an attack on the native-language schooling of children of the local nationality,[23] a second facet of the proposal made it optional to study the local language as a subject in Russian-language schools, or the Russian language in native-language schools. Since in practice there was little likelihood of Russian-language learning being curtailed, this meant that the study of non-Russian languages by Russian and other children was put into jeopardy.

The non-Russians—including many members of the republic CPs—reacted with an unprecedented flood of criticism, most openly expressed by the leaders of Azerbaijan and Latvia. Thus V. T. Lācis, the chairman of the Council of Ministers of the

Latvian SSR, told a party activist meeting in Riga that the discontinuance of the compulsory study of both the local language and Russian would "hardly promote the strengthening of the friendship of peoples,"[24] and the then second secretary of the Latvian CP, A. Pelše, gave a speech at the 24 December session of the Supreme Soviet of the USSR, stating that the thesis had been widely discussed in Latvia and that "The workers of the republic, especially at parents' meetings, unanimously express the necessity to continue in our republic the teaching of both languages—the Latvian and the Russian."[25]

In spite of such expressions of popular will, the centrally initiated new educational policies were pushed through in the end. In Latvia and Azerbaijan this solution necessitated the purging of the local party and state leadership[26] which, in the Latvian case, had begun to raise additional linguistic demands such as that all residents of Latvia holding official positions should learn Latvian. The central interpretation of these demands is well summarized in Kholmogorov's study published one decade later:[27]

Great harm to the cause of linguistic convergence of the socialist nations is done by violation of the voluntary principle in study of languages, manifested in the compulsory study of any language of the peoples of the USSR. In 1959 the Party struck down a tendency evident in several union republics, expressed in the adoption of special decrees requiring everyone to learn some particular language within a stated period of time. Thus, the Seventh Plenum of the Central Committee of the Communist Party of Latvia condemned in 1959 errors of a nationalist nature expressed in the fact that the non-Latvian population of the republic was required to learn Latvian in a stated period of time.

As noted, the differential approaches to language policy reflect a basic perceptual gap between the local non-Russians and Russians, with the interests of the latter typically being safeguarded by the central authorities. In their view pressures for the study and use of the republic languages are an unjustified expression of nationalism, while the republic nations view the alternative stress on Russian as an unjustified expression of "Great Russian chauvinism."[28] This contrast of perceptions exists in other multinational federal states as well, and so does the underlying clash of principles. While the smaller nation typically claims the group right to safeguard its collective cultural identity, members of the majority nation and their representatives argue in terms of individual rights as well as the precedence of a unionwide collective identity.[29] In other words, this is a case where interests at the individual and central level clash with those of the intermediate republic level.

Taking into account the latter, it should come as no surprise that the non-Russian nationalities have not welcomed the new language policy, emphasizing Russian, inaugurated in the late 1970s. To date the best-known protests have occurred in Georgia, where thousands of demonstrators took to the streets in April 1978 to demand that the draft of their new republic constitution be revised to restore Georgian to its former status as the state language of the republic. Apparently recognizing the explosiveness of the issue, the authorities quickly conceded this point, making corresponding revisions in the draft constitutions of Armenia and Azerbaijan as well.[30] This incident has not remained isolated, however, and there have been numerous other accounts of language-based protests in Georgia as well as in other republics.[31] The Baltic and the Caucasian nations are most sensitive to any endangerment of their linguistic and cultural integrity. As a Soviet scholar has noted, the "linguistic atmosphere of inter-ethnic intercourse" is especially similar in the case of Georgia and Estonia.[32]

Last but by no means least, language policy is closely linked to the safeguarding of socioeconomic interests. This is clarified in various comparative ethnic studies,[33] but underemphasized by Soviet analysts for whom such a link is a major ideological embarrassment. In one exceptional case the Soviet ethnosociologist L. M. Drobizheva has outlined how the professional and career interests of non-Russian writers, linguists, historians, artists, and literary scholars are closely tied to the specific "national interests" (*sic*) of their people, including the scope of local language use.[34] Although she does not say so, the same holds true for intellectuals for whom Russian is a major medium of their work. To the extent that language policy promotes the usage of one or the other language it also advances the professional interests of those who have the best facility in that language, which typically are native-language speakers.

Language facility is also linked to social mobility. When republic nationals show concern over the progressive curtailment of the use of republic languages in local VUZy (Russian acronym for Higher Education Institutions), this is not just a cultural or political concern, but also one that is closely tied to the issue of educational access as well as the successful completion of studies. Many non-Russian college-age youths, especially those coming from rural areas, do not have a fluent command of the Russian language.[35] To the degree that Russian language facility plays a role in the competitive entrance examinations or as a language of instruction it constitutes a special educational access barrier for these youths. While changes in language policy represent one possible remedy, another one constitutes special arrangements for non-Russian students. As this type of policy is implemented new problems arise, however, and this is the topic to be discussed in the following section.

Ethnic Favoritism v. Discrimination: Access to Higher Education

In multiethnic states perceptions of ethnic favoritism or discrimination are among the most volatile political issues, and the Soviet Union is no exception. While there is cadre competition in many spheres, the question of access to higher education has increasingly come to the forefront of controversy and there is every reason to believe that the problem will accelerate in the future.

As in other developed societies, higher education represents one of the main pathways to social mobility and economic success and as a result competition for admission to the VUZy is fierce. Our data suggest that nationality plays a much larger role in the selection process than previously recognized, and that this has far-reaching consequences. Replies to the question "who do you think is most easily admitted to higher educational institutions" were among the most surprising in our entire Soviet German interview project. When the question was first formulated, it was anticipated that various criteria would be mentioned, but as it turned out most respondents pinpointed nationality as the one decisive factor. Usually the point was made directly, without much elaboration: "native cadre are preferred," or "each republic its own cadre," or "of course, every nation gives preference to its own people." Others provided details such as "the largest percentage is given to the Kirghiz . . . there is no doubt, there are fixed percentages [for ethnic groups]" (124, from Kirghizia), and sometimes included modifications such as "the people belonging to the respective republic nationality are admitted more easily to VUZy, but if somebody wants to study very much, he will also achieve his thing" (28, from Kazakhstan).

Table 2.3   *Criteria Mentioned as Facilitating Access to Higher Education*

Percentage of respondents mentioning	Region				
	Kazakh-stan, N = 66 (%)	Central Asia, N = 34 (%)	Baltic, N = 28 (%)	Other,* N = 18 (%)	RSFSR, N = 30 (%)
Nationality only	82	68	39	50	33
Nationality and other factors	7	12	4	11	17
Other factors	11	20	57	39	50
Totals	100	100	100	100	100

* Includes Moldavia (N = 12), Ukraine (N = 4), Belorussia (N = 1), and Georgia (N = 1).

Since the basic thrust of replies coincides, categorization is easy: there are those respondents who stress nationality as the decisive factor, those who mention both nationality and something else, and those who cite only other admissions criteria such as membership in the Komsomol, social background factors, *blat* (the use of influence), good grades, or work experience (Table 2.3 gives the summary data). As can be seen from the table, there are major differences between republics and regions, the two opposite ends of the spectrum being held by Kazakhstan and the Baltic republics. Chapter 3 will elaborate reasons for this such as the differential degree of ethnic assertiveness between the western and southeastern Soviet republics in the contemporary period. It is the predominant perception of our respondents that the preferential treatment of republic nationals is due to decisions and arrangements at the republic level.[36] While the origin of the policy certainly is important, it is more crucial to ask about its consequences and effect.

An indication is again provided by our respondents since a follow-up question about the reaction of Russians and other non-locals was posed to those who mentioned the role of ethnicity in admissions. The replies reveal strong resentments as well as feelings of helplessness. The typical reply was: "Of course, people are dissatisfied, but what can they do." Others explained how individuals try to accommodate the situation: "Everybody is angry, but nobody dares to say so openly ... If one doesn't get in, one either loses hope, or tries again in the next year ... or goes to work. Some go to Russia for studying" (71). The alternative of seeking an education elsewhere appears to be quite common: "The Russians now frequently move to Siberia for studying . . . Everybody runs where there are their own people" (178, from Kazakhstan).

Various explanations were given for the pervasive feeling of helplessness and frustration. Some point to apathy or systemic factors: "We have no rights to say anything" (84); "the Russians will suffer everything" (23) or "what is there for the Russians to say, if you talk too much you are likely to end up in jail" (21) being typical comments. Others feel that it is hopeless to complain in light of concrete experience: "They are very upset—Russians as well as Germans . . . They try to get justice, but nothing comes of it. A German girl who always was a very good student was told that she had numerous mistakes in her exam paper: 'show me' [she said] and they said 'we can't'—she didn't get in" (95, from Kazakhstan).

Also frequently stressed is the aggressiveness of the local nationals in claiming that they have a right to preferential treatment within their republic, and "if you don't like it, go back to Russia" (32, from Estonia, and others from other republics). Such sentiments have led to open conflict in at least one instance, in 1978, in Alma Ata. Accounts of the incident vary, but it appears to have been triggered by Kazakh claims that too few of them were admitted to Alma Ata University: "Last year there was a big quarrel in the university; the Kazakhs say, there should be many more of their own people, not the Russians, or others . . . Because that's their land, they say . . . Now things are getting more difficult [for non-Kazakhs]" (4). The clash escalated to physical violence and shouting of various slogans: "the students shouted that the Russians should leave Kazakhstan . . . They beat up everybody and attacked people with their knives" (8, and others).

This incident highlights the emotional and symbolic implications of ethnic preferences in university admissions and it illustrates that controversy over this—or similar issues—can easily escalate into a broader conflict in which the indigenous nationality attacks the Russian presence *per se*. This suggests one of the reasons why the central Soviet leadership until now has shown little inclination to intervene against the expansive native claims in Kazakhstan and Central Asia. As various precedents— especially the school controversy of 1959—have demonstrated, the center has the power to circumvent local interests and to set the parameters of educational policies in the republics if it chooses to do so, but there is a price to pay.

Central reticence to intervene on the side of Russians and other non-locals living in Kazakhstan and Central Asia may also be explained by other reasons. For one, the ethnic quota system in force is informal and, therefore, hard to control. It also appears that the admissions mechanism includes many illegal aspects such as outright cheating on examination results, *blat*, and various corrupt practices. To launch a major campaign against this system might mean the opening of a veritable Pandora's box. In addition, the subject is very sensitive politically since the Soviet leadership has officially declared to pursue a policy of proportional ethnic representation in education, science, and administration, and can hardly attack a practice which in effect secures this goal for some of the most "backward" nationalities. Another major political constraint is imposed by the tendency of the minority nations to stress the reality of the federal nature of the USSR and to claim separate state rights for their republics. Intriguingly this claim has been accepted by at least some of the non-indigenous inhabitants of the republics. Thus we encountered many respondents who described the preferential treatment of a republic nationality and then added "it is their republic," as if this statement in itself already said all.

Even though some non-native inhabitants of the union republics recognize the unequal access to higher education as a special right of the locals within their republic, they resent it both because it is to their disadvantage and is in conflict with the alternative principle of the unionwide "equal" treatment of every Soviet citizen. The republic nationals for their part are dissatisfied as well since they feel that the gains made are insufficient. Thus the central policy-makers are confronted with a classic dilemma in being bound to arouse resentments in both population groups involved, no matter what policy they choose. The political repercussions of the problem are further aggravated, in that the dissatisfaction with current practices of university access is most strongly felt by the youth. This is evident from our interviews as well as from Soviet ethnosociological studies which pinpoint the competition for higher education as one of the reasons for less favorable ethnic attitudes among younger age groups and especially college students.[37]

The Measurement of Aggregate Ethnic Attitudes

In the era of political science sophistication, and a widespread proclivity for the precise measurement of social phenomena, a scholar analyzing the aggregate quality of ethnic relations in the USSR is at a great disadvantage. While Soviet sources provide some material on ethnic attitudes in the spheres of marriage, friendships, or work relationships, the issue of overall sociopolitical ethnic attitudes and relations is one of the most strictly censored topics in the USSR. At most, one can find allusions to "remnants of nationalist ideology" and similar vague expressions, but little about the concrete content of nationality problems and their manifestation. To the contrary, there is an active publication campaign depicting the harmony between nations, their unbreakable friendship, and the great achievements brought about by their fraternal union. While themes like these are pervasive in Soviet publications—as, for example, is shown by a content analysis of Soviet publications[38]—they reach a high-point during the celebration of events such as the fiftieth or sixtieth anniversary of the formation of the USSR.[39] In contrast to the great mass of propagandistic material, uncensored reports about the quality of ethnic relations are scarce. This bears re-emphasizing since it explains why otherwise unusual sources such as samizdat documents, reports by Western journalists, and emigrant surveys have to be used to fill the void, and why one cannot hope to cover the topic exhaustively.

In addition to being an impediment to a multifaceted scholarly assessment of the situation, Soviet publication policy and propaganda campaigns about the unbreakable friendship of the Soviet peoples communicate to the Soviet citizens that this is a sensitive area in which they should be careful not to take a wrong step. The effect of this message is reinforced by the knowledge that if some individual or group nevertheless ventures forth in an open demonstration of views which do not conform with those of the regime, the consequences can be dire.[40] This means that even though there are some remarkable cases of open ethnic dissent, this form of social expression—which is the one most typically measured by Western social scientists—is severely circumscribed in the USSR. It is more characteristic for ethnic disaffection to be expressed in ways which are less easily identified by the Soviet authorities, and this also means that they are less clearly identifiable by us. Nevertheless, sensitivity to less tangible forms of ethnic attitudinal expression, such as symbolic actions or literary allusions,[41] can go a long way in elucidating the situation. So too can the recognition that anonymous contexts are those in which Soviet citizens are most likely to express unsanctioned attitudes. It is this latter aspect that is to be elaborated here.

There are two main ways in which ethnic disaffection can be expressed in a basically anonymous manner. One of them involves unstructured individual contacts in the course of daily transactions such as shopping or taking a bus, and the other consists of spontaneous flare-ups of group antagonism which most typically occur on the occasion of a public event which includes an element of competition. Known cases of the latter usually involve mass protests about one of the issues outlined above. Thus the Alma Ata riots in 1978 were triggered by the announcement of the results of the competitive university entrance examinations, and the Georgian street demonstrations in the same year occurred after a policy change which enhanced the role of the Russian language at the expense of Georgian. As for opposition to a Russian physical and political presence, in May 1969 Uzbeks in Tashkent engaged in massive and violent disturbances under the slogan "Russians get out of Uzbekistan."[42] This was also one of the themes of reported street riots by Tadjiks on the occasion of the May Day celebration in Dushanbe in 1978[43] as well as during a number of incidents in the Baltic region, the largest and most violent of which took place in Lithuania after the self-immolation of a Lithuanian youth in the spring of 1972.[44]

Other demonstrations, typically by young people, have occurred after soccer or basketball matches and following the cancellation of popular music concerts.[45] Since the late 1970s such events have been reported most frequently from Estonia. The Soviet press typically just refers to such events by decrying the "gross violations of public order," but a group of forty Estonian intellectuals has presented an analysis of the deeper causes of the disturbance. In an open letter to Soviet newspapers they argued that the demonstrations by thousands of young people in the fall of 1980 could not be examined by momentary rowdyism, but originated in widespread dissatisfaction with escalating economic and social problems and, most important, was due to concern over developments in the ethnic area. Here the points mentioned were the large influx of Russians, restrictions on the use of the Estonian language, increased propagation of the use of Russian, and unbalanced industrial development at the expense of the environment. Lengthy comments pinpointed the crucial role of language for Estonian national identity and self-esteem.[46]

While there are instances where pent-up antagonisms erupt in spontaneous mass demonstrations by republic nationals, and while these basically anonymous actions are less dangerous to the participants than organized forms of dissent, both our knowledge of such events as well as their incidence are severely circumscribed by the various means of political control exerted by the Soviet authorities. The latter are aware of the emotional force of ethnic feelings and have also analyzed the contexts in which they accelerate, as indicated by one recent comment in *Pravda* according to which:[47]

> Any type of competitive situation, from athletic contests to competitive entrance examinations for higher schools, may, for a variety of reasons, wound national feelings. Hence, in dealing with questions of nationalities policy in the conditions of developed socialism, it's necessary to take into consideration not only the social aspects of this policy but also its sociopsychological aspects.

Mass eruptions of latent ethnic resentments are relatively rare, but there are numerous minor confrontations in tension-laden daily situations. Quarrels arising between individuals meeting in anonymous settings frequently are expressed in ethnic terms, that is, "you Russian" or "you Latvian" becomes a derogatory term. Such quarrels most easily occur in everyday contact in anonymous and frustrating situations, such as when standing in line or queuing, or when using overcrowded public transportation facilities. Although originating within the context of everyday strains or the competition for goods and services, these confrontations quickly assume ethnopolitical connotations, and in Central Asia and Kazakhstan racial overtones as well. In the words of a Soviet author, "sometimes in emotionally stressful situations (in a shopping-line or on a crowded bus) conflicts arise which are accompanied by comments insulting someone's nationality."[48]

Whenever our Soviet German respondents are the source of illustrations of the quality of daily contacts between nationalities, such comments frequently were volunteered. We also posed two direct questions about the overall quality of ethnic relations the first of which asked about the German population's relations with the indigenous population, and the second one how Russians and the locals got along with each other. (In the case of the RSFSR the questions were adjusted to specify the relationship between Russians and local minorities, be they Tatars, or Komi, or what have you.) Turning first to the latter (Table 2.4), one notes that the specifically friendly character of ethnic relations between locals and Russians was depicted

Table 2.4 *"How Do the Russians and the (Local Nationality) Get Along with Each Other?"*

	Kazakh-stan, N = 66 (%)	Central Asia, N = 32 (%)	Baltic, N = 34 (%)	Other,* N = 21 (%)	RSFSR, N = 22 (%)
Well	6	3	3	0	9
Without problems	39	38	21	57	55
Generally badly	18	9	14	10	18
Badly on the part of the locals	37	50	62	33	18
Totals	100	100	100	100	100

* Includes Moldavia (N = 14), Ukraine (N = 5), Belorussia (N = 1), and Georgia (N = 1).

rarely, and that allusions to a "normal" and problem-free relationship were much more frequent. In this instance there is regional variation suggesting that relations are least strained in the RSFSR, Moldavia, and the Ukraine, and worst in the Baltic republics, followed by Central Asia and Kazakhstan.

The survey question was open-ended, and it is significant that when respondents said that the local nationality and the Russians got along badly, they mostly specified that the hostility originated from the natives. Elaborations coincided with the previously mentioned resentment about the Russian presence or behavior, language problems, and local aspirations. Sometimes verbal or physical fights break out, even more so when competition over girls or alcohol is involved. Respondents were aware that such incidents are not supposed to occur or to be mentioned, thus: "one isn't supposed to say it, but the Tadjiks hate the Russians" (126).

While there is regional variance in the quality of the ethnic climate, differentials also apply to the nationalities involved. Although the focus here is on relations between republic nationals and Russians, there can be no doubt that the ethnic climate also varies among other groups. A survey conducted by Zvi Gitelman among primarily Soviet Jewish emigrants illustrates this well. In one question respondents were asked to characterize the relations between ten pairs of nationalities, and responses show that clear distinctions are made. Thus relations between Latvians and Lithuanians on the one hand, and Russians and

Table 2.5 *Extent of Negative Ethnic Relations, by Region and Nationality*

Relations of local nationality characterized as strained	Kazakh-stan, N = 66 (%)	Central Asia, N = 32 (%)	Baltic, N = 34 (%)	Moldavia and other, N = 21 (%)	RSFSR, N = 22 (%)
With Russians	55	59	76	43	36
With Soviet Germans	18	16	7	0	31

Belorussians on the other, were mostly characterized as "very good" or "good." In contrast, 83 percent called relations between Georgians and Armenians "poor," and a full 92 percent said so in regard to Estonian–Russian relations.[49]

Our survey also included a question which illustrates differentials between nationalities. As noted, we not only asked for a characterization of relations between the locals and the Russians, but also between the locals and the Soviet Germans.

As Table 2.5 illustrates, the Soviet Germans perceived relations between the locals and Russians to be considerably worse than their own relations with the locals. Again there is regional variation, with residents of the Baltic, Moldavia and other Western republics reporting a minimum of negative relationships, and those from the RSFSR mentioning the highest incidence. In light of the limitation of our sample this result cannot be taken as an accurate numerical measure of the respective relationships, but it can serve as an illustration of basic patterns and points such as that the quality of ethnic relations varies both by region and according to the nationalities involved.

Conclusions

This chapter focuses on collective ethnic sentiments and the macrolevel of relations between nationalities. The main finding is that a clear "we–they" differentiation is made both in terms of group designations as well as in the perception of competing and contrasting interests. This is particularly true for the two major population groups found in any non-Russian union republic, the titular nationality and the Russians.

There are numerous sources of ethnic friction, one of the more basic ones being contrasting views about the reasons, justification, and consequences of the Russian presence. For the indigenous populations historical and political memories of the less than voluntary attainment of union with Russia play a role, especially so in the Baltic republics where the term "Russian" typically is used less as an ethnic ascription than as a political shorthand allusion to "occupier."[50] This is in contrast to the perception of the Russian population and representatives of the center who see themselves as liberators and benefactors whose presence is entirely justified. In the case of some of the republics, especially Kazakhstan and Central Asia, these differences in perceptions are heightened by differential interpretations of cultural value and progress. The Russians typically see themselves as the *Kulturträger* who were instrumental in bringing enlightenment and education to these regions, and consequently espouse a paternalistic or even racist attitude. In contrast, the local population values its own cultural heritage, communal identity, and achievements .[51]

In all the republics the titular nations feel that they have special rights within their "own" territory. One of these rights, especially important to the nations of the Caucasus and the Baltic, concerns the inviolable status of the local languages. While there is resentment about the lack of reciprocity of language acquisition on the part of the Russians, the basic problem revolves around daily language competition in every republic context. To the extent that one of the two main languages gains a dominant role it not only poses a danger to the cultural impact of the other, but also puts the other language users and identifiers at a distinct social and economic disadvantage. Again one finds that here as well as in other multiethnic societies members of different nationalities tend to have different evaluations about the justice of linguistic claims and actual policies. In light of Soviet policies promoting the unionwide dominance of the Russian language the republic nations feel encroached upon, which suggests that language conflict will increase.

Socioeconomic competition such as is seen in the case of access to higher education is a further issue straining ethnic relations, and our Soviet German respondents who have resided in the various republics predominantly feel that the overall ethnic climate is bad. There are, however, several factors mitigating against overt demonstrations of ethnic disenchantment the most important of which is the Soviet political control system with all its facets, including press campaigns and resulting social "double-think." People understand that ethnic strife is officially taboo and, as a result, tend to suppress such feelings or to express them in less tangible and anonymous ways.

Notes: Chapter 2

1   See Lewis Coser, *The Functions of Social Conflict* (New York, The Free Press, 1964); and Ralf Dahrendorf, *Class and Class Conflict in Industrial Society* (Stanford, Calif.: Stanford University Press, 1959). For an application of the conflict approach as contrasted to a systems approach to the analysis of ethnic relations see R. A. Schermerhorn, *Comparative Ethnic Relations* (New York: Random House, 1970), pp. 20–59; and Ira Katznelson, "Comparative studies of race and ethnicity," *Comparative Politics*, vol. 5, no. 1 (October 1972), p. 147.

2   This term has also been used in Soviet writings; cf. Iu. V. Arutiunian, L. M. Drobizheva, and V. S. Zelenchuk, *Opyt etnosotsiologicheskogo issledovaniia obraza zhizni* (Moscow: Nauka, 1980), p. 226.

3   For a numerical depiction of the growing Russian physical presence in the borderlands see table A.8, p. 237. For a good account of the influx of Russians to Kazakhstan and Central Asia in the nineteenth and twentieth centuries see Robert A. Lewis, Richard H. Rowland, and Ralph S. Clem, "Modernization, population change and nationality in Soviet Central Asia and Kazakhstan," *Canadian Slavonic Papers*, vol. 17, no. 2–3 (Summer and Fall 1975), esp. pp. 290–4.

4   See, for example, Karl W. Deutsch *et al.*, "Political community and the North Atlantic area," *International Political Communities, an Anthology* (Garden City, N.Y.: Anchor Books, 1966), p. 10. On the way in which various regions were incorporated in the USSR see Richard Pipes, *The Formation of the Soviet Union: Communism and Nationalism 1917–1923* (Cambridge, Mass.: Harvard University Press, 1970); and Boris Meissner, *Die Sowjetunion, die Baltischen Staaten und das Völkerrecht* (Cologne: Politik und Wirtschaft, 1956).

5   In Central Asia the colonization by Russians has been resented from the beginning of the Russian conquest on and was a principal reason in early resistance against establishment of Soviet rule: Geoffrey Wheeler, *A Modern History of Soviet Central Asia* (New York: Praeger, 1964), p. 131; see also Geoffrey Wheeler, "The Russian presence in Central Asia," *Canadian Slavonic Papers*, vol. 17, no. 2–3 (Summer and Fall 1975), pp. 189–201.

6   Walter Kolarz, *Russia and her colonies* (New York: Praeger, 1952), pp. 243, 263–5.

7   Strobe Talbott (ed.), *Krushchev Remembers: The Last Testament* (Boston, Mass.: Little, Brown, 1974), p. 121; allusions to the same event are made in *Kommunist*, 1958, no. 11, p. 18.

8   *Kommunist Sovetskoi Latvii*, 1959, no. 9, p. 13.

9   *New York Times*, 27 February 1972.

10 That this attitude has been ingrained for decades can be illustrated by the deeply shocked reaction of Russians of varying political outlook when confronted by the territorial losses of the Brest-Litovsk Treaty in 1918: Adam B. Ulam, *Expansion and Coexistence: Soviet Foreign Policy 1917–73*, 2d ed. (New York: Praeger, 1974), pp. 51–75.

11 L. M. Drobizheva, *Dukhovnaia obshchnost' narodov SSSR: istoriko-sotsiologicheskii ocherk mezhnatsional'nykh otnoshenii* (Moscow: Mysl', 1981), p. 92.

12   L. M. Drobizheva and A. A. Susokolov, "Mezhetnicheskeie otnosheniia, i etnokul'turnye protsessy (po materialam etnosotsiologicheskikh issledovanii v SSSR)", *Sovetskaia etnografiia*, 1981, no. 3, p. 21.

13   Rein Taagepera, "Baltic population changes, 1950–1980," *Journal of Baltic Studies*, vol. 22, no. 1 (Spring 1981), p. 45.

14   Stanley Lieberson, *Language and Ethnic Relations in Canada* (New York: Wiley, 1970), pp. 9–10.

15   cf. Bill Fierman, "The view from Uzbekistan," special issue on "The changing status of Russians in the Soviet Union", *International Journal of the Sociology of Language*, 1982, no. 3, pp. 71–8.

16   Comments to this effect were made by many of our respondents. See also reports by Western travelers and other observers, for example, Ronald Wixman, "Ethnic nationalism in the Caucasus," *Nationalities Papers*, vol. 10, no. 2 (Fall 1982), p. 146.

17   cf., for example, R. F. Inglehart and M. Woodward, "Language conflicts and political community," in Pier Paolo Giglioli (ed.), *Language and Social Context* (London: Penguin Modern Sociology Readings, 1972), pp. 358–75; and T. Rennie Warburton, "Nationalism and language in Switzerland and Canada," in Anthony D. Smith (ed.), *Nationalist Movements* (New York: St. Martin's Press, 1976), pp. 88–109.

18   Warburton, "Nationalism and language," p. 105.

19   Jonathan Pool, "Mass opinion on language policy: the case of Canada," in Joan Rubin and Roger Shuy (eds.), *Language Planning: Current Issues and Research* (Washington, D.C.: Georgetown University, 1973), pp. 62–3.

20   Arutiunian and Kakhk, *Issledovaniia*, p. 84.

21   See various studies cited by Jonathan Pool, "Language and loyalty," paper delivered at the Eighth World Congress of Sociology, Toronto, 18–23 August 1974, esp. p. 8; and Lieberson, *Language and Ethnic Relations*, pp. 3–9.

22   Bernard Spolsky, "Attitudinal aspects of second language learning," *Language Learning*, vol. 19 (1969), pp. 271–83.

23   Again the parallels to Quebec are striking since there too the locals have intepreted freedom of choice in school enrollments as an attack on the minority culture. Legislature passed in 1977 stipulates that children have to attend schools in their native language: cf. Margaret B. Sutherland, "Comparative perspective on the education of cultural minorities," in Anthony E. Alcock, Brian K. Taylor, and John M. Wetton (eds.), *The Future of Cultural Minorities* (New York: St. Martin's Press, 1978), pp. 54–5; and George F. Theriault, "Separatism in Quebec," in Raymond L. Hall (ed.), *Ethnic Autonomy—Comparative Dynamics* (New York: Pergamon, 1979), pp. 102–3.

24   Yaroslav Bilinsky, "The Soviet education laws of 1958–9 and Soviet nationality policy," *Soviet Studies*, vol. 14 (October 1962), p. 143; and John Kolasky, *Education in the Soviet Ukraine* (Toronto: P. Martin, 1968), p. 30.

25   Cited in Kolasky, loc. cit.

26   Bilinsky, "Education laws," pp. 138, 147. See also the very thorough discussion by Michael J. Widmer, "Nationalism and communism in Latvia: the Latvian Communist Party under Soviet rule," Ph.D. dissertation, Harvard University, 1969.

27   A. I. Kholmogorov, *Internatsional'nye cherty sovetskikh natsii. (Na materialakh konkretno-sotsiologicheskikh issledovanii v Pribaltike)* (Moscow: Mysl', 1970), p. 153.

28   See, for example, the 1972 samizdat letter by seventeen members of the Latvian CP as reported in *New York Times*, 27 February 1972. For the full text see George Saunders (ed.), *Samizdat: Voices of the Soviet Opposition* (New York: Monad Press, 1974), pp. 427–40.

29 For an excellent analysis of the general conflict between individual and group rights see Vernon Van Dyke, "The individual, the state, and ethnic communities in political theory," *World Politics*, vol. 29, no. 3 (April, 1977), pp. 343–69. For case studies compare previously cited sources on Canada as well as Val R. Lorwin, "Belgium: religion, class, and language in national politics," in Robert Dahl (ed.), *Political Oppositions in Western Democracies* (New Haven, Conn.: Yale University Press, 1966), esp. pp. 170–1.

30 See, for example, *New York Times*, 15 April 1978, p. 3, and 25 April 1978, p. 11.

31 On protests about the increasing use of Russian in higher education in Georgia see Michael Binyon, "Soviet Georgians protest college instruction in Russian," *Chronicle of Higher Education*, 9 September 1981, p. 15; and Ronald Suny, "Georgia and Soviet nationality policy," in Stephen F. Cohen, Alexander Rabinowitch, and Robert Sharlet (eds.), *The Soviet Union since Stalin* (Bloomington, Ind.: Indiana University Press, 1980), p. 218. On protests in Lithuania and Estonia see Roman Solchanyk, "Russian language and Soviet politics," *Soviet Studies*, vol. 34 (January 1982), pp. 34–6.

32 Drobizheva, *Dukhovnaia obshchnost'*, p. 98.

33 The impact of the dominant role of English in limiting social mobility of Francophones in Quebec and Canada is mentioned by Kenneth McRoberts and Dale Posgate, *Quebec: Social Change and Political Crisis* (Toronto: McClelland & Stewart, 1976), pp. 135–6. See also Joseph Rothschild, *Ethnopolitics, a Conceptual Framework* (New York: Columbia University Press, 1981), p. 26.

34 Drobizheva, *Dukhovnaia obschchnost'*, pp. 111–13.

35 Thus one recent report published in a pedagogical newspaper in Latvia (*Skolotāju avīze*, 21 March 1979) noted the results of a test in Russian composition given to Latvian high school graduates applying for admission to higher educational institutions. Only 2 percent were graded "excellent," while 20 percent were "good," 51 percent "satisfactory," and 27 percent were unable to complete the examination. Since Latvia is one of the most Russified union republics, one can assume that results are the same or even poorer in other republics.

36 For an elaboration see Rasma Karklins, "Nationality power in Soviet republics: attitudes and perceptions," *Studies in Comparative Communism*, vol. 14, no. 1 (Spring 1981), pp. 86–7.

37 cf. Chapter 5; and Drobizheva, *Dukhovnaia obshchnost'*, p. 116.

38 See, for example, V. K. Mal'kova, "Primenenie kontent-analiza dlia izucheniia sotrudnichestva sovetskikh narodov (po materialam respublikanskikh gazet)," *Sovetskaia etnografiia*, 1977, no. 5, pp. 71–80.

39 See, for example, D. Kunaev, "Velikaia sila druzhby i bratstve," *Kommunist*, 1982, no. 10, pp. 22–35.

40 For data on sentences for activities connected with various types of ethnic protest see *Biographical Dictionary of Dissidents in the Soviet Union 1956–1975*, compiled and ed. S. P. de Boer, E. T. Driessen, and H. L. Verhaar (The Hague: Martinus Nijhoff, 1982).

41 cf. William Fierman, "Uzbek feelings of ethnicity: a study of attitudes expressed in recent Uzbek literature," *Cahiers du Monde Russe et Sovietique*, vol. 22, no. 2–3 (August–September 1981), pp. 187–220; and Rolfs Ekmanis, *Latvian Literature under the Soviets: 1940–1975* (Belmont, Mass.: Nordland, 1978).

42 *Chronicle of Current Events*, no. 8, 30 June 1969; and David C. Montgomery, "An American student in Tashkent, with some notes on ethnic and racial harmony in Soviet Uzbekistan," *Asian Affairs*, vol. 59 (n.s., vol. 3) pt. 1 (February 1972), p. 39. For a fascinating account of an attempted cover-up of the riots see *Kontinent*, 0.38 (1983), pp. 209–20.

43 Several of our Soviet German respondents who had lived in Central Asia independently referred to this incident. The author is grateful to Walker Connor for pointing out that these riots were given great publicity in China (*People's Daily*).

44 *New York Times*, 22 May 1972.

45 Incidents have been reported by the *Christian Science Monitor*, 28 January 1982, p. 8; *New York Times*, 18 October 1980, p. 5; *Soviet Analyst* (November 1980); Radio Liberty Research Paper No. 243, 1977; and *Washington Post*, 31 October 1977.

46 "Estonia: protests and repressions," *Soviet Analyst* (January 1981), pp. 2–4.

47 *Pravda*, 27 August 1982; trans. in *Current Digest of the Soviet Press*, vol. 34, no. 34, p. 4.

48 Drobizheva, *Dukhovnaia obshchnost'*, p. 233.

49 Zvi Gitelman, "Are nations merging in the USSR?" *Problems of Communism*, vol. 32 (September–October 1983), p. 42.

50 Such differentiations are important to prevent misinterpretations. Thus several Western journalists have characterized Baltic attitudes toward Russians as "racist," ignoring the political content: cf., for example, R. W. Apple, Jr., "Latvia is proud to be a world away from Moscow," *New York Times*, 10 December 1980, p. 8; and David K. Shipler, "Soviet Baltic states accept stability over separation," *International Herald Tribune*, 21 March 1979, p. 5.

51 The ethnic pride of Central Asians and Kazakhs in their old cultures has been remarked upon by Montgomery, "Student in Tashkent," pp. 36–9; Fierman, "The view from Uzbekistan," p. 76; and others. The paternalistic Russian and European Soviet attitude is evident in this evaluation of the validity of the indigenous claims, "the young intelligentsia have engaged in national mythology. The official myth in Alma Ata is that the Kazakhs, hitherto known to the world as a race of illiterate nomads, in fact had an important culture in bygone times. In the desert, it seems, are undiscovered cities of the ancestors of the present-day Kazakhs, containing evidence of literacy and high technical achievement. That being so, the Kazakhs are clearly more important than has been supposed. They do not need to be taught culture by anyone, but can themselves set an example in literature, science, and self-government": Mark Popovsky, *Manipulated Science* (New York: Doubleday, 1979), p. 131.

3

Nationality Power: Developments and Trends

As is true for all political relationships, the question of power is at the core of nationality relations in the Soviet Union. No matter what specific aspect a commentator on Soviet nationality relations chooses to focus upon—be it demography, party policy, economics, or linguistic trends—he sooner or later arrives at a point where anything said has to be related to the distribution of power between the center and the periphery, and between the Russians and the non-Russians. The question arises not only about the status quo, but also about future trends. This chapter intends to present such an evaluation based both on general data and the findings of another segment of our interviews with recent Soviet German emigrants.

As will be shown, most of our respondents defined nationality power within republics as being related to access to better jobs and leading positions, educational achievement, demographic change, and the relative position of the two competing cultures. Some also referred to psychological factors such as ethnic pride, solidarity, and assertiveness. There is a strong consensus that currently vastly different trends pertain to individual republics and regions. The most evident contrast is between the Baltic republics where the indigenous nations are seen to be losing in power, and Central Asia and Kazakhstan where the opposite is seen to occur. There the natives are gaining power at the expense of the European population. Since the latter developments are especially volatile and confront the Soviet government with major policy dilemmas, we shall pay special attention to them. In light of the contrast to the Baltic region the latter will be taken as the other major case to be emphasized. The Baltic and the Central Asian republics in many ways represent opposite ends of the

77

broad spectrum of nationality trends in the USSR and thus constitute good case studies for pinpointing the major factors playing a role.

This chapter again focuses on group relations at the union republic level. As argued before, it is within the non-Russian republic context that the most significant ethnic processes occur. Next to providing a sense of the relative power of the basic population groups, we aim at assessing the implications for the quality of ethnic relations at the macrolevel. Can one expect more or less ethnic strife in the coming decade? What are the main forces acting on the situation and what does it suggest for the future of Soviet nationality policy?

Observer Evaluations of Ethnic Trends

The limitations of official Soviet sources for the analysis of the quality of group-level relations between various nationalities have already been discussed; it is for this same reason that we again have to rely on alternative and supplementary data such as those derived from emigrant surveys. This type of material has problems of its own, but at a minimum it can be used to indicate the thrust of popular perceptions. Admittedly such perceptions are subjective, but then one can argue that subjective perceptions play a role in politics and it is, therefore, of interest what they are. In the case of the observations related by our respondents one can also show that they are largely in accord with objective data.

There can be little doubt that the issue of changing nationality power and relationships is a focus of interest for a great number of Soviet citizens, especially so for those living in the non-Russian republics. In the course of our interviews with the Soviet German emigrants many respondents talked about it on their own. This was especially the case among those who had lived in Kazakhstan and Central Asia, who also tended to speak most volubly on the issue, indicating that they had thought about it while still in the Soviet Union. Since most respondents lived in simple circumstances and worked in low-level occupations, the perspective they provide is that of the common man rather than elite members, and references relate mostly to everyday occurrences.

In addition to comments volunteered early in the interview process, the following analysis is based on replies to a question posed to our Soviet German respondents, namely: "You used to

live in . . . [name of republic]; in your view is the power of the
. . . local nationality] increasing, or decreasing, or staying the
same?" If the reply noted either an increase or decrease of local
power, the interviewer followed up with "in what regard?" In
this second part of the question preformulated replies were
deliberately omitted since individual illustrations and interpretations of the vague term "power"[1] were of crucial interest in
themselves, and replies therefore were recorded verbatim. The
open-endedness in this part of the question yielded many statements which were both informative in content and highly
suggestive in form. These findings will be presented in statistical
summaries as well as by direct quotation. In order to communicate the qualitative sense of our findings even further, trans-
lations follow the original wording faithfully and include only
minimal grammatical corrections.

The formulation of an interview question necessarily sets
certain parameters for replies. Thus while nationality power was
deliberately undefined, the wording of our question strongly
suggested that evaluations focus on power relations within
individual union republics rather than on those between republics and the center. There is also an implied dichotomy of
powerholders, namely, republic nationals and "others." As it
turned out, the latter were nearly universally interpreted to be
Russians—and in rare cases "Moscow." The formulation of the
question furthermore asks for comparisons over time, without
specification of a time frame. It would have been more accurate to
provide the latter, but this was omitted since the length of time
individuals had resided in particular republics varied and we
did not want to draw attention off the main point of the question,
that is, whether the respondent did perceive any changes in
power developments.

As will be shown, a majority of respondents noted either an
increase or decrease in the power of the titular nationality of their
respective republic of residence. But before proceeding to a
detailed presentation of these findings, a few comments should
be made about those cases where respondents stated that the
power of the local nationality was "staying the same" or that they
"did not know." A variety of causes account for these two replies.
Thus some of the respondents who said "I don't know" were
simply indecisive, while others genuinely felt that they had no
realistic basis for evaluation. This was typical of individuals who
had little contact with the nationalities—mostly those who had
lived in the Russian areas of the RSFSR—or who had entirely

different preoccupations such as the respondent who said: "I don't know, being an average worker it is impossible for me to say something like that, we were more interested in the availability of food" (28). Others chose "I don't know" as a means of evasion, sometimes adding "this question is too political." Evasion or apprehension about answering a question that might prove politically sensitive also caused a number of the "staying the same" replies, with some adding a standard statement which could be read in the Soviet press such as "one can find persons of all nationalities in high positions" (122, from Dushanbe).

Substantively more interesting are those instances where the "staying the same" category of response was chosen because respondents negated the possibility of a republic nationality ever having real power. This was expressed in statements such as: "They continue as before, they [the locals] do have higher positions, but the power belongs to Moscow anyway" (98); or "they want more [power], but they [the authorities] always keep a rein on them, if somebody acts too extremely, the people are exchanged" (168, from Estonia); and a person who lived in the Ukraine said: "It is their republic, but it is still dependent on Russia, there is no going away from Russia, it is written in the Constitution that they can separate, but that isn't so in reality . . . and they are used to it" (116). There were, of course, also some who genuinely thought that there was no notable change in nationality power such as respondent no. 97 from Moldavia, who said: "in the leadership the leading persons are Moldavian, that is as it used to be."

This kind of response was, however, an exception to the rule since most respondents noted either an increase or a decrease in the power of the titular nationality of the republic they last resided in. A comparison of replies referring to individual republics furthermore reveals striking regional variations in the perceptions of trends (Table 3.1). The most notable difference is that between responses of people who lived in the Baltic republics and those who lived elsewhere; while in the latter case power was more frequently seen to be increasing, the reverse is true for the Baltic. The contrast is most accentuated between the Baltic republics and Kazakhstan, where a majority of respondents chose the directly opposite replies: while 67 percent of those who lived in Kazakhstan thought that native power there was increasing, 59 percent of those who lived in the Baltic perceived it as being on the decrease.

Table 3.1   *Perceptions of Power Changes in Non-Russian Republics*

Nationality power seen to be	Percentage of respondents mentioning				
	Kazakh- stan, N = 66 (%)	Central Asia, N = 36 (%)	Baltic, N = 34 (%)	Moldavia and other, N = 19 (%)	RSFSR,* N = 27 (%)
Increasing	67	39	6	31	19
Decreasing	2	11	59	21	33
Staying same	15	31	18	37	11
Don't know	16	19	17	11	37
Totals	100	100	100	100	100

* In the case of respondents who had lived in the RSFSR the question was reformulated to apply to any larger native nationality in the respective area, or neighboring non-Russian republics.

Note: For the crude data see Table A.8, p. 237.

How can one explain the differences? A first indication is provided by a closer look at the replies to the second part of the interview question, where respondents who had noted increasing or decreasing nationality power were asked to specify what they meant. Since this part of the question was open-ended, and since "power" was undefined, individual responses could in theory have varied considerably. In fact they stayed within a narrow range and allowed categorization. Thus the comments about increasing nationality power can be subdivided into six groups.

(1) The factor mentioned most frequently as a sign of increasing native power is the indigenous nationality holding more and higher positions. This phenomenon was referred to in general terms, such as: "They gather native cadre and hold the higher positions" (20, from Kazakhstan); or more specifically "We think that they are getting stronger . . . There are Kazakhs everywhere, in the shops and as bosses" (110); or "they are promoted at work . . . They feel like the masters" (96, from Moldavia). Other typical and revealing statements were: "Now there are more Kazakhs everywhere, frequently one has a Kazakh as the boss and a Russian on the second place; the Kazakhs don't understand as much and then the Russian does his work" (176); "the highest position is held by a Kazakh, the lower ones may also be held by other nationalities" (43); and "lately the Kazakhs are always

81

getting ahead in the *nachal' stvo*, even if they understand less . . .
The Russians and Germans are rejected . . . They [Kazakhs] rule
. . . The Kazakhs put their own nation in . . . the first one is
Kunaev, there are many Russians on second positions for doing
the work" (7). About Tadjikistan it was said: "Their power is
increasing; in the shops, for example, there were at first only
Russians, now they are all their own [people], the first secretary
is a Tadjik, the third a Tadjik again—it's the same at the very top.
The Tadjiks are ahead now . . . We got there in 1959, then there
was rarely a Tadjik in the police force—it was mostly Russian—
now 70 percent are Tadjiks" (102).

While rising to higher positions is most frequently seen to
occur in the economic sphere, politics and administration are
mentioned as well. Another area of native gains is education:
"Yes, the Kazakhs strive to strengthen everything that is theirs;
also there are more of them now in the universities and more in
higher positions—it is very rare that a Kazakh is a common
worker" (142).

Some respondents felt that they had to explain these developments: "Formerly they lost very much, now they want to reestab-
lish all of that; in the 1950s the training of cadre was neglected
and that is now made up . . . in politics, science, economic
offices—in all places" (166, from Kirghizia). Nevertheless, non-
locals usually resent this cadre policy. When we asked about
reactions of people who do not belong to the republic nationality,
especially Russians, typical replies were: "Just try to say something! If one says something against this, the Kazakhs say 'whose
bread are you eating, on whose land do you live?'" (43); "the
Russians, of course, are angry" (166, from Kirghizia); and "the
Russians don't like it, but what can they do, it is such a thing with
the republics . . . it has been like this for the past ten to fifteen
years that the Kazakhs are preferred everywhere" (176). In some
cases this development is causing the non-locals to leave: "they
all strive towards moving to their own republic" (20, from
Kazakhstan).

(2) The second factor mentioned as a sign of increasing native
power is higher learning: "One can see that in the institute,
wherever there is studying—all are Kazakhs; and, of course,
bosses are not made from workers, but from learned [people]"
(75). Others remarked on the sociopolitical consequences of
higher education: "I think they are getting more powerful, they
study more now; when a person is learned, he demands more" (3,
from Moldavia); "the Kazakhs are getting more and more edu-

cated, and when one is educated one understands more and then, at one moment, they say 'now listen, this is my country'" (47, from Kazakhstan); or "now there are very many learned Kirghiz . . . and if one of them has a high position, he'll try to get Kirghiz all around himself . . . If he has any kin [rod], he'll help, so that many of them come . . . and the Russians get on with much more difficulties then . . . however, those on the very top are only put there by Moscow" (1, from Kirghizia).

Besides individuals getting a better education some of the republic nationalities were perceived as attaining a generally higher level of development, or were "getting more cultured" in the specific Russian idiom. Why this should imply an increase in power is explained in this statement of a young woman from Kirghizia: "They state their dissatisfaction more, are able to take care of themselves, develop culture, study, [go to work] in shops, service organizations, study to be lawyers . . . they are in scientific institutions, doctors . . . now they could get along without the Russians, now they have even surpassed them" (59).

(3) Numerical relationships between nationalists are seen as another indicator of power. This holds true for both increases and decreases in the number or proportional standing of a republic nationality, and in some cases also of the status quo, that is, several respondents noted that a local nationality's power was increasing "because they are in the majority." The increase in numbers, particularly through high birth rates, was most typically mentioned in relationship to Muslim areas: "They have many children, they multiply" (169, from Kazakhstan); or "Oh yes, their power is larger now, other nationalities have three children [per family], but the Kazakhs have large families . . . They have six to seven children, sometimes even up to ten . . . In the place where my daughter worked, the telegraph office, a Russian said: 'It is terrible, the black race takes over'" (4, from Kazakhstan). In two cases it was said that indigenous power increases because more natives move to the cities (63, from Kazakhstan; and 178, from Moldavia).

(4) Respondents measured power not only in concrete terms but many also cited psychological and symbolic aspects such as increases or decreases in ethnic pride or assertiveness. These statements usually were general, such as "national pride is also on the increase" (95, from Kazakhstan), but some gave concrete examples of local nationals, insisting that they have special rights as the "masters" of a republic. Some made comparisons, such as: "Formerly they used to be silent, downtrodden, but now they

shout their songs in the streets. Formerly, the Russians were putting the screw on Kazakhs, but now it is the other way around" (51, from Kazakhstan). Assertiveness and the defense of national rights were said to be expressed in many ways, including physical confrontations (72, 121).

(5) Cultural trends were mentioned on occasion; thus the infrequent use of the Russian language was once cited as an example of increasing native power (94, from Kazakhstan); and in two cases the continued observance of native customs and traditions was noted, which is a theme to be elaborated upon in Chapter 7.

(6) The sixth type of comment is hard to categorize; verbatim quotes best relate their content: "It [Kazakh power] is increasing. For example, if there was a fight between Kazakhs and Russians or Germans, the Kazakhs would be let off without a sentence, but the Russians or Germans would be punished . . . For the Russians too. It is getting difficult to live in Kazakhstan" (35, from Kazakhstan). "I was in a sanitarium where all the others were Turkmen; I heard talk about wanting to secede from the Soviet Union . . . The Turkmen want their people in the leading positions . . . in the district committee of the party one finds only Turkmen, and one Russian." When asked about reactions of the Russians, this same respondent continued: "They are disgusted . . . there are people who see that it isn't according to the statutes—[there was] a Russian woman, she resigned from the local Soviet because she saw that it was wrong, but it isn't possible to do anything . . . The others adjust, dance to their [Turkmen] tune" (71). Or about Kazakhstan: "Formerly they were helped a lot, but now they themselves are high up . . . Now the Kazakhs are more the bosses, they aren't like the Germans, they stick together *very* much . . . The entire large families . . . Kazakhs are very much for everything of their own, are big nationalists, would love to introduce all their own [things]" (127).

While these extensive quotations provide a qualitative illustration of the replies to our question, a quantitative indicator is provided in Table 3.2. It ranks the six types of replies by the frequency that each was mentioned. The ranking shows the difference in the emphasis accorded to various factors.

Table 3.2 also summarizes respondent definitions of increasing nationality power in capsule form. The strong consensus about the meaning of ethnic "power" also applies to respondents citing a decrease in it since the illustrations given largely constitute

Table 3.2   *Aspects of Increasing Nationality Power*

	Total	Kazakh-stan	Frequency mentioned Central Asia	Baltic	Moldavia and other	RSFSR
More native cadre, higher positions	42	26	10	—	4	2
More education, develop-ment	28	11	9	1	4	3
More national pride, assertive-ness	22	12	5	—	1	4
Increase in numbers	16	10	3	2	1	—
Native culture gains	4	2	2	—	—	—
Other	10	7	1	—	—	2

reverses of measures cited for increasing local power. Thus the first example of decreasing local power again concerns cadre policy and the distribution of authority. Typical statements were: "You now find more Russians in responsible positions" (156, from Estonia); and "the Russians have much say, the Lithuanians are mostly in sovkhozes and kolkhozes; those who work as white-collar workers are mostly Russians" (49, from Lithuania). Others focused more on the power relationship between republics and the center: "Moscow now takes every-thing more strictly into its own hands" (25, from Lithuania); or "Moscow has a large influence on the Kirghiz" (39, from Kirghizia).

Negative demographic trends were given as a further indicator of decreasing local power, and again we find that the reverse development was cited as a sign of increasing nationality power. There is a slight difference, however, in that next to changing birth rates many respondents also emphasized the impact of Russian immigration. To cite two statements about Latvia: "Power decreases; the Russians, they come in and it goes down. The Latvians who are in the government are called toadies. Voss [then first secretary of the Latvian CP] is now getting himself ready to go to Moscow . . . People say "they sell Latvia in order to personally get on top' . . . Latvians now join the party as well, in order to be able to hold their country, otherwise there are only Russians in it" (118). "The power of Latvians decreases. Fewer are born, more die, and if one Latvian gets into governing, there are two Russians [there] for him, the Latvian has to dance as the Russians call the tune. Voss now does everything that Brezhnev wants" (119).

Long-term consequences of an increased Russian presence are noted as well, and this leads us to the third measure of decreasing native power, that is, changes in the sphere of culture, language, and tradition: "Because more Russians come, there is a certain assimilation. There used to be only Latvians in our office . . . now all documents are in Russian" (133, from Riga); and "Russians are sent in and fill the highest positions. In the institutions of learning there are now more groups studying in Russian and that is the path to higher positions" (73, from Lithuania).

Numerous other statements suggest a general decline in the position of native cultures; to cite just a few: "Slowly the Russian things are getting rooted everywhere" (197, from Kirghizia); "There is less freedom . . . The people want to stick to it, to religion and [their own] schools, but they are not allowed . . . it isn't respected" (82, from the Ukraine). Or a typical remark about one of the nationalities with the RSFSR, the Udmurts: "They merge more and more with the Russians, take on their beliefs and customs" (153). And finally: "They [Estonians] say that they now have to study more Russian, starting even in kindergarten . . . I think that everything will be more Russian in time" (171, from Estonia). The factors mentioned as illustrating decreasing nationality power are summarized and ranked in Table 3.3.

A comparison of Tables 3.2 and 3.3 shows that although the three aspects of decreasing nationality power are reverses of three aspects of increasing nationality power, the latter has two more categories. This is partly explained by nearly twice as many respondents mentioning increases in native power (see also Table A.8, p. 237), but there is a substantive difference as well. For one, the respondents who thought that nationality power was decreasing had more difficulty in articulating examples—the phenomenon was more difficult to pinpoint. In addition, different aspects are emphasized in the educational and cultural sphere. Thus gains in the educational level of natives are ranked high as a sign of increasing native power, but there is no equivalent category in the illustrations of power decreases.

Table 3.3   *Aspects of Decreasing Nationality Power*

	Total	Estonia	Lithuania	Latvia	Moldavia and other	RSFSR
			Frequency mentioned			
Russians hold decisive positions	18	1	6	5	3	2
Russians immigrate more	16	1	5	8	1	1
Russian culture gains	16	1	3	3	3	5
Other	2	—	—	—	—	2

Instead there is an emphasis on the emasculation of native cultures. This suggest that increases and decreases of nationality power not only refer to different trends as measured on the same scales, but also pinpoint qualitative differences in developments and perceptions.

Analysis of Findings

Having presented the measures of nationality power used by people who have lived in the various regions of the USSR and presented the basic data on perceived trends in its development, the main task of analysis is to explain the considerable variation found in comparisons of regions and republics. As a first step, reflections on the character of our data as well as comparisons with other sources are indicated.

Thus one should recall that the regional distribution of our sample is unbalanced. This is unfortunate but unavoidable in light of the geographic dispersion of the Soviet German population as well as the vicissitudes of Soviet emigration policy. Also since the number of respondents from certain republics is small (cf. Table A.8, p. 237), regional additions and comparisons were made in most instances, leading to an underemphasis of differences between individual republics.

It is also unfortunate that relatively few respondents lived in the RSFSR. We have little basis for comparisons with the smaller ethnic groups living there, as well as few insights about the way in which nationality developments in the non-Russian republics are perceived by people living in Russia.[2]

The relatively small size of our total sample—which results in subgroups of the sample being even smaller—makes it further-more impossible to reliably check for correlations between types of responses and respondent characteristics. Nevertheless, calculations were made in order to identify clear-cut imbalances; the factors examined were age, sex, religiosity, urban–rural distribution, and knowledge of local language. No significant correlations with types of responses were found, with one excep-tion: young people (age 18–30) are overrepresented among those perceiving a decrease in nationality power. A closer look at this group shows that most of them are young males (fourteen out of eighteen), which suggests that their views may have been influenced by service in the armed forces.

In general, however, background characteristics of respon-dents have no apparent influence on their evaluations; this is further supported by individuals who had lived in various regions and who volunteered comparisons which noted the opposing trends. The case of a respondent who had lived in Lithuania for the past three years is typical: in reply to our question he said that native power there was decreasing, but then went on to contrast this to Kazakhstan, where he had lived before and where "the Kazakhs have raised themselves very much" recently (129).

In theory, the findings could also have been influenced by biases of the respondents as a group. Since interview results from other groups are not available on this topic, it is impossible to discount this possibility altogether. But several factors speak against a major impact of bias resulting from group affinities. Thus while it is true that Soviet Germans generally have closer affinities to Balts than to Central Asians, it has also been found that such affinities play a much stronger role in personal interac-tions than in those having to do with work or administrative matters.[3] Since our findings refer mostly to the administrative, occupational, and educational spheres, one may contend that personal sympathies are less influential. More important, it should be reemphasized at this point that power relations within the republics were near-universally defined as those between republic nationals and "others." Although the latter primarily refers to Russians, the category also includes other non-indigen-ous groups, including the Soviet Germans. Thus, to the degree that the Soviet Germans identify their own interests with those of all non-locals, the resulting bias is consistent in its thrust for all republics and, therefore, cannot explain the major intraregional variations in our results.

In sum, it appears that individual background characteristics and group biases of our respondents have little influence on the findings and that the regional variation in perceived nationality trends reflects actual differences in the republics. This is confirmed by other sources dealing with the cited phenomena. Thus the last Soviet censuses show that while the natives are numerically gaining in Kazakhstan and Central Asia, they are losing in the Baltic republics. The number and the proportion of Russian residents has been increasing most dramatically in the urban centers of Latvia and Estonia. In contrast to this trend in the Baltic, urban areas in the other non-Russian republics have become progressively more native (see Table A.1, p. 230).[4] Differential demographic trends among various Soviet nationalities unionwide, as well as within specific republics, have numerous repercussions on ethnic relationships, and it is interesting that residents of the various non-Russian republics are well aware of this. The long-term effect of changing numerical ratios between nationalities is one of the topics most intensely discussed by Soviet and Western experts on nationality problems.[5] Although demographic trends affect the standing of the non-Russian nationalities in many ways, the dramatic growth of the Soviet Muslim population is most consequential since it adds a strong quantitative pressure to native claims for a larger share of the educational, economic, and administrative sector of their republics.

As to objective data on ethnic trends on who holds economic and political positions within various republics, one should first of all mention difficulties of precise measurement. Many of the available Soviet statistics aggregate data for entire republic populations without an ethnic breakdown, or else present unionwide nationality statistics which are not broken down by republics. For our purposes both types of data are inadequate since the main focus is on the relationship of republic nationals and Russians *within* the respective non-Russian union republics. Statistics providing information about the relative occupational, political, or educational status of these two population groups are scarce. As a result, studies of the proportionality of ethnic representation in better jobs, the CPSU, and education frequently rely on unionwide nationality data or on purely regional data.[6]

Due to the data problems as well as complexity of adequate evaluations, only a very general assessment of the "objective" situation can be attempted here. As concerns native representation in republic governmental and party posts, available data do not contradict the observations made by our respondents. Most of the respondents referring to Muslim areas lived in Kazakhstan and Kirghizia, and these are the two republics that had the highest relative indices of national representation among republic elites between 1955 and 1972.[7] Grey Hodnett's finding that natives are assigned to the posts with highest visibility is even more to the point[8] since this practice clearly is reflected in observer perceptions of high native representation.

If one looks at enrollments in higher educational institutions— data which are a good indicator of overall social mobility and attainment[9]—several points emerge. Thus the republic-level ethnic educational data summarized in Table A.10, p. 239, show that during the 1960s Kazakhs and Central Asians were increasing the number of students per 1,000 conationals in their republics, but so were the local Russians. Nevertheless, due mostly to underlying demographic differentials, the relative representation of native students in the student body increased in Uzbekistan, Tadjikistan, and Turkmenistan. It remained the same in Kazakhstan and Kirghizia. While these findings hardly support the perception of major proportional gains for the natives, they do not contradict them either. The data on the three Baltic republics show a decrease in the proportional representation of native students, most notably so in the case of Latvia, where one notes an 18 percent drop between 1960–1 and 1970–1. This supports the perception of local power losses as noted by our respondents.

At this point it should be emphasized that our findings refer to *trends* in nationality power, not its existing level. Also respondents were asked only to evaluate trends in the one republic where they had lived last; the comparisons between republics were made *a posteriori* in our analysis. The spontaneous comparisons suggest that results would not have differed much if we had asked all respondents for such comparisons, but results would probably have differed if the question had focused on the status quo rather than trends. If, for example, we had asked for a comparison of the power that the Estonians hold in their republic today, and the power that the Kirghiz or Kazakhs hold in theirs, the ranking of Estonia would probably have been higher than when asked about trends. The Baltic republics have traditionally been more highly developed than Central Asia and Kazakhstan. Until the early 1970s Central Asians ranked at the bottom on Soviet unionwide statistical comparisons of higher educational attainment, while the Balts ranked at the top (see Table A.9, p. 238). Historical factors such as time of incorporation, achievements during the period of independence,[10] and so on, go a long way in explaining existing differences but they are not the focus of our analysis. Nor is the comparison of the differential "absolute amounts" of ethnic power in individual republics.

The reflections about comparisons of existing levels of educational attainment suggest that the local gains in Kazakhstan and Central Asia can in part be explained as a "catching up" phenomenon and that Baltic and Soviet Asian differences can be related to differential stages in social and economic development. But no matter how one explains the differential trends in nationality developments, these trends pinpoint the locus of the most dynamic contemporary changes to Kazakhstan and Central Asia. What are the sources and the political consequences of these changes?

Ethnopolitical Contexts and Repercussions of Current Trends

A first indication of the politics of current ethnic trends is provided by the replies to another question in our interview schedule, namely, the problem of access to higher education discussed in the previous chapter. As we noted, respondents emphasized that preferential treatment is given to republic nationals, especially so in Central Asia and Kazakhstan. This links up well with the findings on increases in nationality power. Higher education was mentioned as a crucial aspect of power, and it is also closely associated with the other aspect mentioned most frequently, that is, the access to higher positions.

It is crucial to ask about the origin and effect of such a development. In the case of preferential educational treatment it helps to look at replies to two follow-up questions put to those respondents who pinpointed nationality as a prime criterion. The first question asked about the source of this practice, that is, whether it was based on a decision made in Moscow. Of those respondents who did reply in terms of decision-making (N = 73) 82 percent negated this and said that the decision originated in the republic, 7 percent thought that it involved both the republic and the center, and only 11 percent thought that the center was decisive. The formulations used illustrate varying perceptions of the process and power relations involved: "That originates in Moscow, it has given rights to the republic . . . Moscow wants that these [republics] keep up, they formerly were—how should I say, wild . . . [underdeveloped] . . . and they themselves make even more of it: let's say Moscow had arranged it, so that there would be 50 percent Kazakhs [in the universities], then they [Kazakhs] arrange it that there are 75 percent" (2); or "I think so, yes. It is [Moscow's decision], based on a request of the republics, because each republic wants to have its own specialists" (30, from Moldavia); or to quote some statements negating the role of Moscow: "no, it isn't [from Moscow], they of course want that the whites have the upper hand, but now the blacks [sic] take over everywhere . . . The Kazakhs are Kazakhs, they want to raise their people" (127); and "no, they themselves [are decisive] . . . now suddenly the Kazakhs hold their head high" (146); and "something like that can't come from Moscow, it is [decided] on the spot . . . Moscow makes no difference, it must be for equal rights . . . The republics are the ones who look after their own" (103, from Lithuania).

In sum, respondents believed that the preferential treatment of republic nationals was primarily due to decisions and arrangements at the republic level. The Russian and other non-local population feels that they are losing out and resent this policy. It strains ethnic relations and so does any policy and development which increases the social and economic standing of the indigenous populations "at the expense" of the other residents of the non-Russian republics. Further comments on this have been made by other visitors and residents of the non-Russian republics, especially Central Asia and Kazakhstan. Thus a Western doctoral candidate who spent a year in Uzbekistan reports how proudly Soviet officials (both in Moscow and Uzbekistan) spoke of their programs to promote native cadre, but that these same officials tend to ignore the effects this policy is having on ethnic relations. To quote:[11]

> affirmative action has become one of the most divisive forces among the various nationalities in Uzbek life, and has reinforced ethnic identity among all of Uzbekistan's nationalities. It has made ethnic affiliation an essential ingredient, if not the main determinant, of one's ability to advance in Uzbek society.

A Soviet Jewish scientist who before his emigration to the West did much traveling and research work in the various republics makes the same point and supports the European population's evaluation that this policy is unjust, nationalist, and discriminatory. His comments about Central Asian graduate students and scientists include formulations which also indicate his disdain for their scientific ability and cultural level, which he measures against a Russian and European standard. He ridicules doctoral theses of non-Russians who "can't even write grammatical Russian" and notes that "in academic circles in Moscow and Leningrad one may hear many anecdotes about the illiterate scripts received from Central Asian graduates."[12] While giving numerous examples how republic nationals are given preferential treatment in regard to jobs and academic credit, he also says that they have become increasingly assertive—or "arrogant" as he thinks—during the past fifteen years.[13]

In light of all these statements the most pressing question is why Soviet policy-makers do not intervene. Several explanations are possible. The first is that Soviet nationality policy since its inception has been based on a dualistic strategy which, while granting concessions to a few native claims, keeps a strict rein on the politically most crucial structures and processes. Among the latter the strict centralization of the CPSU as well as central power to make political appointments are most important, and this power has hardly been undermined at this stage. To the extent that Central Asian locals have reached high positions in the party and state apparatus the presence of Russian cadre (being formally second in command does not necessarily mean actual secondary power) as well as close ties to the central apparatus act as balancers to any potential diversions from the course as charted by the CPSU,[14] and periodic purges of indigenous communists for "nationalist deviations" have demonstrated the limits of local power in this sphere. Thus the Soviet leaders appear confident that they can contain the most directly political expressions of native assertiveness.

As concerns the building of native social and economic elites, it has always been the official Soviet calculus that a certain extent of "nativization," or *korenizatsiia* as it was called in the 1920s, is to the long-term advantage of the Soviet state since these native elites are expected to be both acculturated and loyal. To the extent that this expectation of harmonious ethnic integration may have been doubted it nevertheless was perceived to be less risky than a policy which blocks the upward mobility of underdeveloped minority groups.[15] And last but not least important, it also has always been a central element of official Soviet nationality policy to rely on the physical presence of a significant number of Russians as a cultural and ethnic safeguard against an escalation of ethnic claims. The crucial question to ask, therefore, is whether this calculus is wrong, or whether any of the expectations it has been built on are not being fulfilled in Central Asia and Kazakhstan.

To date the evidence is ambiguous. Some of our respondents, as well as other sources, believe that the official calculus will emerge as the correct one,[16] and obviously this is also the claim of the Soviet authorities themselves. In light of the history of the CPSU since 1917, and in light of its overall success in containing major ethnic policy challenges, it would be foolish to doubt its political acumen and ability to somehow—for better or worse—find solutions to problems and crises. Nevertheless, the current trends in Central Asia and Kazakhstan suggest that a qualitatively new and complex situation has emerged.

For one, there is the problem of the demographic balance within the region. The demographic trends are unlikely to change significantly in the near future. As noted, the last two decades have been characterized by a rapid natural growth of the indigenous populations as well as their proportional gains over the number of Russians and other Europeans. Since European birth rates in the USSR are low, and since the Soviet Union is characterized by an accelerating labor shortage, it is unlikely that the number of non-natives in Central Asia and Kazakhstan will be significantly raised either through migration or natural growth. To the contrary, it is possible that the labor shortages in other parts of the USSR, as well as the increasingly inhospitable social environment in this region, will lead to European outmigration,[17] which would accelerate demographic change in favor of the natives. The growth of the local population implies that the native claims for more educational and social mobility will increase.

There is only one way in which such demands can be fulfilled without losses on the part of the Russian population, and that is within the context of a major increase in the total sum of educational and occupational opportunities. This does not apply to the region; instead one finds an increasing trend toward a "zero-sum" situation in which the gains of one population group equal the losses of the other. As the experience of other societies has shown, such redistributive scenarios lead to more competition and political conflict.[18] It is this type of situation that is taking place in Central Asia and Kazakhstan.

Theoretically the Soviet authorities have two policy options if they want to prevent this scenario. They could try to influence the demographic balance by changing migration flows, or they could stop the "affirmative action" programs. In fact the two policies are interrelated, as has been noted by the Soviet demographers Litvinova and Urlanis who feel that only a strictly "equal" policy will lead to the migratory pattern favored by the government, that is, the interrepublic exchange of population. To cite:[19]

Migration policy, especially where interrepublic migration is concerned, is related to nationalities policy. The optimization of migration processes is promoted by strict adherence to the principle of national equality and the provision of equal opportunities for social growth (i.e., job promotions and opportunities to receive education or to upgrade job skills) to representatives of any nationality, whichever Soviet republic they live in. The 1970 and 1979 censuses showed an increase in the percentage of people of the indigenous nationality in the majority of union and autonomous republics and a reduction in the percentage of such people living outside their republic. One reason for this is that members of the indigenous nationalities still receive preferential treatment in the area of social advancement in their own republics; this policy was justified during the initial period after the revolution, but it should be changed in the light of current conditions.

The suggested change of policy is, however, difficult to implement and very risky politically.

Turning first to the difficulties of implementation, one should recall that the sources and mechanisms leading to the current practice of preferential treatment of republic nationals in Central Asia and Kazakhstan are only partly related to central policies, and in large part result from the efforts of the natives themselves. In order to intervene effectively the center would have to make a major effort and win numerous bureaucratic skirmishes in thousands of republic admissions and personnel offices. While difficult in practice, such confrontations would be exceedingly sensitive since the indigenous nationals would be bound to argue that they have special rights within "their own" republics as well as a right to "catch up" with the more developed nationalities. The latter argument is hard to refute since it has been a constant theme of Soviet official propaganda, and because statistical disparities persist.

On balance it thus appears that the central Soviet authorities are caught in a classic policy dilemma of "being damned if they do and damned if they don't." If they should try to stop the educational and professional gains of the indigenous populations, they probably will increase the happiness of the local Russian and other European population, but at a high cost in native dissatisfaction and international propagandistic liabilities.[20] But prospects do not appear rosy even in case of a continuation of current policies. The European population resents its gradual loss of ground as the carrier of modernization and economic development and is bitter about actual and imagined cases of preferential treatment of locals.[21] If current trends continue, this dissatisfaction will increase and so will ethnic hostility.

Ironically dissatisfaction is rising among the indigenous population as well, despite its being on the winning side. There are several reasons for this. For one, as has been pointed out by Teresa Rakowska-Harmstone, modernization in a multiethnic context is volatile even if the dominant group allows for a degree of economic and social equalization since the new elites usually perceive that their relative position is changed insufficiently and expectations rise.[22] In addition, the overall level of past socioeconomic disparities and ethnic stratification in Central Asia and Kazakhstan has been such that despite gradual change the status quo gives the native population objective reasons for feeling dissatisfied.[23] But in matters like these subjective perceptions are even more decisive, and in the view of some locals the continued Russian role in high-level political and socioeconomic positions as such poses a problem, and this problem is unlikely to disappear in face of solely incremental change.

In addition, the Soviet Central Asians perceive that advances result from their own efforts rather than from the magnanimity of the "elder brother." They also stress that they have an inalienable right to preferential treatment not only because of the need to catch up, but also "because it is our country." This territorial emphasis[24] has in part been legitimized through the federal structure of the USSR, through periodic campaigns aiming at the "indigenization" of cadre in the non-Russian areas, and by the dialectical rhetoric of Leninist nationality policy and is, therefore, difficult to counter by the central authorities. The legitimate role of the locals as the "masters" of their own republics has become a reality not only to them, but has also been grudgingly accepted by a sector of the European population, adding to its weak position in the face of local power gains.

The situation is different in the Baltic republics. The perception of our Soviet German respondents that there the indigenous nationalities are pushed into an increasingly defensive position is confirmed by overall demographic data as well as by other Soviet statistics such as those on enrollments in higher educational institutions. If one examines the relative weight of Russian and local enrollments within the respective republics (Table A.10, p. 239), one notes that in the decade between 1960 and 1970 the gains of the Russian population have been dramatic, especially so in the case of Latvia and Lithuania. If one again takes these data as a general indicator of socioeconomic standing, there is the clear suggestion that, in the Baltic republics, Russians increasingly assume the leading positions. This trend has been confirmed by Baltic protests and samizdat sources, especially the protest letter of seventeen Latvian communists smuggled to the West in 1972.[25] While such sources indicate the detrimental impact of Russian ascendancy on the ethnic climate in the Baltic region, the same is suggested by some ethnosociological studies to be cited later. Ethnic competition in regard to higher education and high-level jobs can easily lead to ethnic conflict even in those situations where the local population is making some gains, but conflict is much more likely if the opposite trend holds true.[26] Thus one can only conclude that the prospects for ethnic harmony in the Baltic republics is also poor, although for different reasons than in the case of Central Asia and Kazakhstan.

Notes: Chapter 3

1 Interviews were conducted in either German or Russian, depending on the respondents' fluency in either language. The original term used in German was *Macht*, and in Russian, *vlast' i sila*.

2 As indicated in the note to Table 3.1, the interview question was reformulated for respondents who had lived in the RSFSR; the detailed replies are shown in Table A.8, p. 237. Although the sample of people from the RSFSR is relatively small, respondents tended to support the findings made for the other republics such as the perception of power increases in Kazakhstan. In those instances when references were made to the nationalities of the RSFSR, they were seen to be losing power.

3   cf. Chapters 5 and 6. See also Juozas A. Kazlas, "Social distance among ethnic groups," in Edward Allworth (ed.), *Nationality Group Survival in Multi-Ethnic States* (New York: Praeger, 1977), pp. 228–54.

4   See Table A.1, p. 230, as well as Soviet census publications, especially, *Itogi vsesoiuznoi perepisi naseleniia SSSR 1970 goda*, (Moscow: Statistika, 1973), Vol. 4; and *Naselenie SSSR, Po dannym vsesoiuznoi perepisi naseleniia 1979 goda* (Moscow: Politizdat, 1980).

5   For Soviet comments on this point see, for example, A. A. Susokolov, "Vsesoiuznaia nauchnaia sessiia XXVI s"ezd KPSS i zadachi izucheniia natsional'nykh otnoshenii v SSSR," *Sovetskaia etnografiia*, 1982, no. 2, pp. 111–15; and L. N. Terent'eva, "Etnicheskaia situatsiia i etnokul'turnye protsessy v sovetskoi Pribaltike," *Rasy i narody*, vol. 9 (1979), pp. 142–60. For statements of Western analysts linking demographic trends to political developments see especially Hélène Carrère d'Encausse, *Decline of an Empire: The Soviet Socialist Republics in Revolt* (New York: Newsweek, 1979), pp. 48, 86–7, 267; and Michael Rywkin, "Central Asia and Soviet manpower," *Problems of Communism*, vol. 28, no. 1 (January–February, 1979), pp. 1–13.

6   For a recent assessment of regional socioeconomic equality see Donna Bahry and Carol Nechemias, "Half full or half empty?: the debate over Soviet regional equality," *Slavic Review*, vol. 40, no. 3 (Fall 1981), pp. 366–83; for a study basing itself mainly on unionwide nationality statistics, but showing awareness of intrarepublic ethnic differentials, see Brian Silver, "Levels of sociocultural development among Soviet nationalities: a partial test of the equalization hypothesis," *American Political Science Review*, vol. 68, no. 4 (December 1974), pp. 1618–37. On methodological limitations of the latter analysis, as well as numerous similar studies, especially due to lack of age adjustment of data, see Ellen Jones and Fred W. Grupp, "Measuring nationality trends in the Soviet Union: a research note," *Slavic Review*, vol. 41, no. 1 (Spring 1982), pp. 112–22. For a discussion of the conceptual limitations of purely statistical evaluations of ethnic equality see Rasma Karklins, "Ethnic politics and access to higher education: the Soviet case," *Comparative Politics*, vol. 16, no. 3 (April 1984), pp. 277–94.

7   Ellen Jones and Fred W. Grupp, "Modernisation and ethnic equalisation in the USSR," *Soviet Studies*, vol. 36, no. 2 (April 1984), p. 175, who standardize data from Grey Hodnett, *Leadership in the Soviet National Republics* (Oakville: Mosaic Press, 1978), pp. 101–3.

8   Hodnett, *Leadership*, pp. 89–95.

9   cf. Iu. V. Arutiunian, "Izmenenie sotsial'noi struktury sovetskikh natsii," *Istoriia SSSR*, 1972, no. 4, p. 11; and *Sotsial'noe i natsional'noe, Opyt etnosotsiologicheskikh issledovanii po materialam Tatarskoi ASSR* (Moscow: Nauka, 1973), p. 29. More recently Richard Dobson has shown that participation in higher education is positively correlated with the number of skilled mental workers ($r = 0.89$). Richard B. Dobson, "Changes in patterns of ethnic stratification in the Soviet Union: are the Soviet nationalities converging?" paper presented at Annual Meeting of the Pacific Sociological Association, San Diego, California, 21–24 April 1982.

10 For a succinct analysis of factors causing Estonia to be different from the other Soviet republics see Tõnu Parming and Elmar Jarvesoo (eds.), *A Case Study of a Soviet Republic, the Estonian SSR* (Boulder, Colo.: Westview Press, 1978), esp. pp. 1–5.

11 Nancy Lubin, "Assimilation and retention of ethnic identity in Uzbekistan," *Asian Affairs*, vol. 12, pt. 3 (1981), p. 283.

12 Mark Popovsky, *Manipulated Science* (New York: Doubleday, 1979), p. 121.

13 ibid., pp. 130–3.
14 John Miller, who has studied the personnel policy of the CPSU in the nationality areas speaks of a carefully designed system in which Russian and native officials act as a check on each other: see John H. Miller, "Cadres policy in nationality areas. Recruitment of CPSU first and second secretaries in non-Russian republics of the USSR," *Soviet Studies*, vol. 29, no. 1 (January 1977), p. 34, 3–36, *passim*. Key jobs related to personnel affairs and security are dominated by non-natives: see Hodnett, *Leadership*, p. 95.
15 cf., for example, Jerry F. Hough, *Soviet Leadership in Transition* (Washington, D.C.: Brookings Institution, 1980), pp. 33–4; and Vernon V. Asparturian, "The non-Russian nationalities," in Allen Kassof (ed.), *Prospects for Soviet Society*, (New York: Praeger, 1968), p. 196.
16 Thus the former Soviet sociologist Zil'berman talks of a "pseudo-nationalization" of the governments and party apparati in the non-Russian republics which cannot by any means be regarded as a victory for nationalist principles: David Zil'berman, *"Ethnography in Soviet Russia,"* *Dialectical Anthropology*, 1976, no. 1, p. 150.
17 Rywkin, "Central Asia and Soviet manpower," pp. 11–13; and Popovsky, *Manipulated Science*, p. 134.
18 Daniel Bell, "Ethnicity and social change," in Nathan Glazer and Daniel P. Moynihan (eds.), *Ethnicity: Theory and Experience* (Cambridge, Mass.: Harvard University Press, 1975), p. 147.
19 G. I. Litvinova and B. Ts. Urlanis, "Demograficheskaia politika Sovetskogo Soiuza," *Sovetskoe gosudarstvo i pravo*, 1982, no. 3, p. 45. On Soviet "indigenization" policy in the first decades of Soviet rule see William K. Medlin, William M. Cave, and Finley Carpenter, *Education and Development in Central Asia* (Leiden: E. J. Brill, 1971), esp. pp. 69–70.
20 Soviet Central Asia has consistently held a special place in Soviet foreign propaganda and policy: see Rasma Karklins, "The nationality factor in Soviet foreign policy," in Roger Kanet (ed.), *Soviet Foreign Policy in the 1980s* (New York: Praeger, 1982), pp. 58–76.
21 Next to our previously cited sources this is confirmed by Russian samizdat of the right which has emphasized that Russian nationalism is promoted by the preferential treatment afforded to ethnic minorities; cf. various sources cited by Victor Zaslavsky, "The ethnic question in the USSR," *Telos*, vol. 5 (Fall 1980), p. 73.
22 Teresa Rakowska-Harmstone, "The study of ethnic politics in the USSR," in George W. Simmonds (ed.), *Nationalism in the USSR and Eastern Europe in the Era of Brezhnev and Kosygin* (Detroit, Mich.: University of Detroit Press, 1977), pp. 22–3.
23 cf. Robert A. Lewis, Richard H. Rowland, and Ralph S. Clem, "Modernization, population change and nationality in Soviet Central Asia and Kazakhstan," *Canadian Slavonic Papers*, vol. 17, no. 2–3 (Summer and Fall 1975), pp. 295–300, as well as previously noted data on educational levels.
24 Republic nationals tend to emphasize the beneficial role of such policies as well as the sovereign nature of their republics: for example, James Critchlow, "Nationalism in Uzbekistan in the Brezhnev era," in George W. Simmonds (ed.), *Ethnic Politics in the USSR*, pp. 309–15; and Teresa Rakowska-Harmstone, "Nationalism in Soviet Central Asia since 1964," in ibid., p. 287. For a recent Soviet article emphasizing the sovereign character of the union republics see V. M. Chkhikvadze, "Pravovye osnovy sblizheniia sovetskikh natsii," *Sotsiologicheskie issledovaniia*, 1982, no. 3, pp. 3–11.
25 George Saunders (ed.), *Samizdat: Voices of the Soviet Opposition* (New York: Monad Press, 1974), esp. pp. 430–5.

26 cf. Chapters 5 and 6. For specific references to negative repercussions on ethnic relations if "the educational level of the Russian population component rises further relative to that of the indigenous nationality" see A. A. Susokolov, "Vliianie razlichii v urovne obrazovaniia i chislennosti kontaktiruiushchikh etnicheskikh grupp na mezhetnicheskie otnosheniia (po materialam perepisei naseleniia SSSR 1959 i 1970 gg.)," *Sovetskaia etnografiia*, 1976, no. 1, p. 110; and Iu. Arutiunian, "Konkretno-sotsiologicheskoe issledovanie natsional'nykh otnoshenii," *Voprosy filosofii*, 1969, no. 12, p. 137.

4

Ethnicity in Institutional Settings: Schools and the Armed Forces

This chapter discusses the degree to which Soviet educational institutions and the armed forces have an ethnically integrative role. These two all-encompassing state institutions are the objects of much governmental planning and organization; how exactly are ethnic relations structured within them and what are the consequences of organizational arrangements? By their nature schools and the armed forces primarily involve young people and thus have a formative impact on ethnic perceptions and relations: what are the notions these young people attain? Is, for example, official policy toward language rights and ethnic stratification in these institutions seen to be equitable or not and what, if any, are the consequences of such popular perceptions?

Soviet schools and the military are good cases for the study of the relationship between the structural and attitudinal dimensions of ethnicity since varying approaches have been tried over time. Among these the two extreme "models" are the ethnically bifurcated school system in place in the non-Russian union republics until 1959, and the centralized all-union military service existing since the end of World War II. Although slowly changing in the case of the schools, a basically opposite organizational pattern persists in the contemporary Soviet Union: in most cases general education is segregated according to the language of instruction, and as an indirect consequence, by nationality as well; in contrast, recruits from all nationalities serve in ethnically mixed units, in which the Russian language is the only official language of command and communication.

What are the consequences of each of these contrasting approaches? Does, for example, institutional mixing and the dominance of one state language enhance the quality of ethnic interactions and attitudes, or is the opposite true?

This is a core question both theorists and practicians have long faced in multiethnic states. While choices are affected by calculations of practical feasibility, the assumptions about ethnopolitical consequences of either choice have been decisive in most instances. As to what the consequences might be, comparative theories of ethnic relations present two opposing views, which for the sake of simplicity will be called the "assimilationist" and the "pluralist" schools.

It is the contention of the "assimilationist" thinkers and politicians that the promotion of a "state language" and of ethnic contact within unitary institutions enhances ethnic and political integration. Usually the decrease of particularism is also expected to be a concomitant of modernization.[1] In contrast, the "pluralist" school of integration analysis has argued that acceptance and safeguarding of institutional and linguistic diversity—and even accepting a certain degree of conflict—is the approach most conducive to state integration as well as positive relations between nationalities.[2] The empirical cases cited in support for the latter argument are primarily Switzerland as an example of successful integration—as well as a whole sequence of negative examples of historical and temporal state disintegration due to overemphasis of functional homogenization. In contrast, the assimilationist school of thinking has emerged mainly from the American experience which has led critics to point out that generalizations from this immigrant society should be dealt with very carefully.[3]

Although using a different vocabulary, Soviet nationality policy over time has reflected the thinking of both schools. Being above all a practical politician, Lenin argued for a basically "pluralist" agenda after the October revolution,[4] and policy in the 1920s reflects this argument. The assimilationist approach has gradually but consistently gained ground since then. Gradual change has also taken place in the school system, but educational cultural pluralism for the primary nationalities was basically in place until the late 1970s, which is the temporal cutoff point for most data available for this study. As noted, language competition at the group level is one of the core issues in ethnic relations and various nationalities have diverging views about what is equitable. The non-Russian nations have shown that

102

education in native languages is valued highly. They have reacted sensitively to encroachments in this sphere, and one could go so far as to say that within the non-Russian republics the system of bilingual education is a cornerstone of the ethnic and political equilibrium.

As will be shown in this chapter, the experience with a limited number of integrated schools and with the integrated military service has been mixed. Although attitudes toward service in the unitary armed forces are difficult to discern, findings on language dissimulation and offduty ethnic grouping suggest that the integrative impact is limited at best. Our discussion, moreover, illustrates the role of language facility and attitudes in determining both the formal and informal emergence of mono- and multiethnic entities.

Educational Institutions

Next to the granting of a degree of territorial autonomy through the federal state structure, education is the main sphere in which the Soviet regime has made accommodative concessions to its non-Russian populations. Although there have been gradual changes over time, the use of native languages in general education has been pervasive among the larger nations inhabiting their own union republics. The motives for this have been twofold. For one, the question of language use in education has always been at the core of non-Russian ethnic concerns resulting in considerable political pressure. Soviet leaders, primarily under the influence of Lenin, recognized early on that their only hope of reaching the nationalities with their political and social message was to present it in a "national form," especially as it applies to language. This strategy was both practical—the great majority of non-Russians knew no Russian—and, at the same time, sensible in political–psychological terms. As Stalin said at the Twelfth Party Congress in 1923:[5]

> To make the Soviet regime in the republics understood and ingrained [and] . . . not merely Russian but also multinational . . . it is necessary that not only the schools but also all institutions, all organs—both Party and government—should become national step by step . . . should operate in the language understood by the masses.

The recognition of the role of native languages as a major tool and link to successful political and social integration bears emphasizing since it implies that any departure from this policy carries the risk of negative repercussions. Ethnic protests have occurred whenever inroads on native language education have been made, most notably so at the time of the educational reform of 1958–9. As a result, general education in native languages has largely stood its ground, with a significant decline occurring only among lower-status nationalities, especially those in the RSFSR.[6]

The status of non-Russian languages in Soviet education is an important topic in its own right, but the main reason for it being discussed here is its link with ethnic relations. Interethnic contact in schools and universities is limited if instruction is carried out in varying languages. In multiethnic states educational language policy inadvertently determines the extent of physical and institutional segregation of students, and we thus have to inquire about the specifics in the USSR.

Turning first to general education, one finds that it is typical for the non-Russian union republics to have a dual system of primary and secondary schools, each using its own language of instruction. It is also typical for the majority of schoolchildren to attend schools where instruction is given in their native language. Consequently most children of the republic nationality attend schools in the republic language, whereas Russian students—as well as most members of dispersed nationalities— attend schools where instruction is in Russian.[7] While this is the general rule, some change away from it has occurred since the educational reform of 1959 which provided the formal right of parents to choose which type of school their children would attend. When this reform was first proposed in 1958, it was widely interpreted as a measure jeopardizing the long-term viability of native-language education, triggering an unprecedented flow of open criticism on the part of the non-Russian nations. Thesis 19, as the reform proposal was to become known, was attacked in the press of the union republics and led to a heated debate in the Supreme Soviet of the USSR on 24 December 1958. After a temporary concession by the central authorities, most provisions of Thesis 19 were implemented unionwide in 1959.[8]

The issue of language use in schools has remained a sensitive one and it is indicative that it is difficult to find statistics about the number of students of each nationality enrolling in schools with one or the other language of instruction. As far as can be determined, there again is considerable variation between the republics with the number of republic nationals attending schools where the medium of instruction is Russian ranging between 5 and 35 percent. The lowest percentage of native children attending native language schools (approximately 65 percent) has been cited for Kazakhstan; calculations suggest that Belorussia is the next lowest, followed by the Ukraine. Latvia and Kirghizia hold an intermediate position, with the three remaining Central Asian republics, the three Caucasian republics, Lithuania and Estonia ranking at the top.[9]

As the enrollment pattern as well as the controversy over Thesis 19 indicates, the majority of non-Russians in the union republics prefer to have their children educated in native language schools. Another illustration for this is provided by a Soviet survey asking non-Russians about the preferred language of instruction in general education schools. As Table 4.1 shows, the majority of Moldavians, Estonians, Uzbeks and Georgians surveyed favor the native languages, with the percentage of pro-Russian sentiments in this context being especially low among Georgians and Estonians. It is notable that a relatively high percentage of urban Estonians (17 percent) and urban Uzbeks (14 percent) refused to answer at all. High refusal rates usually suggest that respondents view a question as too sensitive. Since the appropriate rates for rural Estonians and Uzbeks are lower than for their urban counterparts, one may assume that language policy is more controversial in cities than in the countryside. The argument that urbanization can increase conflict over ethnic issues is also found in the theoretical literature on ethnic relations. It is in the cities that ethnic contact occurs most frequently and where latent pressures for increased non-Russian enrollments in Russian-language schools are strongest.

For the time being most indigenous non-Russians in the union republics do, however, attend native-language general schools. The linguistic bifurcation of instruction has the inadvertent effect of physical ethnic segregation of schoolchildren, an effect which the Soviet authorities have tried to overcome by establishing a number of so-called "bilingual" schools. In this type of school parallel classes in both the local language and Russian are taught under one roof, but students are separated in their classes only during instruction, all other school activities being held together. Thus the children mix during recesses, in assemblies, school circles, and in the meetings of the school branches of the Pioneers and the Komsomol. Officially it is the purpose of these

Table 4.1 "In your Opinion, in What Language Should Children Be Taught in School?"

Preference	Moldavians urban (%)	Moldavians rural (%)	Estonians urban (%)	Estonians rural (%)	Uzbeks urban (%)	Uzbeks rural (%)	Georgians urban (%)	Georgians rural (%)
In the native language	53	72	70	71	54	65	n.d.	80
In Russian	23	11	3	3	29	20	n.d.	12
Use the native language in elementary grades; Russian in higher grades	12	8	10	12	2	3	n.d.	4
No answer	n.d.	7	17	13	14	3	n.d.	3
Totals*	86	98	100	99	99	91	n.d.	99

* The source does not provide any explanation why some of the totals do not add up to 100 percent.
Source: M. N. Guboglo, Razvitie dvuiazychiia v Moldavskoi SSR, Kishinev, Shtiintsa, 1979, p. 116.

schools to provide children with circumstances where they learn to speak the language of the other nationality more easily and, at the same time, acquire a more internationalist outlook.[10] In actuality the linguistic effect is one-sided, in that local children attending these schools learn more Russian since it is recognized that in such schools the "common language of the pupils in all extra class activities is Russian, which is the language of school administration."[11]

While the mixed schools achieve their linguistic purpose only in part, it is also doubtful that they fulfill their role of enhancing the "friendship of peoples." For one thing, there is little indication that the number of these schools has increased since the mid-1960s when they were first promoted unionwide.[12] There have also been reports by travelers suggesting that ethnic relations in the "internationalist" schools are less friendly than among students attending separate schools. Thus a teacher who works in a mixed school in Latvia recounted an incident in early 1982 which involved a fight between a Latvian and a Russian student. The militsia was called in and took the Latvian student to its station, from which he was released after having had his hair shaved off. When his Latvian fellow students saw what had happened, they all solidarized themselves by shaving off their own hair.[13] In instances like this bilingual schools hardly enhance ethnic harmony.

Soviet survey data for their part are inconclusive on the effect of mixed schools. While the Arutiunian survey of the Tatar ASSR shows that Tatars who have graduated from mixed or from Russian schools have "more favorable attitudes and enter into personal interethnic contact more often,"[14] this finding in itself does not prove a causal relationship since it is entirely possible that children attending such schools are more internationalist to begin with, or come from mixed families. Results of surveys conducted in Estonia support this point since it was found that when people were asked about their attitudes toward mixed bilingual schools, more favorable attitudes were found to be correlated with mixed parentage as well as bilingualism.[15]

The mixed schools notwithstanding, the structural organization of general primary and secondary education in the non-Russian union republics limits the extent of interethnic contact among students of different nationalities. The same is true for higher education, but to a lesser degree. It is again difficult to provide exact numerical measures since Soviet sources do not provide us with such. Rough calculations show, however, that while 65–95 percent of local youths in the non-Russian republics attend primary and secondary schools in their native languages, the appropriate percentage rate for higher education fluctuates between 20 and 80 percent, depending on the republic. University-level education in native languages is most prevalent in those republics that have a strong tradition of indigenous higher education such as Georgia and Armenia and the formerly independent Baltic states of Estonia, Latvia, and Lithuania. In these five republics the rate of native-language university attendance is close to the 80 percent mark, while the lower percentage rate of approximately 20 percent applies to the Central Asian republics as well as Kazakhstan and Belorussia. Azerbaijan, the Ukraine, and Moldavia appear to hold an intermediate position.[16]

Other data show that the contrast between higher education in Central Asia and the Baltic republics is indeed striking. Out of six higher educational institutions in Turkmenistan only one, the Pedagogical Institute, uses Turkmen as the medium of instruction. Russian is also used, while at the Baltic universities the majority of courses are taught in the local languages. This is not to say that courses in Russian aren't offered there as well, but few natives will enroll in them unless it is the only course available.[17] In those instances where programs and courses are taught in both the local languages and Russian it typically occurs according to the *dvo potoka* (two streams) principle of parallel courses being taught within the same institution. This means that—as is the case in the bilingual general schools—students are segregated during class instruction but mix in university assemblies and organizations.

Little is known about the quality and quantity of this extracurricular mixing, but our interviews with emigrants who have attended Soviet higher educational institutions suggest that contact generally is limited. All of our Soviet German respondents had attended programs taught in Russian. While the student body was mixed in some cases, in most it was predominantly Russian. When respondents were asked to characterize the relations between students of different nationality both in their educational institutions as well as within the city they live in, the great majority (over 80 percent) said that relations were non-problematic. The typical response was rather short, just noting "relations were normal," or "relations were good." Some individuals gave short explanations such as "when one is studying, nationality doesn't make any difference, all have the same goal, to study" (25); and "I didn't notice anything, everybody

108

was only thinking about exams." Some others indicated that this was not true in every situation: "That was okay, wherever there are only whites, it's okay" (1, from Frunze); "Relations were friendly . . . It's impossible for any conflicts to arise, but in the shops, in the city, a Kirghiz will let another Kirghiz go ahead when standing in line" (59); and "In those times [1920s and 1930s] no differences were made" (134).

In those few instances where respondents mentioned strains in interethnic relations most referred to students of a certain nationality keeping to themselves. A respondent from the Udmurt region of the RSFSR described relations like this: "The Tatars know how to get along well with other people . . . The Udmurts, however, are looked down upon" (153). Among those noting bad relations between students three comments stand out: "In Latvia one finds more quarreling among students" (130); "Nowadays there constantly are conflicts between Russians and Kazakhs, especially among the students" (21); and "Everyone looks down on the Kirghiz, they are the most backward, dumb, and dirty" (59).

Such pejorative remarks about the "backwardness" of Kazakhs or Central Asians were by no means infrequent and appear to be characteristic of a certain segment of the "white" population of the USSR. This can also be seen in the way the problem of ethnic discrimination or favoritization during the course of studies in colleges was referred to. While only one respondent said that a nationality was disfavored—the Udmurts in the RSFSR—all others stated that the respective republic nationality was favored. Some said so in general terms: "the group of students from the republic—they had unwritten privileges" (19); or "Estonians are favored" (32). But others gave specifics, such as: "The Kirghiz have a harder time studying, and therefore are helped more, so that they can graduate . . . More is required from the Russian students . . . we accept that, the Russians as well, everybody knows that the Kirghiz have a harder time studying . . . They speak Kirghiz among themselves, and when instruction is in Russian, they don't understand as well" (1, from Frunze).

Other respondents mentioned that when somebody knows Russian badly, he is let through examinations easier (173) or that no difference is made "except for the blacks, they [the instructors] ask less of them, because they know that they are less gifted" (144). The latter quote again illustrates Soviet European perceptions of Central Asians as backward. To the degree that this attitude is evident to the indigenous population it is bound to be detrimental to harmonious ethnic relations. The same applies to the perception of the locals being favored, which is a theme already discussed in Chapter 2. It is worth noting here that there is a link between "affirmative action" and language policy since admissions and other examinations are in part made easier for non-Russians because they do not know Russian that well. In so far as instruction in native languages is available the need for such special arrangements decreases and so do the divisive images of backwardness and favoritism.

Two additional characteristics of the Soviet system of VUZy (Russian acronym for Higher Educational Institutions) influence ethnic relations. Thus contact among students is limited if they are enrolled in evening or correspondence courses, which is the case for nearly one-half of the student body.[18] Ethnic mixing of students is, on the other hand, intensified in those instances when a student leaves his or her native region to study elsewhere such as at one of the more prestigious universities of the RSFSR. While some students may venture out on their own, there is a program encouraging non-Russian students to study at the elite universities of the USSR. Exact data are again hard to obtain, but it is clear that such a program has existed since the 1920s and that it involves special admission quotas and fellowships. According to current practice, the USSR Ministry of Higher and Specialized Education reserves a number of study places for members of specific nationalities and then the appropriate number of students—for example, Tadjiks who have successfully gained admission in one of the local universities in Tadjikistan—are delegated to the reserved slots at the central universities.

Since students who have completed their studies under this program are assigned work in their native territories,[19] its underlying political rationale seems to be the training of native elite members who will be socialized to be loyal to the central system. In one defense of this program a Soviet education official also argues that it promotes the national development of non-Russian nationalities, and another calls it one of the forms of cooperation and mutual aid of Soviet republics.[20] Nevertheless, there are indications that this program is unpopular among at least some of the non-Russian nationalities; thus in 1980 a Georgian newspaper article entitled "Would you like to study in Moscow?" noted that there were insufficient applicants for the reserved places at VUZy outside of Georgia even though there were four candidates per slot within Georgia.[21] Language facility again plays a role since poor knowledge of Russian—especially among non-Russian youths from rural areas—has been pinpointed as a barrier for their participation in educational programs outside of their native republics.[22] Other motives are the general reluctance of many non-Russians to leave their native republics as well as past experiences of minority students not always being well-treated at Russian universities.[23]

Thus one can summarize the situation in regard to higher educational institutions by saying that the great majority of republic nationals study within their own republics, where they constitute a large segment of the student body. If programs are available in Russian as well as in the local languages, this results in a division of the student body in ethnically differentiated groups and institutional subsectors. Where this is the case—and the arrangements differ significantly from republic to republic—students tend to mix relatively little.

The situation may be changing, however, since in the course of the new language policies pursued since the mid-1970s the increasing use of Russian in the VUZy has been emphasized. Although this is not spelled out, one of the results will be more ethnic mixing of the student body. Thus the recommendation to broaden the practice of teaching some courses only in Russian[24] implies that non-Russians and Russians will attend the same courses more frequently. While there is the prospect of increasing interethnic contact in the universities, there is however, little guarantee that this will lead to increasing ethnic integration and harmony. The problems involved can be elaborated upon by a survey of experiences with ethnic integration in the Soviet armed forces.

The Armed Forces

The multiethnicity of the Soviet armed forces has been studied surprisingly little. The few existing studies focus on the implications of ethnic diversity on the effectiveness of the Soviet military in fulfilling its primary role of safeguarding external and internal security.[25] Yet the armed forces also represent a major state institution which affects the lives of the young male population of the USSR and its impact as a tool of socialization has both a calculated and an uncalculated side. The question we want to focus on concerns its formative impact on ethnic relations and perceptions.

According to official Soviet precepts, the armed forces should be—and are—a highly integrative institution and a school of internationalism.[26] This goal is promoted through structural arrangements, cultural policy, and political socialization. More specifically the policy is one of having young conscripts from all nationalities serve in ethnically mixed units, in which Russian is both the only official language and the lingua franca, and exposing them to intense political indoctrination which emphasizes the love for the common motherland and the brotherhood of all Soviet nations. As is true for all politics and social planning, however, the key question concerns the relationship between intentions and reality. Is service in the armed forces really contributing to integrating the multinational Soviet population?

ETHNIC GROUPINGS AND ENVIRONMENTS

In the first decades of Soviet rule some nationalities had their own military units within the Soviet armed forces, but after a short revival during World War II, the monoethnic military formations were relegated to history.[27] In the postwar period all that official Soviet sources tell us about ethnic structuring within the military forces is that men of all nationalities serve together in ethnically mixed units. Nevertheless, there are indications that there is both a pattern of deliberate formal ethnic stratification and structuring as well as informal clustering resulting from social factors and the spontaneous behavior of the soldiers.

Since ethnic stratification within the armed forces is a sensitive issue, it is not unusual for the governing elites of multiethnic states to be uncommunicative about it[28] and to leave analysts to their own devices. In our case the needed original research consists primarily of interview questions put to those of our Soviet German respondents who had served in the Soviet military since 1964.[29] This source suggests that although the demographic reality of the USSR could theoretically lead to three types of units being formed, namely, units that are dominated by Russians, units that are dominated by a specific non-Russian nationality, and units that are ethnically mixed to the degree that no one nationality holds the majority, in practice only the first and third type exist. Our interviews furthermore suggest that the units in which there is no one majority frequently are extremely mixed. Respondents who had served in such units were unable to specify their national composition, typically saying "there were too many nationalities, I don't know" or "it was international, everything conceivable." Soviet press reports similarly emphasize the intensity of ethnic mixing in various units. In contrast, it is the finding of an interview study conducted under the auspices of the Rand Corporation that subgroups of draftees from specific nationalities and regions serve together as a result of the induction system,[30] which suggests that some clustering of nationalities is prearranged.

Rough demographic calculations show that strongly mixed units in which Russians constitute a minority are by no means rare since, according to the 1979 Census, Russians constitute just 52 percent of the Soviet population, and less than that among the draft-age cohort. Although it is difficult to prove any official ethnic policy of assignments, there are indications that a *de facto* pattern exists according to which the units with fewer Russians are those that have non-combat roles, whereas combat units include more Russians and other Slavs. As a rule of thumb, it is safe to say that the more sensitive or the more technologically sophisticated the service branch or task a unit is assigned to, the higher is the percentage of Russian soldiers.[31]

Several conclusions may be drawn from this for the purposes of our analysis. Only a minority of non-Russian draftees serve in units numerically dominated by Russians, and those that do typically have a higher educational and technological level as well as a better command of Russian. The young men with lower skills end up in units that ethnically are highly mixed. Presumably the differential experiences and environment have a differential impact on these subgroups of non-Russians as well as on the Russians. For many conscripts military service provides the first intensive exposure to the multiethnic reality of the Soviet state, and the pattern of assignments suggests that one of the notions they will take away with them is that being Russian is associated with being assigned more responsible roles.

Ethnic mixing in the Soviet armed forces not only affects national groups, but also territorial assignments. There appears to be a pattern according to which units with a Russian majority are predominantly stationed in the borderland non-Russian republics and, as a result, the "internationalist" mixed units are more frequently found in the RSFSR. This practice increases the overall exposure of both the Russian and non-Russian conscripts to "other ethnic" environments during their military service: whenever soldiers are on furlough or otherwise come into contact with the local population, they tend to encounter people of a nationality other than their own.

Next to patterns of ethnic assignments and stationing, ethnic stratification is the most important structural dimension affecting social processes within a multiethnic state institution such as the Soviet military. According to all indications, there is little ethnic differentiation between soldiers and non-commissioned officers, but a major gap exists in regard to the officer corps which is dominated by Russians. Nearly all (83 percent) of our respondents said that Russians formed a clear majority among their superior officers. This finding is confirmed by other sources who also concur with our survey, in that those few officers who come from a non-Russian background are strongly Russified. This is partly due to the exclusive role of the Russian language in all official training and transactions, but adjustment goes beyond pure linguistic facility.[32] Thus one of our respondents mentioned that "there was a Latvian officer, but he had become like a Russian . . . he wanted to get ahead" (119); and another former serviceman said that he could not distinguish of what nationality his officers were: "they spoke Russian and looked like them . . . just try to ask about it" (52). Thus even those officers who are not Russian do little to limit the Russian image of the officer corps. This has implications for ethnic relations within the military, as well as in society at large, since it shows that advancement and integration within a unionwide state institution require extensive cultural Russification and outward merging with the dominant state nation.

In contrast to the strongly Russian officer corps, men of various nationalities serve as non-commissioned officers. When we asked our respondents about the nationality of their sergeants and whether they thought that nationality played a role in the promotion to sergeant, the typical response was "no, there was no difference" and "I was a sergeant myself" or "education is decisive." Nobody indicated that selections were made on the basis of nationality, the one exception being self-selection. Certain individuals were said to be more eager to become sergeants and, as a result, would be chosen more frequently. Several said this to be true for Ukrainians, but one also mentioned Caucasians and another said: "those are mostly Germans . . . whoever knows how to command, nationality doesn't play a role; there was also a Turkmen" (82). The point about Germans appears to be well taken since quite a few of our respondents were in that role.

While there seems to be little ethnic stratification in the case of non-commissioned officers, two additional points should be kept in mind. For one, there are distinctions between professional sergeants who remain in the military for extended service and conscripts who are promoted to sergeants while serving their legal term of duty. The latter type wields less power and are, in the case of non-combat construction units, little more than the leaders of workteams. Nearly all our Soviet German respondents fall into the second category. Thus it appears that while this junior sergeant role is open to all nationalities, the professional sergeants are predominantly drawn from Slavs, especially Ukrainians.[33]

Although our limited data do not allow definitive conclusions, all this implies that significant ethnic clustering and stratification occurs within the formal organizations of the Soviet armed forces. There are strong suggestions that informal clustering also takes place since the soldiers try to keep within their ethnic groups in their personal and offduty relations. Even though all new recruits are warned against the dangers of "national cliquism" (natsional'naia gruppovshchina),[34] it nevertheless is widely practiced among non-Russians as well as Russians. The latter bears reemphasizing since there is a tendency for people to think of "ethnic" characteristics and behavior, only affecting non-majority nations.

The tendency of soldiers to stick together as much as possible with their coethnics has both a communal and a linguistic basis. The prevalent notion among our Soviet German respondents was that it was natural for each nationality to "keep with its own." The statement, "The Kirghiz kept to themselves, and the Uzbeks, everybody. During offduty time everyone keeps together [with their own], it isn't international as they write; a human being is a human being and to each his own are closer" (168), is typical. In the rare (25 percent) cases where respondents thought differently they usually said that soldiers stick together according to the year they enter the service. There is a pervasive custom according to which the older soldiers harass new conscripts, but even here nationality intervenes at least on some occasions: "Of course the black nation kept together. The Russians ridicule their first-year soldiers, harass them, but the Kazakhs defend their young draftees . . . The Kazakhs and Tatars always stand for the other, go on furlough together" (61).

THE ROLE OF LANGUAGE

In a highly centralized and ethnically mixed institution such as the Soviet armed forces the use of language takes on a special significance. In this instance the official Soviet line has been unequivocal and uncompromising, in that Russian is the one and only language of command, training, and socialization. This policy is so consistent that it risks becoming impractical since even though language deficiencies among non-Russian soldiers—of whom a considerable number enter the service with a limited knowledge of Russian—are noted and lamented in the Soviet press, the language problem is not formally recognized in the sense that no special language-training programs exist within the armed forces.[35] The official Soviet rationale appears to be that the formal dominance of Russian as well as the intense mixing of nationalities will provide its own solution to the problem, in that the non-Russian draftees will "automatically" absorb enough Russian to function effectively. While this partly may be true in the case of military task fulfillment—several respondents noted that one does not need to speak much and quickly learns whatever is needed—there are consequences for ethnic grouping and integration.

The level of Russian-language knowledge influences the unit and task assignments, in effect enhancing structural ethnic segregation as outlined above. Informal clustering is enhanced as well since the linguistically alien environment makes non-Russian soldiers even more eager to seek out conationals and to spend as much time with them as possible. Our interviews indicate that the use of non-Russian languages during offduty time is widespread in all types of units, including those where Russians form a numerical majority. There are even cases when the use of native languages spills over into onduty conversations either because a conational is asked to translate something from Russian or simply because many ethnics prefer to converse with each other in their native language. While such practices may alleviate the language problem as such, the use of non-Russian languages by subgroups of soldiers has the effect of aggravating ethnic tensions since Russian soldiers often object to not understanding conversations, or else ridicule the non-Russians for their weak command of Russian.

Former Soviet servicemen now living in the West state that some of the non-Russians only pretend not to know Russian even if they do. Thus "there was an Uzbek about whom it was said that he didn't want to speak Russian and pretended not knowing it. I taught him 'say *mina*,' but he said 'Nina' . . . I tried to explain to him that that is a girl's name, but to no avail . . . He was transferred to the kitchen crew" (82). The desire to be

116

assigned to easier duties is only one of the perceived reasons why language dissimulation occurs. Other explanations are that some non-Russians are reluctant to serve at all, or use language as a means of expressing general attitudes. To cite one example, "although Estonians are not hostile people, Estonian recruits treat Russians and the Russian language in a hostile manner."[36] Negative attitudes related to the use of language are not restricted to non-Russians. As was noted, some Russians react negatively to the use of languages they don't understand. Moreover, the perception of language dissimulation itself may reflect a certain bias which assumes that the non-Russians understand Russian better than they actually do. This leads us to the question about the general state of ethnic relations within the military context.

ETHNIC RELATIONS

While there is good evidence that soldiers stick together according to nationality during offduty time as well as use their native languages, it is more difficult to determine the overall quality of inservice ethnic relations and the long-term impact of military service on ethnic identity and consciousness. The issue is analytically complex and there are severe data problems. While emigrant surveys again provide some insight, they do not provide definitive proof. Soviet sources, on the other hand, are of no help at all since they do not go beyond slogans about the spirit or internationalism and brotherhood prevailing throughout, and being strengthened through military service.

The Rand Corporation interview study, for one, claims the opposite of the officially presented picture of harmony. It cites numerous respondents giving examples of ethnic and racial tension which not only suggest the widespread use of ethnic slurs and verbal attacks, but also physical violence. To cite a summary conclusion:[37]

In the Soviet peacetime armed forces, ethnic conflict is frequent, perhaps prevalent, and occasionally severe. In most cases, we believe that the Soviet armed forces fail to bring about a homogenization of interests and a leveling of ethnic consciousness. To the contrary, national distinctions in many cases, probably a majority, appear to be enhanced by military experience.

117

Our own interview data are only partly in accord with this finding. Ethnic disharmony and antagonisms certainly exist, and especially so between Russians, other "whites" (a classification used by respondents) and Soviet Central Asians. It is not unusual to hear comments, such as: "the Kazakhs and Uzbeks were nationalists, nobody got along with them" (16); or "the Kazakhs—and generally all the blacks—were looked down upon" (18); and "the Russians were contemptuous toward the Asians and the same was true the other way around" (21). But there were other statements about the equality of treatment and about ethnic slurs being punishable.

The diversity of views is furthermore evident in the replies of the Soviet German respondents when asked to provide an evaluation whether "serving in the military strengthens mutual understanding among the nationalities." Of the thirty-four individuals who had experienced military service, 64 percent replied affirmatively, 28 percent negated the proposition, and 6 percent passed. Of those who said yes, most commented on the general integrative effect of the service experience, such as: "You are in a group together, are trained together" (60); "Yes, we all ate from the same pot, we had to be unified" (16); "Yes, in the army a command is a command, there one doesn't look at nationality" (27); "One goes together through all difficulties" (158); "You work together, get to know each other . . . Some know Russian badly, [but] learn it in two years" (159); "You meet very many, find some friends" (58); "In the service all are unified . . . they turn toward the Russian culture" (173); and "Mostly yes, it is different only in those cases where there are many Russians, or many from the Caucasus, then there might be some disunity, but in general the Russian army is very strong, there are many polit-workers; those always see to it that nothing happens" (144).

Of those who said that military service does not enhance ethnic understanding, most commented on a specific ethnic problem: "No, it gets even worse . . . The Russians are more on top . . . Before that, I too thought that all are equal in the service the way they tell it to you, but it isn't" (168); "You learn to know each other, but not to understand each other . . . The Kazakhs and generally the blacks were regarded as much lower beings" (18); "The Russians and Germans did not get along with the Asians; one gets angry, they pretend to be fools, don't want to work, one had to do their work—we beat them up, that helped" (94); "No, conflicts occur. The Armenians and Tatars keep in groups. The Russians keep with the Germans and Ukrainians, are more

118

unified" (93); and "No. It shows who has lived in what society. The nationalities stick together" (61).

Although our sample is small (N = 34) and results must remain inconclusive, it appears that this diversity of evaluations could be related to the differential composition of the units respondents had served in. Those giving negative evaluations of the integrative effect of the military experience mostly served in strongly mixed units, whereas those providing a more positive view had served in predominantly Russian units (most had served in Russian-dominated units, that is, twenty out of thirty-four). The comments also suggest that political control and lecturing, the logic of institutional task fulfillment, and the social experience of serving together do—at least to some degree—enhance interethnic understanding. And sometimes the experience of an alien environment makes for new ties between individuals, who although from different ethnic groups, come from the same village or town. Thus "I had Kirghiz friends there, we are from the *kolkhoz* . . . I looked for them, we were from the same place and it was very interesting when someone received a letter" (109); "[I kept together] with Kazakhs, we were from the same place, I knew them" (121); and "If he is your *zemliak*, then even if he is a Turk, you stick together with him" (163). This notion of a special tie of friendship due to a common place of origin emerging within the context of a new and "foreign" environment suggests that, under certain conditions, new factors begin to influence ethnic relations.

One thus finds that while some ethnic schisms are widened during military service, others are narrowed. Levels of relations again play a role. The narrowing of ethnic gaps as described by our respondents refers primarily to the personal level, whereas the politically more relevant level of group relations remains a question mark.

Conclusions

In a comparative study of the impact of military service on intercommunal relations Cynthia Enloe concludes that while modern mass societies conventionally portray their armed forces as grand integrators and schools of national citizenship, this image is frequently misleading in the case of multiethnic states. For the integrative goal to be achieved certain minimal conditions have to be fulfilled: there must be upward mobility for all objectively qualified members, all groups should be equally subject to military service, there must be complete mixing in various subunits, soldiers of all groups should be trusted enough to be assigned even the most sensitive tasks, and "the language of training and military socialization in general should not be employed so as to impose the culture of the politically dominant group on recruits from all other communities."[38]

As the preceding discussion has illustrated, these five conditions are by no means fulfilled in the Soviet case. The officer corps is dominated by Russians and by a few minority nationals who do not care if they become indistinguishable from Russians. Upward mobility is more extensive in the ranks of non-commissioned officers, but this opportunity is apparently mostly taken advantage of by Ukrainians. One also finds that while all nationalities are subject to military service, there is a *de facto* tendency for the non-Russians to serve in non-combat units such as construction battalions and railroad and guard units. There can be no doubt that the Russian language is altogether dominant. While the officially promoted bilingualism is at least minimally reciprocal at places of work and elsewhere, its sole interpretation within the military is the learning of Russian by non-Russians.

As the conditions for an integrative effect of military service as set by Enloe are not fulfilled, what are the consequences? Drawing again on the experience of numerous multiethnic societies, Enloe finds that in circumstances like these many ethnic identifiers leave the military with a keener sense of the salience of their own ethnicity. She also notes that demobilized soldiers returning to their communities are generally less willing to accept set forms of subservience that traditionally minimize interethnic hostilities and are more willing to interact with the elites for the sake of improving their own communities' well-being.[39] In the Soviet case one should also take into account that the demobilized soldiers have acquired certain skills and experiences which make them more adept at interacting with the system since they typically improve their knowledge of Russian and their competency in referring to official themes of equal ethnic opportunity and status, and have experienced the workings of a major Russian-dominated institution. It is the official Soviet expectation that this socialization will lead to the young men being more closely integrated into the existing system; it is equally possible, however, that it leads to its rejection or to a strategy of intrasystem change.

As one tries to clarify the sociopolitical consequences of the military service experience on non-Russian youth it is useful again to differentiate between subgroups of nationalities, differing ethnic environments, and levels of interaction as well as between functional and attitudinal integration.

The latter distinction was first made by Teresa Rakowska-Harmstone when she evaluated ethnic integration within the Soviet armed forces a few years ago.[40] "Integration" is one of the vaguer terms in political science, and it is helpful to differentiate between its functional aspects related to objective attributes such as language facility and ease of cooperation, and subjective attributes such as values and political attitudes. The relationship between the two is complex; "assimilationist" thinkers and practitioners tend to assume that it entails a positive correlation, whereas the "pluralists" contend that the correlation can be negative, even more so if the "functional" change is involuntary.

As one applies these concepts to the evaluation of the integrative effect of military service in the USSR, one first notes a qualitative gap between the two types of ethnic environments within the Soviet armed forces. In the Russian-dominated units functional integration is strong,[41] and for at least some groups and nationalities attitudinal integration also appears to be considerable. As will be noted in the next chapter, knowing Russian better is associated with more "internationalist" attitudes among blue-collar workers. Ukrainian dissidents for their part have lamented that many Ukrainian conscripts lose both their cultural and emotional link to their native community.[42] The military experience also appeared to have been mostly integrative for a segment of our Soviet German respondents, especially those who served in Russian-dominated units. Thus Slavic nationalities as well as smaller and territorially dispersed groups are those for whom functional and attitudinal integration is most likely to go hand in hand.

The data about other nationalities do, however, tend to substantiate the claim made by Rakowska-Harmstone that those nations who have a pronounced historical national identity, such as Balts, Georgians, and Armenians, remain emotionally unaffected by functional integration and frequently even react in the opposite direction, namely, with increased resentment about the pressures to Russify.[43] This is primarily a political reaction and does not exclude the possibility that on an individual level conscripts from these nationalities too form new interethnic friendships and feelings of camaraderie. Here more detailed data

121

would probably reveal a pattern of friendship formation similar to the one relating to intermarriage (see Chapter 6), that is, that nationals from similar cultural and religious backgrounds are most likely to get together.

While integration is only partly successful in units dominated by Russians, it is even less so in the internationalist units in which a majority of non-Russians serve. Social fragmentation along ethnic lines appears to be widespread, and the use of Russian is less pronounced, especially in offduty conversations. Consequently "functional" integration is less effective, and attitudinal integration is even more questionable. At a minimum this intense contact experience with a variety of other nationalities enhances ethnic self-awareness; one should not forget that this is also the case for the young Russian conscripts.

Thus we find that although the Soviet armed forces are the formally most integrated unionwide institution of the USSR, their integrative impact is uncertain. To the degree that the Soviet leaders reappraise their ethnic calculus they may consider alternative approaches such as an increased emphasis on single nationality units as were used in the early Soviet period. Such units are said to have "strengthened fraternal relations among the peoples of our country, promoted the liquidation of inequality among them in the military sphere, and helped to eliminate suspicion toward the Russian people."[44] This statement appeared in a 1982 Soviet Kazakh article on the Kazakh Red Army units existing during 1922–38. It shows that the notion of the positive role of territorial military formations has not been relegated to the historical past, in spite of the omission of the pre-1977 constitutional references to the right of each union republic to have its own military formations.[45]

It also helps to remember the "lessons" learned from the experience with various types of educational structures. On balance it appears that the granting of education in the native languages to the union republic nations has been successful from the integrative point of view. First, it has, at least in part, fulfilled its original aim of serving as the expeditor of political socialization since the "socialist content" of the Soviet message would have had a much lower impact if it had not been couched in the "national form" linguistically. Secondly, the high degree of preference for native-language schools among non-Russians, as well as their intensely negative reaction to any encroachments in this sphere, shows that the acceptance of the multilingual education system on the part of the central authorities has prevented

122

an escalation of ethnic antagonism. In other words, "preventive medicine" is very good medicine. And finally, it bears reflecting on the underlying integrative rationale of this approach to multiethnicity and multilingualism. The institutionalization of cultural pluralism through the system of bilingual education is a strategy which through preserving diversity aims at building and enhancing a more comprehensive unity.[46] The experience of both the USSR and other multiethnic countries suggests that it is a valid strategy which can be changed only at a high cost.

Notes: Chapter 4

1   cf. Milton M. Gordon, *Assimilation in American Life* (New York: Oxford University Press, 1964), esp. chs. 4 and 5; and Hubert Blalock, Jr., *Toward a Theory of Minority-Group Relations* (New York: Wiley, 1967), ch. 2.
2   R. A. Schermerhorn, *Comparative Ethnic Relations* (New York: Random House, 1970), p. 84.
3   See Cynthia Enloe, *Ethnic Conflict and Political Development* (Boston, Mass.: Little, Brown, 1973), esp. chs. 3 and 7.
4   cf. Hélène Carrère d'Encausse, "Determinants and Parameters of Soviet Nationality Policy," in Jeremy R. Azrael (ed.), *Soviet Nationality Policies and Practices* (New York: Praeger, 1978), pp. 41–7; Isabelle Kreindler, "Lenin, Russian, and Soviet language policy," *International Journal of the Sociology of Language*, 1982, no. 33, pp. 129–35; and V. Stanley Vardys, "Language, Lenin, and politics," ibid., p. 125. For an excellent analysis of Lenin's dialectical thinking on this matter see Walker Connor, *The National Question in Marxist–Leninist Theory and Strategy* (Princeton, N.J.: Princeton University Press, 1984), pp. 201–5.
5   Cited after Jaan Pennar, Ivan I. Bakalo, and George Bereday, *Modernization and Diversity in Soviet Education* (New York: Praeger, 1971), p. 167.
6   Brian D. Silver, "The status of national minority languages in Soviet education: an assessment of recent changes," *Soviet Studies*, vol. 26, no. 1 (January 1974), pp. 28–40; for a good historical summary of changing trends in native language education see Yaroslav Bilinsky, "Education of the non-Russian peoples in the USSR, 1917–1967, an essay," *Slavic Review*, vol. 27, no. 3 (September 1968), pp. 411–37.
7   This is especially true for Ukrainians living outside of the Ukraine, as well as for dispersed nationalities such as Soviet Germans and Jews. In some cases, such as that of Lithuanian Poles, schools in a language other than Russian and the republic language are available. See, for example, Iu. D. Desheriev, *Zakonomernosti razvitiia literaturnykh iazykov v sovetskuiu epokhu* (Moscow: Nauka, 1976), pp. 65–6.
8   Yaroslav Bilinsky, "Soviet education laws of 1958–9 and Soviet nationality policy," *Soviet Studies*, vol. 14, no. 2 (October 1962), pp. 143–7; see also Chapter 2.
9   M. A. Prokof'ev, "V protsesse sblizheniie natsii," *Russkii iazyk v natsional'noi shkole*, 1979, no. 4, p. 12, states that "on the whole nearly 1/3 of students in our country study in their native (non-Russian) languages, but in the Uzbek, Georgian, Azeri, Lithuanian, Tadzhik, Armenian and Turkmen union

republics—more than 80% of the students." Jonathan Pool, "Soviet language planning: goals, results, options," in Azrael (ed.), *Soviet Nationality Policies*, p. 229, cites a Soviet source on 68 percent of Kazakhs in 1966/7 attending native-language schools; see also ibid., p. 30, for calculations giving approximate rates for other nationalities. Desheriev, "Zakonomernosti," p. 39, cites 5·5 percent of Azeris in Azerbaijan attending Russian-language schools in 1968/9. For some data suggesting that no radical changes have been occurring in this regard see Iu. V. Bromlei, *Sovremennye etnicheskie protsessy v SSSR* (Moscow: Nauka, 1975), p. 270.

10 See, for example, *Pravda*, 5 April 1966, p. 8, and 4 January 1974; and more recently *Sovetskaia etnografiia*, 1982, no. 1, p. 165.

11 *Narodnoe obrazovanie*, 1965, pp. 3, 9. See also Prokof'ev, "V protsesse," pp. 19–20.

12 Statistics are again hard to obtain. In the case of Latvia 247 such schools existed in 1966 and one-third of the republic's schoolchildren were attending them: *Pravda*, 5 April 1966, p. 8; but in 1982 only 130 such schools were said to exist: *Padomju Latvijas Komunists*, 1982, no. 8, p. 33. Desheriev, "Zakonomernosti," p. 39, mentions that in 1968/9 24 percent of students in Azerbaijan were enrolled in bilingual schools, and another source mentions that one-third of all schoolchildren were in Kirghizia: I. S. Puchkov, and G. A. Popov, "Sociodemographic characteristics of science personnel," *Soviet Sociology*, vol. 17, no. 4 (Spring 1978), p. 40.

13 Personal communication.

14 cf. Table 6.1, p. 156.

15 Iukhan Kakhk, *Cherty skhodstva* (Tallinn: Eesti Raamat, 1974), pp. 95, 99.

16 This analysis is based on the reading of a large variety of sources most of which allow only this type of broad estimate. In one unusual case of exact data being cited for some republics it may be concluded from a sequence of data that close to 70 percent of Azeri students and 90 percent of Lithuanian students receive higher education in their native languages: A. N. Baskakov and V. Iu Mikhal'chenko (eds.), *Razvitie natsional'nykh iazykov v sviazi s ikh funktsionirovaniem v sfere vysshego obrazovaniia* (Moscow: Nauka, 1982), pp. 34–9, 78–81.

17 ibid., pp. 77–82, 159–160, 225–6.

18 Evening and correspondence school enrollments amounted to 56·5 percent of the total in 1960, and to 45 percent in 1970. See N. S. Egorov, "Main trends in the development of higher education," *Soviet Review*, vol. 19, no. 4 (1978–9), p. 25.

19 See Leonid Novikov, *Hochschulen in der Sowjetunion* (Frankfurt-on-Main: Deutsches Institut für Internationale Pädagogische Forschung, 1981), pp. 57–8; and Bilinsky, "Education of non-Russians," p. 428.

20 *Vestnik vysshei shkoly* (December 1963), p. 78; and V. A. Shpiliuk, *Mezhres publikanskaia migratsiia i sblizhenie natsii v SSSR* (L'vov: Vishcha shkola, 1975), p. 127.

21 *Akhalgazrda komunisti*, 19 July 1980, and 8 September 1980.

22 *Pravda*, 27 January 1981, p. 2.

23 See, for example, Mark Popovsky, *Manipulated Science* (New York: Doubleday, 1979), *passim*.

24 For a good summary see Roman Solchanyk, "Russian language and Soviet politics," *Soviet Studies*, vol. 34, no. 1 (January 1982), p. 32.

25 cf. S. Enders Wimbush and Alex Alexiev, *The Ethnic Factor in the Soviet Armed Forces* (Santa Monica, Calif.: Rand Corporation, 1982); for a contrasting view assigning less significance to ethnicity on Soviet military capability see Ellen Jones, "Manning the Soviet military," *International Security*, vol. 7, no. 1 (Summer 1982), pp. 105–31.

26 See, for example, V. Samoilenko, "Druzhba narodov—istochnik mogushchestva vooruzhennykh sil SSSR," *Kommunist vooruzhennykh sil*, 1982, no. 15, p. 15; S. Kurkotkin, "V dukhe druzhby narodov," *Kommunist vooruzhennykh sil*, 1970, no. 16, p. 23; and V. Zinovyev, "The army of the friendship of peoples," *Soviet Military Review*, 1979, pp. 45–6.

27 For more details see Susan L. Curran and Dmitry Ponomareff, *Managing the Ethnic Factor in the Russian and Soviet Armed Forces: An Historical Overview* (Santa Monica, Calif.: Rand Corporation, 1982).

28 cf. Cynthia H. Enloe, "The issue saliency of the military–ethnic connection: some thoughts on Malaysia," *Comparative Politics*, vol. 10, no. 2 (January 1978), pp. 267–86.

29 Our sample included thirty-four young men. Although only a few questions about ethnic integration in the military were asked, the responses were most suggestive. The Rand study conducted by Wimbush and Alexiev was based on interviews with 130 former Soviet servicemen.

30 Wimbush and Alexiev, *Ethnic Factor*, p. 8.

31 While there are indications that nationality as such plays a role in assignments, our respondents also mentioned other criteria for assignments to non-combat units such as lower level of education or technical skill, bad health, a criminal tendency, or strong religious belief; see also Wimbush and Alexiev, *Ethnic Factor*, esp. pp. 12–15, 25.

32 cf. Teresa Rakowska-Harmstone, "The Soviet army as the instrument of national integration," in John Erickson and E. J. Feuchtwanger (eds.), *Soviet Military Power and Performance* (London: Macmillan, 1979), pp. 142–4; Herbert Goldhamer, *The Soviet Soldier* (New York: Crane, Russak, 1975), p. 189; and Timothy J. Colton, *Commissars, Commanders and Civilian Authority: The Structure of Soviet Military Politics* (Cambridge, Mass.: Harvard University Press, 1979), p. 261.

33 cf. Wimbush and Alexiev, *Ethnic Factor*, pp. 20–1

34 *Serzhanty i starshiny vooruzhennykh sil SSSR* (Moscow: Voenizdat, 1973), p. 54, as cited by Rebecca V. Strode and Colin S. Gray, "The imperial dimension of Soviet military power," *Problems of Communism*, vol. 30 (November–December, 1981), p. 13.

35 On the extent of Russian-language knowledge among non-Russians see Table A.4, p. 233. Although available sources indicate a lack of special language courses or training within the armed forces, the recent emphasis on a general increase of a study of Russian is expected to have an ameliorating effect. Special evening classes have also been organized for young men in the pre-induction stage. For examples from Uzbekistan see *Pravda Vostoka*, 31 January 1979, and 22 May 1983.

36 Cited in S. Enders Wimbush and Alex Alexiev, *The Ethnic Factor in the Soviet Armed Forces: Preliminary Findings*, Rand Note (May 1980), p. 40.

37 Wimbush and Alexiev, *Ethnic Factor*, 1982, p. 37.

38 Cynthia Enloe, *Ethnic Soldiers: State Security in Divided Societies* (Athens, Ga.: University of Georgia Press, 1980), p. 202; see also J. Bayo Adekson, "Military organization in multi-ethnically segmented societies," *Research in Race and Ethnic Relations*, vol. 1 (1979), pp. 109–25, who makes a special point about the importance of avoiding structural segmentation.

39 Enloe, *Ethnic Soldiers*, p. 203.

40 Rakowska-Harmstone, "The Soviet army," pp. 144–8.

41 This is confirmed by Soviet surveys showing that service in the army is the third most important factor in Russian-language learning (after schools and contacts with Russian-speakers): see S. I. Bruk and M. N. Guboglo, "Faktory rasprostraneniia dvuiazychiia u narodov SSSR," *Sovetskaia etnografiia*, 1975, no. 5, pp. 17–30.

42 Ivan Dzyuba, *Internationalism or Russification? A Study in the Soviet Nationalities Problem* (London: Weidenfeld & Nicolson, 1968), p. 137.

43 Rakowska-Harmstone, "The Soviet army", pp. 145–8.

44 K. P. Amanzholov, "Iz istorii formirovaniia kazakhskikh natsional'nykh chastei krasnoi armii v 1922–1938 gg.," *Izvestiia Akademii nauk Kazakhskoi SSR, Seriia obshchestvennykh nauk*, no. 4, p. 12.

45 The 1936 Stalin Constitution was amended in 1944 by a reference to such a right (articles 14-g and 18-b); this clause was omitted from the 1977 Constitution; cf. A. Shtromas, "The legal position of Soviet nationalities and their territorial units according to the 1977 Constitution of the USSR," *Russian Review*, vol. 37 (July 1978), p. 271.

46 For a comparative discussion of this concept see the introduction to this chapter and E. Glyn Lewis, *Bilingualism and Bilingual Education* (Albuquerque, N. Mex.: University of New Mexico Press, 1980), p. 241.

5

Ethnicity and the Workplace

This chapter discusses the role of ethnicity at the workplace. In most cases work requires people to interact in small subgroups, and we want to know whether and how ethnicity matters in this specific sphere of life. Do people feel that it makes a difference whether a work collective is multiethnic or monoethnic? How do they explain their evaluations? Are the reasons given mainly attitudinal, or are there other more "functional" factors as well? Furthermore, what are the consequences of ethnic mixing at work, are the Soviet policy-makers right when they say that this is a major avenue toward closer ethnic integration?

As is true for ethnicity in general, many questions can be asked about ethnicity in the working environment, but by necessity a selection has to be made. Since Soviet ethnosociologists have focused on personal preferences in regard to the nationality of coworkers and supervisors, and on whether ethnicity makes any difference in work, the same topics were emphasized in our interviews with Soviet German emigrants in order to secure comparative data. The original intent was to phrase our questions exactly as the Soviet scholars had, but this unfortunately turned out to be impossible. Few Soviet ethnosociologists report the wording of questions, they differ among each other, and some formulations are problematic in light of methodological criteria established in the West.[1] Thus one cannot attempt to compare results of Soviet and Western surveys in detail; nevertheless, it is useful to compare conclusions. Often the two types of studies complement each other.

One such broad comparison that can be made concerns the variance between attitudes toward intermarriage and attitudes toward coworkers and supervisors of a different nationality. These two microlevel interaction preferences have been the focus of most Soviet ethnosociological research and consequently are also emphasized here (intermarriage is discussed in Chapter 6). The Soviet surveys have found that the percentage of individuals who view the nationality of coworkers and supervisors as insignificant is considerably larger than the percentage of people regarding nationality to be insignificant in marriage. The differential fluctuates, but the average is around twenty percentage points.[2] The same range of difference was found in our survey: while depending on the nationality concerned, only approximately 25 percent of the Soviet German respondents thought that nationality was insignificant for marriage, 55 percent thought that it did not matter in regard to coworkers, and 65 percent thought so in regard to supervisors (cf. Tables 6.8, 6.9, and 5.3).

Even though the range of difference is comparable, the raw percentage of "internationalist" attitudes cited in Soviet surveys usually is higher than in ours. But as was noted in the Introduction, percentage rates as such are rarely meaningful since they are a function of the type of sample used, and neither our nor Soviet samples are representative of the entire Soviet population.

What can be seen from our data is variance, and it shows that ethnicity is perceived to be significantly more important in the personal and familial sphere than in work relationships. Yet there are quite a few people for whom ethnicity also plays a role in the job. Why? What reasons are mentioned by the respondents themselves, and what conclusions can one draw from crosstabulations of individual variables?

Besides a human tendency to have personal ethnic preferences—primarily in regard to one's own national group—six factors are significant or, in the jargon of social science, there are six "independent" variables. These are exposure to multiethnic collectives, language commonality, work-related traditions, economic self-interest, the transference of dissatisfaction, and cultural and political values. While the last three variables are psychological or political, the first three are experiential and functional in nature. As will be shown, the latter emerge most prominently when one asks about ethnicity and ease of cooperation. The same "functional" factors play a less noticeable role when one speaks about personal ethnic preferences at the workplace. Here the pursuit of self-interest, the psychological transference of general dissatisfaction, and cultural and political values are more decisive.

Finally, we shall discuss the meaning of our findings for overall ethnic developments in the USSR such as the relationship between the functional and the attitudinal/political clusters of variables. It seems that they are in part associated with each other in a contrary manner, and that a lower score on the functional measures can be associated with a higher score on the attitudinal indicators. The transference of dissatisfaction is also significant since it demonstrates how general social and economic problems can lead to increasing ethnic tension. There is also evidence, however, that job-related ethnic preferences do not form a single syndrome with other ethnic attitudes since they are in part specific to the work situation. This applies to both the positive and negative attitudes, that is, if an individual accepts or rejects multiethnicity at work, this does not necessarily mean that he will also accept or reject multiethnicity in marriage, or on the political macrolevel.

Factors Associated with Preferences in Job-Related Ethnic Contacts

EXPERIENCE WITH MULTIETHNICITY AT WORK

Surveys asking about attitudes toward interethnic contacts at the workplace typically include respondents who themselves have worked together with people of a nationality other than their own, and others who have had no such experience. Does past exposure influence expressed preferences, and in what way?

Turning first to Soviet surveys, one finds that while they refer to multiethnic work collectives enhancing internationalist attitudes and the formation of the new Soviet community,[3] specific data are scarce. This is true even for a sociological study conducted in Estonia which devotes a full chapter to "multi-national working collectives." While one of the dimensions analyzed reportedly was the impact of the ethnic composition of the workforce both at the enterprise and the brigade level, and while surveys were conducted both in factories with Estonian and with ethnically mixed workforces, the summary of findings nevertheless is skimpy. The most concrete reference is to a survey of Estonians in Tallinn; it reports that individuals who seldom had working contact with other nationalities were twice as likely to think that it is harder to work in multinational collectives than those who had more contact with other national-ities.[4] In a similar finding from Georgia it is said that compared to people who worked in monoethnic collectives respondents who had worked in multiethnic groups were by one-fifth more likely to think that the nationality of their coworkers made no difference.[5] Thus Soviet surveys suggest an association between exposure to multiethnic workgroups and the "it makes no difference" response.

Our Soviet German interviews allow a more detailed evaluation, the first conclusion being that findings are closely linked to the formulation of survey questions. This point is basic in all survey research. Soviet surveys have asked two types of questions, one about the respondent's ethnic preference regarding his supervisor or coworkers, and the other asking more generally whether the ethnic composition of a work collective is significant or not.[6] The reports do not say whether findings differ if one or the other formulation is used. We asked both questions and found that it does matter. If one asks about the general effect of multiethnicity, the "no difference" category is chosen more often than if one asks about a personal preference in the nationality of coworkers (see Tables 5.1 and 5.2). For our sample the differential is largest for persons who worked primarily with Russians; while 80 percent said that the mixed composition of the collective had no influence in general, only 48 percent chose the "no difference" reply when asked about personal preferences in coworkers. This gap illustrates that even though work may go smoothly in a mixed collective, personal preferences can still prevail. Conversely, respondents may not have any personal preferences, but may still identify a functional difficulty in working with other nationals.

The terms "multiethnic" and "monoethnic" can be ambiguous and have to be used with care. While it is easy to see that strongly

Table 5.1 *Evaluations of Multiethnic Workgroups According to Type of Group Respondent Worked in*

| Evaluation of multiethnicity | Dominant nationality in work collective | | | |
	German, N = 17 (%)	Russian, N = 25 (%)	Native, N = 16 (%)	Mixed, N = 55 (%)
No difference	35	80	69	69
Negative influence	59	20	31	27
Positive influence	6	—	—	4
Totals	100	100	100	100

Note: The question was "Scientists here in the West and also in the Soviet Union frequently study the interaction in multiethnic work collectives—what is your experience, does the multiethnic composition of a workgroup have any influence, and if so, is this influence positive or negative?"

mixed groups are multiethnic and that groups made up entirely of one nationality are monoethnic, both terms can be used if two or more nationalities are present, but one is in the majority. The analysis of our Soviet German survey suggests that it is most appropriate to call such collectives multiethnic as well, reserving the term "monoethnic" for cases where the respondents' nationality dominates.

Using these categories for an analysis of the effect of multiethnicity on work, one sees that "no difference" was the dominant reply among respondents who had last worked in one of the three types of ethnically mixed collectives, while only 35 percent of respondents who had worked in "monoethnic" German collectives chose the "no difference" category (cf. Table 5.1). The findings are similar in regard to the question "would you yourself have preferred coworkers of a specific nationality?" As Table 5.2 shows, the ratio of those replying with "no difference" is again larger if respondents worked in multiethnic collectives of one type or another. What can we conclude from this?

It is striking to find such a strong overlap between personal preferences and actual work experience: does this mean that the experience of having worked in a German brigade caused these evaluations, or is it the other way around, and persons with certain attitudes and experiences sought out workgroups in which Germans dominated? Our data are insufficient to answer this question, but if the latter is true, it is an intriguing example of autonomous group formation in the working environment. In the same vein one could assume that those

Table 5.2 *Ethnic Preference Regarding Coworkers According to Type of Group Respondent Worked in*

| | Dominant nationality in work collective | | | |
| | German, N = 17 (%) | Russian, N = 25 (%) | Native, N = 16 (%) | Mixed, N = 60 (%) |
Coworker preference				
No difference	29	48	63	67
Prefer Germans	71	48	25	23
Other preference	—	4	12	10
Totals	100	100	100	100

Note: The question was "Would you yourself have preferred coworkers of a specific nationality, or didn't it make any difference to you?" If a preference was expressed, the follow-up questions asked "who?" and "why?"

Table 5.3 *Ethnic Preference Regarding Supervisor and Coworkers*

Preference	Supervisor, N = 159 (%)	Coworkers, N = 136 (%)
None	65	55
Germans	20	39
Republic nationals	12	2
Russians	3	2
Reject locals	—	2
Totals	100	100

people who were more prepared to work in multiethnic collectives did end up working in them. It is uncertain whether this is so, and it is also possible that the experience in a multiethnic collective caused its acceptance. But no matter what the causal chain, we can conclude that there is a significant association between past exposure to multiethnic workgroups and their acceptability.

Interethnic contacts on the job not only involve relations between coworkers, but extend to relations between employees and supervisors. There are indications that Soviet scholars have asked both about coworkers and supervisors, but their reports say nothing about potential differences in the degree that ethnicity is seen to play a role. In the case of the Soviet Germans the nationality of bosses emerges as somewhat less significant than that of coworkers. But compared to coworkers there is

Table 5.4 *Ethnic Preference Regarding Supervisor in Non-Russian republics*

Preference	Nationality of Respondents' last supervisor	
	Local, N = 44 (%)	Non-local, N = 89 (%)
None	52	67
Local	29	5
German	17	25
Russian	3	3
Totals	100	100

more preference for republic nationals as superiors (see Table 5.3). In part this is related to the experience of having worked under a native boss since, as can be seen in Table 5.4, the preference of local bosses is higher among respondents who worked under them. This suggests that in this instance a specific interaction experience has enhanced a positive ethnic preference.

Economic Calculus and Work Traditions

When respondents have an ethnic preference regarding their coworkers, it nearly always concerns persons of their own nationality. The explanations given vary and it is by no means possible to categorize all—or even a majority of reasons—as attitudinal. Functional reasons relating to smooth interaction within the group and "getting the job done" were cited often, and so were work-related traditions and financial considerations.

Thus some personal preferences in coworkers or negative evaluations of multiethnic work collectives focus on differences in earnings. Respondents felt that because Germans work harder, the brigades in which they dominate earn more: "There are German construction brigades, and they earn more" (144); "There were three of us working together, but our pay was calculated together and we didn't want to take any lazy blacks [in our group]" (144); and "There are quarrels about earnings if it [the brigade] is mixed" (186). The practice of calculating earnings on the basis of the performance of brigades rather than individuals apparently can lead to strife and negative perceptions of other ethnic groups, although the reverse also can apply in that some nationalities may be perceived especially positively if they work well. The Germans themselves thought that their industriousness improved attitudes toward them, but one should of course interview members of other nationalities to confirm this notion.

There were other, at least partly "functional," explanations of differing evaluations of mixed workgroups. Some respondents explained their negative view of multiethnic workgroups by stating that work goes smoother among people of one nationality: "If one has to help each other with the work, then it isn't the same anymore [in a mixed group]" (156); and "When it is mixed, it is worse both in work and in discipline, everybody tries to put blame on others" (35). Ethic rivalries, differential behavior patterns, and differences in work ethic were also seen as influential. To cite just one example: "There is some quarreling, some-body always thinks that he knows more . . . The Tadjik women have a baby once a year—they don't work, take leaves" (69).

Similar reasons were adduced by Uzbek workers in Tashkent, who were interviewed by Soviet ethnosociologists who had noticed that they had chosen to work in a subdivision of their own. The Uzbeks stated that it was easier for them to work with each other because of common traditions and an understanding of the expected norms of interaction such as showing respect for older people or inquiring about the welfare of family members before starting a business conversation.[7] The influence of "manifestations of old customs and habits" on the lack of multiethnic collectives in the Chechen-Ingush province in its part has been mentioned by *Pravda*.[8] These examples suggest that workers' ethnic preferences do in fact influence the type of workgroups formed and that the relationship between the two phenomena is symmetric.

Commonality of Language

Ethnosociological studies undertaken in the USSR as well as in the West indicate that the lack of a common language is one of the more significant reasons why people state that ethnicity makes a difference in work relationships. Language barriers impede com-munication needed for task fulfillment as well as in personal interactions; thus, quite naturally, monolingual persons are more likely to state a preference for coworkers and supervisors of their own nationality as well as for those of another nationality who know their language.

The best Soviet data clarifying this point are in the study undertaken in the Tatar ASSR by the Arutiunian team. The publications resulting from this research repeatedly pinpoint language facility as a major variable associated with differing evaluations of the significance of nationality in interethnic con-tacts at work or in the familial sphere (see also Chapter 6). The special importance of language knowledge for relations at work are highlighted by the emphasis that monolingual Tatars place on the role of ethnicity at work: while it is as a rule typical for a lower percentage of people to say that ethnicity is important at work than in marriage, the reverse is true for Tatars knowing only Tatar since only 66 percent "ascribe no importance to nationality of supervisors and coworkers," while 69 percent

Table 5.5 *Knowledge of Russian and Crossnational Attitudes of Tatars*

Question: "If you were able to choose your immediate supervisor, which would you prefer?"	Knowledge of languages		
	Tatar, N = 1220 (%)	Russian, N = 52 (%)	Both, N = 252 (%)
Would prefer a person of the same nationality as myself	12·0	3·6	3·2
Supervisor's nationality makes no difference to me if he knows Tatar	16·4	3·6	14·7
Nationality of supervisor makes no difference at all	65·7	85·7	79·0
I have difficulty in answering this question	2·4	7·1	0·8
No answer	3·5	—	2·3

Source: Iurii V. Arutiunian, "Konkretno-sotsiologicheskoe issledovanie natsional'nykh otnoshenii," *Voprosy filosofii*, 1969, no. 12, p. 133.

stated that nationality made no difference in marriage (see Table 6.5). Such a departure from the typical pattern of response indicates the influence of a special factor, in this case the lack of knowing Russian.

The Arutiunian team was sensitive to the significance of language in ethnic relations from the inception of its study on. Thus when formulating the answer categories to the question "if you were able to choose your immediate supervisor, which would you prefer?" they included the option "supervisor's nationality makes no difference to me if he knows Tatar." As can be seen from Table 5.5, this response category was most frequently chosen by Tatars knowing only their native language and no Russian; these same respondents also have the highest incidence of responses (12 percent) preferring a supervisor of their own nationality. The data in Table 5.5 are significant, in that they do not solely pinpoint the respondents' lack of knowing Russian as a source of less favorable interethnic contact attitudes, but also highlight the two-sidedness of the relationship by clarifying that the supervisor's knowing Tatar can also make a difference. While logic tells us that commonality of language can equally well be arrived at through bilingualism among Russians as among non-Russians, this point is underemphasized by Soviet analysts, especially if they write for political purposes.

Even Arutiunian, while providing the data in the table, concludes his pathbreaking article by stating only that "knowledge of Russian and familiarization with Russian culture at school age has a particular high social effect and to some degree insures against resurgence of nationalist moods."[9] The analytical one-sidedness of underscoring the significance of bilingualism only among non-Russians is due to the official language policy which has increasingly emphasized the integrative effect of non-Russians learning Russian since "in the Soviet Union Russian constitutes the language of interethnic communication."[10] In light of this politicization of the issue Soviet ethnosociologists are circumspect in their statements, but a careful perusal of their work reveals other instances illustrating the benefits of reciprocal language learning.

Thus a study of ethnic relations in major industrial enterprises in Estonia notes that bilingualism makes a difference not only in the case of Estonians, but also among Russians and inmigrants of other nationalities. While stating this as its own finding, the study also asserts that the workers of enterprises with an ethnically mixed workforce understand this in light of the "high degree of democratism in the relations between workers of different nationality and a respectful attitude towards language differences."[11] Commonality of language is important in work and even more so in the promotion of friendly personal relations among coworkers.[12] Surveys conducted among Russians living in Estonia and Georgia show that among those knowing the local languages, favorable attitudes toward interethnic contact at work are by one-third higher than among those without such a language facility,[13] and even Kholmogorov's comparatively superficial research conducted in Latvia during the 1960s mentions that language problems were cited by many of those respondents stating that it was difficult to work in multinational collectives.[14]

The impact of language barriers on job-related and personal relations at work is also evident from our survey with Soviet German emigrants. Only a relatively small subgroup (N = 16) had worked in groups dominated by non-Russian republic nationals, but among those who had, several mentioned the lack of a common language as one of the primary reasons for negative evaluations of the multiethnic composition of work collectives: "Negative, if you don't know their language" (80); "When I was working a shift with Moldavians only, they spoke in their language and I remained on the side" (84); "It is bad, I don't understand any Latvian, and they don't understand

German" (118); and "If one doesn't understand the language, one sits alone" (70). Those respondents who had lived in the Baltic republics especially often said that some knowledge of the local language was crucial for effective and friendly interaction. It was pointed out that many Latvians, Lithuanians, and Estonians do not speak Russian well, or do not want to use it; a truck driver who lived in Latvia explained, "There was one boss who always said, if one lives in Latvia, then one should learn Latvian" (119). This is an example where language facility is more than a "functional" need and a cultural–political attitude surfaces.

The significance of language barriers is also evident in the case of some respondents who explained their lack of ethnic preference in coworkers or their views that multiethnicity of work collectives was insignificant by saying that "there was no difference, everyone spoke Russian" (23, 58, 62, 98). In the same vein those who did express an ethnic preference mentioned that they preferred Germans—and in some instances Russians—because of the commonality of language. The role of a common language can also be discerned in the relatively few cases where local coworkers were preferred: in the three cases where this occurred all the respondents spoke the local language fluently. A similar association can be observed in the case of ethnic preferences in regard to supervisors since our data show that among those who have some or a good knowledge of the respective local language the tendency to prefer native bosses is higher than among those who do not know the language (Table 5.6).

Table 5.6   *Language Skill and Ethnic Preference of Supervisor in Non-Russian Republics*

	Respondent knows local language		
Preference	Well, N = 19 (%)	A little, N = 20 (%)	Not at all, N = 119 (%)
None	58	70	64
Other Germans	21	5	21
Locals	21	15	9
Russians	—	10	4
Totals	100	100	100

Note: Ethnic preference was measured by the question "If it had been possible for you to choose your immediate superior, would you have preferred a specific nationality, or wouldn't it have made any difference to you?"

137

Table 5.7 *Evaluation of Multiethnic Collectives, by Knowledge of Russian*

	Respondent's knowledge of Russian		
	Good,	Medium,	Poor,
Evaluation of	N = 45	N = 55	N = 30
multiethnicity	(%)	(%)	(%)
No difference	71	64	63
Negative	29	33	33
Positive	—	3	4
Totals	100	100	100

Until now the main emphasis of discussion has been on non-Russian languages, but what about Russian? It is logical to assume, and numerous Soviet authors have stated it to be a fact, that a better knowledge of Russian among non-Russians is associated with more favorable attitudes toward multiethnic contacts on the job. Nevertheless, the relationship is complex. Our data from the Soviet German emigrant survey show a slight indication of a better language facility in Russian being associated with more favorable views in the sense of a prefer-ence for Russian supervisors or coworkers; but the overall rate of such a preference is low (see Table 5.8). "More favorable views" can, however, also be interpreted to mean an increment in the rate of respondents saying that nationality makes no difference. In this regard our data suggest some interesting points.

As Table 5.7 illustrates, the "no difference" response is cho-sen somewhat more frequently by respondents knowing Rus-sian well if they are asked about the general influence of the multiethnicity of work collectives. This is not the case, however, if the question is formulated in terms of a personal preference of coworkers or supervisors (Table 5.8). Here the association between the "no difference" category and degree of Russian-language knowledge is negative in both cases, with those respondents having a poor knowledge of Russian actually emerging as the most "internationalist." This suggests a rever-sal of the previously noted patterns of association. How can one explain this phenomenon?

For one thing, attention should be paid to the thrust of the question and the meaning as compared to the question on the role of ethnicity at work *per se*. It appears that those knowing Russian better acknowledge the limited functional role of

Table 5.8   *Preference of Coworkers and Supervisor, by Knowledge of Russian*

	Respondent's knowledge of Russian		
	Good, N = 53 (%)	Medium, N = 57 (%)	Poor, N = 28 (%)
1 *Preference of coworkers*			
No difference	45	59	61
Prefer Germans	41	37	32
Prefer Russians	4	2	—
Prefer locals	4	2	—
Reject locals	6	—	7
Totals	100	100	100
	N = 67 (%)	N = 61 (%)	N = 32 (%)
2 *Preference of supervisor*			
No difference	61	64	69
Prefer Germans	19	18	22
Prefer Russians	8	2	3
Prefer locals	12	13	6
Other	—	3	—
Totals	100	100	100

ethnicity in reply to the one question, but personal preference is comparatively higher than among those who know Russian less well. A similar finding was noted above (see p. 101 and Tables 5.1 and 5.2), namely, that those individuals who had worked in collectives dominated by Russians assigned least significance to the multiethnicity of work collectives, but at the same time had the highest degree of personal preferences.

This underlines the importance of differentiating between the various dimensions of interethnic relations at work; it also suggests that the functional evaluation of the role of ethnicity and personal ethnic preference are by no means congruent, and may even be negatively correlated with each other. This is in accord with the findings of the Arutiunian survey (see below), although Arutiunian notes this phenomenon only for professionals and white-collar employees. In the case of our data no such separate association exists, which may be due to the ethnic concern pinpointed by Arutiunian as applying to the Tatar "intelligentsia"—namely, concern for the cultural heritage of the nation—applying to all occupational groups of Soviet Germans.

As an extraterritorial nationality with practically no cultural autonomy the Soviet Germans face the acute danger of losing their linguistic and cultural identity. One may hypothesize that those individuals knowing Russian best are most aware of this danger and, therefore, react by a stronger attitudinal preference for job contacts with Germans.

Socioeconomic Aspects

A number of Western theorists of ethnic relations have drawn attention to the role of economic factors in promoting integration as well as in aggravating or even causing conflict. Thus it has been argued that both individuals and groups tend to transfer job dissatisfaction to the ethnic sphere, that economic competition can easily attain an overtone of ethnic politics, and that there are ways in which stages of economic development are associated with accelerating nationalism.[15] Although there have been some Western scholars who have tried—usually by extrapolation and based on a few empirical data—to examine the relevance of such arguments in the case of the multiethnic Soviet Union, Soviet analysts have tended to reject any such notions by proclaiming them to be irrelevant in light of the socialist character of Soviet society. Nevertheless, a close look at the findings of Soviet empirical ethnosociologists as well as Western surveys suggest that economic aspects can and do affect the quality of ethnic relations in the USSR.

The survey undertaken by the Arutiunian team in the Tatar ASSR was the first concrete sociological analysis undertaken in the USSR to refer to links between ethnicity and socioeconomics. It found that next to language knowledge, occupation and social stratum is the other major factor associated with differing evaluations of interethnic contacts. Among the people surveyed professionals and white-collar workers have more negative interethnic attitudes than other social strata, and while this applies to both marriage and job contacts, the percentage of those stating that nationality makes a difference for work is actually higher than that saying so in regard to marriage.[16] Since this is a reversal of the usual pattern of response, it suggests that these people are especially aware of or are affected by multiethnic interaction at work. Why?

The first consideration concerns professional interests and the type of work this stratum of people is engaged in. Although the Arutiunian study does not subdivide the professionals and white-collar workers into subgroups, it is clear that they include a considerable portion of persons in whose work cultural differences play a special role; to provide an illustration from another study undertaken in Latvia, Kholmogorov pinpoints teachers and "workers in the arts" as having the lowest percentage of positive attitudes toward interethnic work contacts.[17] A study conducted in Moldavia is even more precise:[18]

> While for the administrative, industrial, and the scientific–technical intelligentsia the appraisal of the work situation is not transferred into the national sphere (they do not have any special professional reasons for that), the work interest of the scientific–humanistic and artistic–creative parts are directly linked to the national literature, language, history, art, and this is reflected in the needs of these people.

Or in other words, people working in the arts and humanities tend to have more negative evaluations of the value of "interethnic contact at work" because their own professional interests are tied to specific cultures.

The Moldavian study also shows that this principle applies to all nationalities in the USSR, including the Russians. Among the Russians in Moldavia who belong to the creative and humanistic intelligentsia the percentage saying that "the ethnic composition of the collective has no significance" is an abysmal 57 percent compared to the already low 74 percent for the same Moldavian professional group.[19] What the local Russians are saying is that they can work with more ease and better if their coworkers are Russians as well. This meshes well with our overall findings, but it is a rare instance that a Soviet source provides confirming data about the ethnic preferences of Russians. In most instances ethnic processes in the USSR are discussed as if they affect only non-Russians.

Besides being concerned about their own professional interests members of the intelligentsia tend to be at the forefront of national strivings. Thus a commentator on the results of the Tatar study states:[20]

> the general level of culture and concern for creation of ethnic intellectual values make precisely the professional people the most active voice of national self-awareness. They are the category most sensitive to the historical past of the nation and its culture.

The same author adds a little later that "some members of the professional and intellectual categories" of minority peoples are hostile toward the loss of national distinctiveness brought about by urbanization and modernization and espouse a "striving to preserve ethnically distinctive features of lifestyle and culture."[21] This striving again pinpoints political and cultural values and is strong despite the professionals being in close contact with other cultures and people of other nationalities; this is in contrast to the white-collar individuals who also have a high level of "philistine prejudices" whose life style is much more ethnically self-contained.[22] This brings up a point to be elaborated upon in Chapter 6, namely that contact with other ethnic groups is by no means unilinearly associated with more favorable interethnic attitudes.

Disappointed socioeconomic aspirations are a further cause of the high incidence of negative interethnic attitudes among professionals and white-collar personnel. Arutiunian shows that respondents who used to do mental work but were engaged in physical work at the time of the survey have a high rate of negative ethnic attitudes, and he also makes the generalization that "whenever social 'expectations' are not wholly realized, a dissatisfaction appears that is projected upon interethnic attitudes."[23] Drobizheva elaborates on the same point when she says: "where factors of competition on the social scale are present (for example, in admission to higher educational institutions or assignments to jobs), some show an inclination to introduce an ethnic factor into their explanations of the successes or failings of a given individual."[24] Such disappointments have an especially pronounced effect on the age group between 18 and 22. The untypically high rate of negative interethnic attitudes among both rural Tatars and Russians falling into this age group (see Table A.5, p. 234) has been associated with "concrete conditions of life" and more specifically with resentments about failing to pass competitive entrance examinations to higher educational institutions, and in the case of Russian youths with dissatisfaction with the conditions of rural life and problems of moving to towns.[25] Other Soviet surveys also show an unusually low percentage of younger age groups (20–24-year-old Uzbeks, 18–24-year-old Ukrainians living in Moldavia, and 25–29-year-old Siberian Tatars) stating that "nationality makes no difference at work,"[26] but they do not venture explanations. The projection of dissatisfaction with other aspects of life presumably again plays a role.

Other Soviet studies have arrived at similar conclusions. The survey conducted among industrial workers in Estonia links dissatisfaction with work, conditions at the place of work, and relations with management to negative evaluations of working in ethnically mixed collectives. Although the research report fails to provide details, it mentions that among persons who are dissatisfied with their work "positive orientations towards interethnic contacts" decrease by two-thirds,[27] and to cite from another part of that same study:[28]

National feelings arise when the socio-psychological climate is adverse, when people are dissatisfied with the general conditions in the work collective. In the case of a maritime repair enterprise one finds that those who said that the ethnic composition of a collective does make a difference (4·8% of respondents) also tended to negatively evaluate the inter-relationships in the brigade ($-·084$ as compared to an average of $+·309$) as well as in the shop ($-·167$ as compared to an average of $+·266$). Analysis shows that the reasons for dissatisfaction are related to the organizational–technical and social conditions and were just transposed to the sphere of ethnic feeling.

In a similar vein the analysis of a survey undertaken among Moldavian workers in Kishinev concluded that "the connection between attitude toward interethnic contacts and satisfaction with work is indisputable."[29] The author of this study also interprets this as a psychological transfer phenomenon.

Next to professional rivalry the transference of socioeconomic dissatisfaction to the ethnic sphere thus is the major material factor influencing ethnic attitudes at the workplace. In addition, some of our Soviet German respondents indicate that among blue-collar workers calculations of earnings in a brigade sometimes affect preferences in coworkers. Otherwise little socioeconomic influence can be detected in the case of our sample, the one exception being a somewhat higher degree of negative evaluation of multiethnic workgroups by persons with the highest level of education (50 percent negative evaluation as compared to an average of 35 percent for the total sample). The highest educated group also has the highest degree (22 percent) of people preferring republic nationals as their bosses.

Regional and Ethnic Variance in the Role of Ethnicity in Job Contacts

As the Soviet Germans are a secondary ethnic group, one must be careful in implying that a finding about them may be pertinent for a broader population. We assume, however, that if we can show the impact of a variable—for example, language knowledge—on preferences expressed by the Soviet Germans, the basic type of relationship is also likely to hold true for other nationalities in the Soviet Union. In their role as observers of other nationalities the Soviet Germans can also provide insights about the larger ethnic groups.

In the context of on-the-job relations we asked only one question in regard to the "others," namely, whether the respondent thought that the ethnicity of the supervisor made a difference to their coworkers. Affirmative replies were more frequent than in the case of the respondents' own preferences: while 65 percent of the respondents stated that to them the ethnicity of their supervisor made no difference, the percentage in this category dropped to 59 percent when reporting about coworkers. This suggests that extraterritorial groups, such as the Soviet Germans, may in some regards be more "internationalist" than other nationalities. Since the highest rate (64 percent) of perceived preferences refers to the Baltic republics—where the Germans worked in collectives dominated by the indigenous nationalities—these data also suggest that the Balts (and maybe republic non-Russian nationalities more generally) have stronger preferences in this realm than smaller groups or the Russians (see Table 5.11). This assumption is supported by some data from the Kholmogorov survey conducted in Latvia, which shows that in regard to positive attitudes toward multinational workforces the indigenous Latvians rank lowest (Table 5.9).

Table 5.9 *Attitudes toward Multinational Work Collectives, Various Nationalities in Latvia*

Opinions	Latvians (%)	Russians (%)	Belo-russians (%)	Poles (%)	Ukrainians (%)	Jews (%)
Positive	84	92	94	90	93	91
No answer	9	6	4	8	6	6
Negative	7	2	2	2	1	3

Source: A. I. Kholmogorov, *Internatsional'nye cherty sovetskikh natsii. (Na materialakh konkretno-sotsiologicheskikh issledovanii v Pribaltike)*, Moscow, Mysl', 1970, p. 172.

Ethnic differentials are also evident in other Soviet surveys, such as one conducted in western Siberia which indicates that— similarly as will be shown in regard to marriage data—the Ukrainians who have migrated there have the most internationalist outlook, whereas it is lowest among local Kazakhs (Table 5.10). As Table 5.10 also illustrates, the Kazakhs have the highest percentage of respondents saying that it is harder to work in an ethnically mixed group.

Some of the reasons why ethnicity does or does not make a difference at work emerge from verbatim explanations of our Soviet German respondents. A typical comment about the nationality of the boss making no difference was "as long as he knows the job, it doesn't matter" (105). Thus the primary explanation for ethnicity not being significant is job-related. Among those specifying preferences of their coworkers a frequently encountered statement was that people just prefer a boss of their own nationality: "Lithuanians would prefer Lithuanians, and Russians would prefer Russians" (100), or "of course everybody

Table 5.10 *Ethnic Attitudes of Rural Population of Western Siberia (Percentage of Respondents)*

| | Ethnic group | | | |
| | Siberian Tatars, N = 4,967 | Kazakhs, N = 894 | Shors, N = 549 | Ukrainians, N = 820 |
Attitude	(%)	(%)	(%)	(%)
Believe ethnic make-up of work associates makes no difference	86	78	89	93
Believe it is harder to work in an ethnically mixed group	7	15	8	1
Take positive attitude toward ethnically mixed marriages	62	32	80	78
Favor marriages to persons of own nationality	32	65	14	14

Source: N. A. Tomilov, "Sovremennye etnicheskie protsessy v iuzhnoi i sred- nei polose Zapadnoi Sibiri," *Sovetskaia etnografiia,* 1978, no. 4, p. 15.

wants their own" (167). Another respondent related this experi-
ence: "Our boss was a Ukrainian. The Kazakhs didn't like him,
but they liked the Kazakh [who was boss before]. When the
Ukrainian was boss, the Russians would come to work on
Sundays [to fulfill the plan], but when the Kazakh was boss, the
Muslims came to work on Sundays" (82).

A second point coincides with explanations the Germans gave
about their own preferences in regard to coworkers and supervisors, that is, language was pinpointed as a major reason for
preferences, especially in the Baltic area. Thus a lorry driver who
had lived in Latvia said: "If a Russian is the boss, one has to speak
in Russian" (119), and another respondent said that Russians
prefer to have a Russian boss "because they do not understand
the Latvian language" (130).

A further explanation why colleagues preferred a boss of their
own nationality was that "it is their native country." This reply
underlines the perception of an indigenous republic nationality
having special rights and strivings within its republic, a political
argument also encountered in replies to other questions in our
interview schedule (cf. Chapters 2 and 3). The RSFSR is perceived
as being an exception in this regard. Thus one respondent
commented on the prevalence of non-Russians aspiring to have
supervisors of their own national background by saying: "In
Russia there is no difference; it is different in Kirghizia, there
they want their own, in Estonia too, but in the RSFSR it doesn't
matter" (168). This difference between the RSFSR and the non-
Russian union republics is also evident from the regional comparison of stated preferences, which are lowest both in the case
of our respondents who lived in the RSFSR as well as the
perceived preferences of their co-workers (Table 5.11).

Next to regional and nationality-related differentials the most
noteworthy finding is that white-collar workers were considerably less likely than blue-collar workers to report that the
ethnicity of the boss made no difference to their coworkers (48
and 64 percent respectively). A further analysis of these data
shows that this tendency is most pronounced in the case of
non-Russian white-collar workers. While this finding must
remain tentative in light of the relatively small sample in our
survey, it is nevertheless suggestive by being in accord with the
findings of the Arutiunian survey noted earlier. Since both
modernization theory and current trends in the social development of the non-Russian nations suggest that the ratio of native
white-collar workers will increase during the next decades, this

Table 5.11 *Ethnic Preference in Regard to Work Supervisors: Respondents' Own Preference (1) Compared to Evaluation of Preference of Coworkers (2)*

| | Kazakhstan and Central Asia | | Baltic* | | Moldavia and other | | RSFSR* | |
	(1) N = 89 (%)	(2) N = 64 (%)	(1) N = 27 (%)	(2) N = 22 (%)	(1) N = 17 (%)	(2) N = 15 (%)	(1) N = 26 (%)	(2) N = 19 (%)
Specific nationality is preferred	35	31	41	64	53	40	19	27
No difference	65	59	59	36	47	60	81	74
Totals	100	100	100	100	100	100	100	100

* The regional differentials indirectly reflect differentials in the composition of work collectives and thus the ethnicity of the coworkers referred to. Thus 75 percent of the collectives in the RSFSR were composed mostly of Russians, and 75 percent of those in the Baltic republics were dominated by Balts.

likelihood of the significance of ethnicity increasing concurrently.

Conclusion and Questions for Further Study

Both Soviet as well as Western survey data leave no doubt that at least a part of the Soviet laborforce (depending on the Soviet survey referred to, a minimum of 5·6 percent and a maximum of 54 percent)[30] have ethnic preferences in regard to coworkers and supervisors. Similarly, a significant proportion of the laborforce believes that the ethnic composition of a work collective "makes a difference." In both cases the explanations given or derived through data analysis indicate that a host of factors play a role. While it is the immediate suggestion of the question formulation that we are dealing with personal attitudes pure and simple, personal likes and dislikes recede into the background once one has a closer look at the data.

A significant part of the replies are based on evaluations of the ease of cooperation with individuals of the one or other nationality. A common language is the prime example of a factor affecting ease of cooperation, others are related to work traditions and compatibility. Blue-collar workers for whom individual earnings are based on the performance of the entire brigade are concerned about the diligence of their coworkers. White-collar workers for their part, and especially professionals involved with the humanities and the arts, perceive a close link between their professional interests and the position of their particular ethnic groups. More broadly one finds that negative experiences in competitive socioeconomic situations, downward social mobility, and job dissatisfaction are easily transposed to the ethnic sphere. In addition, one notes the impact of group-based cultural and political values which are most clearly expressed in verbal arguments that one or the other language or ethnic group should be given a dominant position in the entire society, including the place of work.

As already indicated in the previous chapters, the inquiry about the implications of ethnic stratification in the USSR has been greatly underdeveloped in the past. Both our own data and the comparative literature on ethnic relations pinpoint ethnic stratification at a place of work or nationwide as a major source of ethnic discontent and conflict.[31] While Soviet sources rarely mention stratification as such, they make references to the general role of economic competition and the lack of job satisfaction enhancing negative ethnic attitudes. The politicization of ethnicity in light of economic strains perceived either individually or by whole ethnic groups is of major consequence. The link between economic satisfaction and ethnic harmony suggests that any decrease in the former can cause a decrease in the latter.

A further dimension requiring more study concerns the consequences of ethnic preferences in work relationships. There are indications that these preferences influence the formation of work collectives both on the part of people choosing where to apply for work and on the part of people doing the hiring. Although our interview schedules did not include a question about why people choose to apply for specific jobs, several voluntary statements suggest that the ethnic composition of the workforce does play a role. Thus a Latvian respondent in a pilot study noted that she did not apply to work in a laboratory because the majority of technicians were Russians (L6), and one of the Soviet German respondents stated that Latvians are reluctant to take jobs in places where the boss is Russian (60). As regards hiring practices, there have also been suggestions by respondents that ethnicity plays a role,[32] but more research is needed to explore specifics.

Many more questions than have been touched on in this chapter could be asked about the role of ethnicity at places of work. Thus one might differentiate between working relations *per se* and overall social relations at the place of work, especially as they relate to contacts during lunchbreaks, at meetings and after-hours contacts. The results of some fragmentary research along these lines suggest that differing patterns of interrelationships apply to these two spheres. Where work itself is concerned, respondents tend to emphasize that people are task-oriented and that overall relations are "normal" and friendly. Once relations move into the more personal social sphere, however, it appears that people seek out conationals and that a certain grouping occurs.[33]

It was noted in the introduction to this chapter that interethnic contacts are accepted more easily at work than within the family; the subsequent discussion noted exceptions to this rule and identified the factors associated with individual subgroups deviating from this pattern. A point still to be discussed is whether ethnic attitudes in various spheres of life constitute an attitudinal complex or whether they are wholly or in part independent of each other.

Our findings about the significance of functional factors in the ease of cooperation on the job suggest some of the work-related attitudes apply to this sphere alone. So in part do the professional economic interests, although they can be the source of broader macrolevel ethnic perceptions. In contrast, cultural and political values and psychological transference on their part clearly are not purely work-related.

Soviet ethnosociologists contradict each other as to whether ethnic attitudes form a syndrome. In commenting on the survey conducted in the Tatar ASSR Drobizheva has stated that:[34]

There was a particularly close correlation between the answers to such questions as attitude toward mixed marriages and attitude toward work on a multinational staff. Our data make it possible to trace the following regularity. Among Russians, Belorussians, and Ukrainians, responses to the question about mixed marriages were consistent in more than 70% of the cases, and in some groups in more than 80% of cases to answers to the question about attitude toward work in a multinational work force; while among Tatars and Kazakhs, the frequency with which responses coincided was somewhat rarer (from 60% to 70%). The findings in the Tatar ASSR yield the following picture: if a person does not ascribe importance to nationality when marrying, then as a rule he or she will have a positive attitude as well toward work in a multinational work force. However, among those with favorable attitudes toward interethnic contacts on the job one encounters people with a negative attitude toward ethnically mixed marriages or with no firm set toward them. Thus questions pertaining to attitude toward mixed marriages and interethnic contacts at work are not interchangeable.

While this suggests that interethnic attitudes form a syndrome in part, other Soviet scholars argue that they are affected by separate independent factors. In one of the few Soviet studies employing correlation analysis, rather than just bivariate crosstabulations and comparisons of percentage rates, Susokolov finds that "attitudes toward familial and on-the-job interethnic contacts are mutually independent in a considerable proportion of the population,"[35] and that the main association instead is the one between job satisfaction and work-related ethnic attitudes. He also explicitly suggests that "the two kinds of attitudes under examination are under the influence of different factors."[36]

Arutiunian draws a similar conclusion when summarizing his own research over the years. In a rare comment on the high degree of endogamic preference among the peoples of Central Asia he argues that these attitudes are related only to the intimate personal sphere and that they "are not as such an expression of interpersonal ethnic attitudes in the broader sense of the concept" since work-related ethnic attitudes in the same region are "distinguished by the highest degree of internationalism."[37]

All of this confirms the basic thrust of the findings of our own and other Western surveys on ethnic attitudes of people from the Soviet Union. Interethnic preferences and evaluations in the various spheres of life do not constitute a single syndrome that can be measured on a predictive attitudinal scale such as a Guttman scale since different factors affect each of them. This conclusion is reinforced by a survey of the role of ethnicity in familial and communal relations discussed in the next two chapters.

Notes: Chapter 5

1 The questions used by Kholmogorov—although not reported in detail—are especially problematic. Thus when asking about the effect of multiethnicity of the workforce, he uses a double-barreled question and asks about two factors at once, that is, the effect of multinational composition upon work and interpersonal relations: A. I. Kholmogorov, *Internatsional'nye cherty sovetskikh natsii (Na materialakh konkreno-sotsiologicheskikh issledovanii v Pribaltike)* (Moscow: Mysl', 1970), pp. 168–70.

2 See, for example, Iurii V. Arutiunian, "Konkretno-sotsiologischeskoe issledovanie natsional'nykh otnoshenii," *Voprosy filosofii,* 1969, no. 12, pp. 129–39, esp. tables 2 and 3; and L. M. Drobizheva, "Sotsial'no-kul'turnye osobennosti lichnosti i natsional'nye ustanovki (po materialam issledovanii v Tatarskoi ASSR)," *Sovetskaia etnografiia,* 1971, no. 3, pp. 3–15, table 5. While these two studies report on Tatars and Russians, a study of four non-Russian groups living in Western Siberia also found that the percentage with a positive attitude toward mixed marriages typically was smaller than the percentage who believe that multiethnicity of a work collective has no significance. The differential was between 9 and 46 percent: see N. A. Tomilov, "Sovremennye etnicheskie protsessy v iuzhnoi i srednei polose Zapadnoi Sibiri," *Sovetskaia etnografiia,* 1978, no. 4, p. 15.

3 D. Kh. Aibazov, "Opyt sotsiologicheskogo issledovaniia internatsional'nogo vospitaniia trudiashchikhsia v mnogonatsional'nykh trudovykh kollektivakh," *Sotsiologicheskie issledovaniia,* 1980, no. 3, p. 169.

4 Iu. Arutiunian and Iu. Kakhk, *Sotsiologicheskie ocherki o Sovetskoi Estonii* (Tallinn: Periodika, 1979), p. 75.

5 L. M. Drobizheva, *Dukhovnaia obshchnost' narodov SSSR: istoriko-sotsiologicheskii ocherk mezhnatsional'nykh otnoshenii* (Moscow: Mysl', 1981), p. 214.

6 The Soviet surveys rarely report the exact formulation of their questions, but it is clear that at least in the case of supervisors, specific nationalities (Tatar

or Russian) were mentioned in the Arutiunian survey (cf. Table 5.5). Questions about coworkers apparently were phrased in terms of choices between answer categories stating that the (*a*) ethnic composition of the collective has no significance, (*b*) multiethnic collectives are preferable, or (*c*) monoethnic collectives are preferable: cf. Iu. V. Arutiunian, *Sotsial'noe i natsional'noe, Opyt etnosotsiologicheskikh issledovanii po materialam Tatarskoi ASSR* (Moscow: Nauka, 1973), p. 286, as well as the row headings in Table 5.10.

7   Drobizheva, *Dukhovnaia obshchnost'*, p. 104.

8   *Pravda*, 8 October 1983, p. 2.

9   Arutiunian, "Konkretno," p. 134.

10 L. M. Drobizheva and A. A. Susokolov, "Mezhetnicheskie otnosheniia, i etnokul'turnye protsessy (po materialam etnosotsiologicheskikh issledovanii v SSSR)," *Sovetskaia etnografiia, 1981, no. 3*, p. 18.

11 Arutiunian and Kakhk, *Sotsiologicheskie ocherki*, p. 84.

12 ibid., p. 81.

13 Drobizheva, *Dukhovnaia obshchnost'*, p. 92. In another publication the same author also mentions that 80 to 90 percent of Uzbeks feel that nationality makes no difference in work relationships "assuming that the people know the language of each other." L. M. Drobizheva, "Sblizhenie kul'tur i mezhnatsional'nye otnosheniia v SSSR," *Sovetskaia etnografiia*, 1977, no. 6, p. 17.

14 Kholmogorov, *Internatsional'nye cherty*, p. 170.

15 On the latter point see especially Karl Deutsch, *Nationalism and Social Communication* (Cambridge, Mass.: MIT Press, 1953). The economic transfer phenomenon has recently been discussed by Joseph Rothschild, *Ethnopolitics: A Conceptual Framework* (New York: Columbia University Press, 1981), *passim*. For an earlier analysis, see Hubert Blalock, Jr., *Toward a Theory of Minority Group Relations* (New York: Wiley, 1967), ch. 2.

16 Arutiunian, "Konkretno," p. 339; see also Table 5.5.

17 Kholmogorov, *Internatsional'nye cherty*, p. 170.

18 Iu. V. Arutiunian, L. M. Drobizheva, and V. S. Zelenchuk, *Opyt etnosotsiologicheskogo issledovaniia obraza zhizni* (Moscow: Nauka, 1980), p. 220.

19 ibid., p. 221.

20 Drobizheva, "Sotsial'no-kul'turnye osobennosti;" trans. in *Soviet Sociology*, vol. 13 (Summer–Fall 1974), p. 87.

21 ibid., p. 88.

22 ibid., p. 86–7.

23 Arutiunian, "Konkretno," p. 342.

24 Drobizheva, "Sotsial'no-kul'turnye osobennosti;" trans. in *Soviet Sociology*, op. cit., pp. 89–90.

25 ibid., p. 77.

26 Drobizheva, *Dukhovnaia obshchnost'*, pp. 87, 94; Arutiunian *et al.*, *Opyt*, p. 203; and N. A. Tomilov, *Sovremennye etnicheskie protsessy sredi sibirskikh tatar* (Tomsk: University of Tomsk Press, 1978), p. 170.

27 Arutiunian and Kakhk, *Sotsiologicheskie ocherki*, p. 100. Similar findings from surveys in Uzbekistan, Georgia, Estonia, and Moldavia are cited in Drobizheva, *Dukhovnaia obshchnost'*, pp. 96–9, 201.

28 Arutiunian and Kakhk, *Sotsiologicheskie ocherki*, p. 85.

29 A. A. Susokolov, "Neposredstvennoe mezhetnicheskoe obshchenie i ustanovki na mezhlichnostnye kontakty," *Sovetskaia etnografiia*, 1973, no. 5, pp. 73–8; trans. in *Soviet Sociology*, vol. 13 (Summer–Fall 1974), p. 152; and see also Arutiunian *et al.*, *Opyt*, pp. 206–7, 223–4.

30 The 5·6 percent are cited in N. A. Tomilov, "Sovremennye etnicheskie protsessy u tatar gorodov Zapadnoi Sibiri," *Sovetskaia etnografiia*, 1972,

no. 6, p. 27; the 54 percent refers to elderly urban Uzbeks, see Drobizheva, *Dukhovnaia obshchnost'*, p. 87.

31 The most recent theory along these lines is that of "internal colonialism" developed by Michael Hechter and others: Hechter, *Internal Colonialism* (Berkeley, Calif.: University of California Press. 1975), *passim*.

32 Rasma Karklins, "Ethnic interaction in the Baltic republics: interviews with recent emigrants," *Journal of Baltic Studies*, vol. 12, no. 1 (Spring 1981), p. 27.

33 ibid., pp. 28–9.

34 Drobizheva, "Sotsial'no-kul'turnye osobennosti;" trans. in *Soviet Sociology*, op. cit., p. 74.

35 A. A. Susokolov, "Neposredstvennoe mezhetnicheskoe;" trans. in *Soviet Sociology*, vol. 13, no. 1–2 (Summer–Fall 1974), p. 148–9.

36 ibid., p. 151.

37 Iu. V. Arutiunian, "O nekotorykh tendentsiiakh kul'turnogo sblizheniia narodov SSSR na etape razvitogo sotsializma," *Istoriia SSSR*, 1978, no. 4, p.103.

6

Ethnic Intermarriage

Next to the outlook on multiethnicity at the workplace intermarriage attitudes are the main dimension Soviet ethnosociologists have singled out for measuring the strength of ethnic perceptions in Soviet society. This precedent is followed here in order to make use of the Soviet data and because intermarriage constitutes a prime case for the assessment of ethnic preferences and interactions applying the perspective from "below." It represents voluntary behavior in the purest sense. Although politics may affect intermarriage rates indirectly by promoting migration and other kinds of demographic mixing, marriage remains one of the core life decisions made by individuals. To what extent do members of the various Soviet nationalities accept or reject each other in their most intimate sphere of life and what are the factors associated with preferences?

While the practice of intermarriage is determined by individuals, the outlook on it is influenced by families and communities, and the consequences are also felt by the latter. Thus there is a link between the individual and the group level of ethnic relations. This has been recognized by Soviet politicians and scholars who have paid increasing attention to ethnically mixed families as a vehicle for promoting the "new historical community of people—the Soviet people."[1] They see the family as a "microenvironment for ethnic integration and natural assimilation,"[2] and highlight its link to the macroenvironment and the whole of Soviet society, that is, "mixed marriages play a major role in the internationalization of the Soviet people."[3]

Since mixed marriages are seen as a progressive phenomenon, they are praised and encouraged, and the more propagandistic writings emphasize that they already are widespread and are bound to become even more so in the future. What in fact is happening? As will be shown, both Soviet and Western research

154

suggests extensive variance between categories of nationalities and pinpoints religion, the strength and uniqueness of communal tradition and culture, and specific types of environments as the major factors making a difference. The study of both actual behavior and attitudes also shows that, since marriage is a two-sided relationship, the identity of both partners has to be specified if meaningful conclusions are to be drawn. Social distance and attraction scales fluctuate a great deal with intermarriage being easily accepted in some cases and strongly rejected in others. Since there are so many ethnic groups in the Soviet Union, variance is tremendous. More important, the consequences of intermarriage are hardly such as to change the essence of the existing nations and to lead to the creation of the qualitatively different and new Soviet nation as envisaged by the official Soviet social theorists.

The topic deserves a book-length study, and more detailed analysis than is possible here. Our goal is limited to pinpointing the basic patterns of ethnic interactions in the familial sphere and to analyzing the implications for overall ethnic relations. As will be shown, the tenacity of nationality is impressive in this one sphere where the merging of peoples is most concrete.

Intermarriage Behavior

RATES OF INTERMARRIAGE

Before reviewing surveys of attitudes, it is useful to assess intermarriage behavior. It is suggestive that despite Soviet assertions that ethnic intermarriage in the USSR demonstrates the increasing internationalism of the Soviet population, official unionwide statistics on actual intermarriage rates have not been published. Available partial data and indices derived by Soviet sociologists studying the archives of ZAGS (Registry Offices) in individual regions suggest that the existence and identity of the larger territorially based nationalities is in no case seriously threatened and that endogamy continues to constitute the norm.

One useful, although indirect, indicator of intermarriage is the proportion of individuals living in ethnically homogeneous families. As Table 6.1 illustrates, in 1969 this rate fluctuated between 74·7 and 94·1 percent, depending on nationality. The groups listed represent the great majority of the Soviet population, namely, the titular populations of the fifteen union republics. As other data indicate (see below), intermarriage is more

Table 6.1   *Measures of Intermarriage, Union Republic Nationalities within Own Republics*

Nationality	Percentage of members of families living in ethnically homogeneous families, 1970*	Index of endogamy, 1969†
Kirghiz	92·5	95·4
Kazakhs	91·1	93·6
Turkmens	93·9	90·7
Azeris	92·7	89·8
Uzbeks	93·0	86·2
Georgians	92·0	80·5
Estonians	76·7	78·8
Tadjiks	91·2	77·3
Lithuanians	84·3	68·2
Moldavians	83·5	62·0
Latvians	74·7	61·4
Belorussians	80·2	39·0
Ukrainians	78·2	34·3
Armenians	94·1	33·4
Russians	81·6	n.d.

* Calculations based on data from the Soviet 1970 Census; for more details see Wesley A. Fischer, *The Soviet Marriage Market: Mate-Selection in Russia and the USSR*, New York, Praeger, 1980, pp. 222–5.

† The range of this index is from 0 to 100, with 0 indicating a random choice of marriage partner disregarding nationality and 100 indicating totally non-random selection. This index was developed and calculated by the Ukrainian demographer M. V. Ptukha; for details see Liubov' V. Chuiko, *Braki i razvody*, Moscow, Statistika, 1975, pp. 71–7.

prevalent among secondary ethnic groups, that is, the smaller extraterritorial groups as well as branches of the larger Soviet nations living outside of their titular republics, but these cases are atypical.

Table 6.1 illustrates both the generally low rates of intermarriage among the primary ethnic groups (first column) as well as the strength of their respective tendency toward endogamy (second column). The latter is provided since percentage rates indicating actual intermarriage are useful only as a measure of the extent to which national groups are affected by it, they are less meaningful in gauging the weight of ethnicity in marital choice since they are not *prima facie* indicators of the opportunity to meet and select mates of one nationality or the other. In light of the uneven regional distribution of nationalities this theoretical opportunity varies and has to be taken into account in evaluations of the strength of endogamous tendencies.

There have been several attempts to calculate indices reflecting the weights of opportunity and deliberate selection; the most straightforward of these was developed by the Ukrainian demographer Ptukha (see Table 6.1, column 2). This index of endogamy measures the ethnic randomness of marital unions; the data indicate a decided tendency for the major non-Russian nationalities to marry within their own national groups, although this proclivity varies in strength. It is most pronounced among the traditionally Muslim nation as well as among the Georgians; it is strong among the Balts; and is least pronounced among the Belorussians, Ukrainians, and Armenians. The Armenian case may constitute a statistical fluke since there are few non-Armenians in Armenia and intermarriage with this small group of people weighs heavily in the calculation of the index. The low endogamy index is more convincing in the case of the Belorussians and Ukrainians, although as will be explicated below, their exogamous tendency primarily reflects an ease of intermarriage with other Slavs.

The emphasis on marriage within their own nationalities as measured by the high index of endogamy among all of the six major Soviet Muslim nations, that is, the Kirghiz, Kazakhs, Azeri, Uzbeks, Turkmen, and Tadjiks, has also been noted in qualitative sources, among them our own interviews with Soviet Germans who have lived in close contact with these people (see Chapter 7). Our respondents and most other sources relate this phenomenon to the influence of traditions and religion[4] as well as to strong communal ties and identity. For the Muslims marriage is much more of a communal and group-related decision than for the traditionally Christian nations where the individual is paramount. Replies to a survey question about whether one should ask one's parents' approval for entering into marriage illustrate this well: while 88 percent of the Uzbeks said yes, only 22 percent of the Estonians did.[5] The gap in the extent of communal influence is also expressed by another Soviet source which states that in Estonia "traditions do not set such a severe taboo against interethnic marriage as is the case among the Muslim nations".[6]

Actual intermarriage rates as well as the proclivity toward it not only differ by nationality, they also differ according to the ethnic environments in which people reside. Intermarriage is more prevalent in large urban centers than in small towns and in rural areas. While 14 percent of all families in Estonia are mixed (the USSR average is cited as being 13 percent), 29 percent of marriages registered in the first and third quarters of 1975 in Tallinn were mixed. This ratio is said to be typical for the entire USSR, that is, the rate of binational marriages in cities is double that of the countryside.[7] Findings of Soviet scholars about the role of this and other demographic factors have been succinctly summarized by Krivonogov:[8]

> The pattern of ethnic settlement is an important factor influencing the process of formation of ethnically mixed marriages. The number of such families is particularly large in zones of ethnic contact.

And another Soviet ethnosociologist specifies three such zones of ethnic contact:[9]

> The first zone is constituted by the peripheries of the settlement areas of specific peoples. The second zone consists of large cities, new housing complexes, and "Virgin lands" areas. It is known, for example, that the indigenous population has numerically been surpassed by other nationalities in several large cities (Kazan, Ashkhabad, Vilnius, et al.). The third zone consists of regions where penetration by other nationalities puts an end to the compact settlement of certain ethnic groups.

In specific locales the frequency of intermarriage differs within subregions, and also by nationality. Thus one finds that within Tashkent it is useful to differentiate between the old part of the city which has traditionally been inhabited by Uzbeks and the "new town" inhabited mostly by European nationalities; the overall rate of intermarriage is twice as high in the latter as in the former.[10] Again the differential ethnic propensity to intermarry would be measured most accurately by an index of endogamy taking account of the local opportunity structure, but detailed statistics are hard to obtain. Rough estimates suggest that the differentials are considerable.

The data on Northern Kazakhstan, presented in Table 6.2, are a case in point. Thus the intermarriage rate of Kazakhs is much lower than that of Russians, although at least twice as many Russians lived in the listed cities. The intermarriage rate for the other two Slavic groups, the Ukrainians and the Belorussians, also appear disproportionately high. Similar tendencies can be

Table 6.2 Intermarriage Patterns in Northern Kazakhstan, 1940–70

City*	Percentage of marriages mixed	Percentage of mixed marriages among									
		Kazakhs		Russians		Ukrainians		Belorussians		Germans	
		men	women	men	women	men	women	men	women	men	women
Kokchetav	36	17	2	26	26	72	70	76	77	48	58
Kustanai	40	21	4	29	30	67	69	79	82	45	53
Pavlodar	37	13	1	26	27	65	67	87	83	53	61
Tselinograd	34	14	1	23	27	68	62	80	79	37	44

* Data on the ethnic composition of these cities are not available, but oblast-level data suggest that in 1970 Russians in all instances constituted some 40 percent of the inhabitants, Kazakhs 20 percent, Ukrainians 10 percent, and Germans between 5 and 10 percent, the rest being made up by other groups.

Source: Yu. A. Evstigneev, "Interethnic marriages in some cities of northern Kazakhstan," Soviet Sociology, vol. 13, no. 3 (Winter 1974–5), pp. 3–15.

noted in other locales which suggests that it is not just a question of being an extraterritorial group. Thus the Ukrainians residing in the Omsk oblast of Western Siberia intermarry at a rate of 83 percent, while the Kazakhs of the area—also a minority— intermarry only at a rate of 4 percent.[11] This very low figure illustrates Muslim resistance to intermarriage even in environments where they are heavily outnumbered and do not enjoy any of the cultural and social advantages of union republic status.

PATTERNS of INTERMARRIAGE

In those instances where marriage across ethnic barriers occurs, certain patterns of nationality combinations predominate. One may summarize these patterns by stating that when nationalities intermarry they tend to do so with culturally fraternal peoples.

Again this community-oriented proclivity is strongest among Soviet Muslim groups. In those few instances where Tadjiks, Uzbeks, Kazakhs, Azeri, Ingushi, and so on, intermarry, they typically marry another Muslim. In some of these cases it is even questionable whether it is accurate to talk of "mixed marriages" since many of the current national subdivisions and designations represent creations of the Soviet period and remnants of the pre-Soviet all-encompassing Islamic identity survive. This is especially true for the smaller ethnic groups of the northern Caucasus and the indigenous people of Central Asia.[12]

Although Soviet sources fail to emphasize that intermarriage has many variants and that their respective incidence varies, some of the data they present illustrate this point. Thus the studies of intermarriage in Northern Kazakhstan show that Kazakhs intermarry most frequently with Tatars. The other major ethnic combination here and in other regions involves Russians, Ukrainians, and Belorussians as well as smaller Slavic groups living in the USSR.[13] In this case intermarriage is facilitated by linguistic and cultural affinity; in addition, the Slavs have been at the forefront of the migratory population movement in the USSR and intermarriage is much higher among migrants than among residentially rooted groups.

Citing the influence of "religious inhibitions, language barriers, and the survival of certain prejudices," one of the few Soviet sources analyzing variants of ethnic combinations in marriage notes that other more frequent combinations include marriages between Latvians and Lithuanians (linguistic closeness) and Latvians and Estonians (Lutheran affinity) as well as

Table 6.3 Prevailing Combinations in Ethnically Mixed Marriages, Selected Cities of the USSR (in Percentages)

Intermarriage pattern	Kiev, Ukrainian SSR	Minsk, Belorussian SSR	Kishinev, Moldavian SSR	Vilnius, Lithuanian SSR	Riga, Latvian SSR	Tallinn, Estonian SSR	Ashkhabad, Turkmen SSR	Petropavlovsk, Kazakh SSR	Kazan, Tatar ASSR	Cheboksary, Chuvash ASSR	Saransk, Mordvinian ASSR
Basic local nationality with Russians	72	61	21	14	25	36	11	2	33	67	52
Basic local nationality with other nationalities	15	21	20	17	12	7	10	5	11	4	4
Russians with Ukrainians	—	11	35	17	23	23	29	47	26	14	24
Russians with other nationalities	10	5	14	36	28	16	33	34	28	14	18
Other variants	2	2	11	16	12	18	17	12	2	1	2
Total	100	100	100	100	100	100	100	100	100	100	100

Source: For Petropavlovsk, A. P. Egurnev, "Mezhnatsional'nye braki i ikh rol' v sblizhenii natsii i narodnostei SSSR," Nauchnyi kommunizm, 1973, no. 4, p. 30; for other places, L. N. Terent'eva, "Forming of ethnic self-consciousness in nationally mixed families in the USSR," in Sociological Studies: Ethnic Aspects, Moscow, Papers presented at the Eighth World Congress of Sociology, Toronto, Canada, 1974, p. 47: the data refer to the parents of 16 year-olds receiving their first passports between 1960 and 1969.

Table 6.4 *"Attraction" and "Repulsion" Indexes Calculated from Interethnic Marriages in Latvia, 1976 (in Percentages)*

Nationality		Marriage index	
husband	wife	in urban area	in rural area
Latvian	Russian	−64·9	−55·4
	Ukrainian	−70·1	−56·1
	Belorussian	−65·3	−54·0
	Jew	−91·8	—
	Lithuanian	+1·4	−21·4
	Pole	−33·8	−41·4
Russian	Ukrainian	+8·6	+2·5
	Belorussian	+2·7	+5·5
	Jew	−24·5	—
	Latvian	−68·9	−57·3
	Lithuanian	−15·0	−36·2
	Pole	−12·6	+5·0
Ukrainian	Russian	+6·7	+6·2
	Belorussian	+6·2	+5·9
	Jew	−46·6	+5·4
	Latvian	−65·0	−54·0
	Pole	+2·0	−99·9
	Lithuanian	−33·1	+1·8
Belorussian	Russian	+4·2	+7·2
	Ukrainian	+2·5	+3·7
	Jew	−86·2	—
	Latvian	−55·4	−63·4
	Lithuanian	−56·7	−16·6
	Pole	+3·2	+6·7

Source: A. Lapin'sh, "Brachnaia izbiratel'nost' v Latviiskoi SSR," *Sotsial'no-demograficheskie issledovaniia sem'i v respublikakh sovetskoi Pribaltiki,* ed. P. Gulian, A. Kelam, N. Solov'ev, E. Tiit, and P. Eglite, Riga, Zinatne, 1980, p. 60.

Belorussians and Poles.[14] The role of religious background is furthermore highlighted in Armenia, where Armenians are much more likely to intermarry with Russians than with Azeri.[15]

The prevalence of specific combinations in intermarriage can also be illustrated by the data in Table 6.3. In most of the cities listed the Russians and the respective indigenous nationality constitute the two largest population groups. The theoretical likelihood of these two groups intermarrying is thus the largest, but the actual distribution suggests that choices take on different patterns. In all the non-Slavic capitals listed, as well as in Petropavlovsk and Kazan, the rate of marriages of Russians to other non-locals is higher than to the locals. Marriages within the Slavic group again constitute a dominant pattern both in these instances and in the case of Kiev and Minsk.

Several conclusions can be drawn. For one, great care should be taken when making inferences based purely on geographically defined intermarriage rates; while people tend to assume that such rates reflect the exogamous behavior of the indigenous nationality, this is true only in part. Moreover, the behavioral tendency toward exogamy is affected by many of the same factors as will be noted for intermarriage attitudes, namely, that differentiations are made between groups and that those most easily accepted are the ones that are closest in religious or cultural terms. Ideally, if an extensive data bank on intermarriage behavior subdivided by both locale and nationalities were available, individual "indices of endogamy" could be calculated to measure the strength of differentiation.

In an exceptional case such a calculation has been published for Latvia in 1976. The data support our conclusions, in that ethnic attraction, as expressed by the numbers with plus signs in Table 6.4, is evident nearly exclusively among culturally fraternal nations, that is, Balts and Slavs respectively. Similarly, the so-called "repulsion index" is high in all Baltic–Slavic combinations. One may conclude that intermarriage rates differ among subgroups of nationalities and that variance is associated to a host of factors among which religious tradition, cultural and linguistic identity, and political–historical love/hate prejudice appear to be the most important.[16]

Attitudes toward Intermarriage

SOVIET SURVEYS

Since the late 1960s the Soviets have published a number of articles and books which include data on intermarriage attitudes. The reports differ in the thoroughness in which they cite the actual survey results and methods, and they also differ in the quality of analysis. To this day the best and most extensive work is that undertaken in the Tatar ASSR by Arutiunian and his team from the Institute of Ethnography of the Academy of Sciences of the USSR, and this section will consequently emphasize this research.

The Arutiunian study stands out among Soviet ethnosociological work in being more conscientious in reporting its
methods. It is a standing rule in survey research to report the
exact wording of questions since it is closely linked to the results
obtained and is crucial for a clear understanding of their meaning. Nevertheless, Soviet reports on surveys typically do not cite
the wording of questions, leaving it up to the reader to try to
deduce it from the text or from headings in statistical tables.
Since such formulations are more inexact, the reader may be
misled. Thus even the Tatar study, which has been summarized
many times, included in its initial reports tables in which the
most positive statement about intermarriage was cited as "regard
nationality as insignificant for marriage,"[17] but later publications
referred to the same results as "have favorable view of mixed
marriages."[18] The two are not the same. The formulation of the
survey question and the answer categories used show that the
version used in the initial reports was the exact one:[19]

Question: Do you approve of marriages of Tatars to Russians?
What would be your attitude if one of your nearest relatives
(son, daughter, brother, or sister) made such a marriage?

I regard such a marriage as undesirable.
I would prefer a person of my nationality, but would not object
to such a marriage.
Nationality makes no difference; the most important thing is
the person's individual qualities.
I find it difficult to say.
No answer.

A close reading of the answer categories shows that while there
is a category specifying that intermarriage is regarded as "undesirable," no category specifies the opposite view of it being
"desirable." The most positive response provided is that
"nationality makes no difference." Interpreting the latter as a
"favorable view of mixed marriage" (see Table 6.6) is inexact, to
say the least.

Caution is similarly advisable in the interpretation of other
tables (some of which are reproduced in this study) if they use
the category "have negative attitude toward mixed marriages."[20]
While this is an accurate characterization of the attitude expressed by those respondents who chose the first answer category, it
might also reasonably be used to characterize the second one,

although the switch from attitude to behavior adds some ambiguity. Nevertheless, the second response category typically is omitted in those tables focusing on negative views of intermarriage (for an exception, see Table 6.7).

Even though it is advisable to be circumspect in the use of Soviet survey results, they can be useful in the analysis of variance which serves to pinpoint factors that are associated with differing attitudes and behavior. Thus one finds that while the percentage of respondents stating that nationality makes no difference in marriage typically is in the 70–80 percent range, this benchmark figure changes upwards or downwards depending on the subgroups examined in analysis. In the case of the Arutiunian study the lowest percentage cited concerns 52 percent both for the subcategories "Tatars over the age of 50," and "urban white-collar Tatars in Kazan." The highest rate given is 84 percent for both "female Tatar professionals living in villages with a predominantly Russian population" and "male Tatar farmhands living in Russian villages."[21] Thus the prevalence of neutral attitudes about intermarriage is associated with the sociodemographic characteristics of respondents, but it is difficult to disentangle the influence of individual factors. The reports are extremely meager in citing their raw data, and since one cannot recalculate and independently interpret results, one has to use the findings as presented by the Soviet specialists.

As one searches for evidence about significant associations between intermarriage attitudes and other factors, it is found that religion, age, and gender are the least complex. Many Soviet reports note that religious identity and belief is associated with a preference for endogamy. In the words of Arutiunian's original report on the Tatar ASSR "the closest connection is seen between ethnic attitudes and religion."[22] Women reject intermarriage more often than men, and age plays a role as well, although the latter may be less straightforward than is suggested. While there is a tendency for older people to reject intermarriage more often, some younger age groups have also been associated with more negative attitudes.[23] Occupation appears somewhat associated with interethnic attitudes; in one listing farm equipment operators emerge as the most, and white-collar workers as the least, indifferent to interethnic marriages within their closest family (see Table 6.7).

Next to occupation, gender, age, and religion, which are standard sociodemographic variables examined in sociological analyses, there are two special factors associated with ethnic

Table 6.5 *Relationship of Tatar Attitudes in Interethnic Relationships to Language of Schooling and Character of Ethnic Contacts in School*

Language of schooling and character of contacts in school		Attitudes	
		Regard nationality of coworkers and supervisor as insignificant (%)	Regard nationality as insignificant for marriage (%)
Tatars who know Russian	Graduates of Russian-language school	87	82
	Graduates of Tatar-language school	82	74
Tatars who know only their native tongue		66	69

Source: L. M. Drobizheva, "Sotsial'no-kul'turnye osobennosti lichnost' i natsional'nye ustanovki" (po materialam issledovanii v Tatarskoi ASSR), *Sovetskaia etnografiia*, 1971, 3, p. 10.

attitudes, namely, language facility and intensity of ethnic contact. Thus knowledge of a language other than the native one is positively correlated with less exclusive ethnic attitudes. While this is true on the whole,[24] a large number of Soviet socioethnological studies have focused on the significance of non-Russians knowing Russian. Thus the Arutiunian study includes several tables according to which Tatars who do not know Russian are more likely to state that nationality makes a difference in marriage as well as in regard to coworkers and supervisors than Tatars knowing Russian—especially those who have attended Russian-language schools (Table 6.5). This general tendency has been corroborated in other studies, the one exception being professionals and semi-professionals, or to use the Soviet term, the "intelligentsia." As already noted in Chapter 5, this exception is most pronounced in attitudes related to ethnic contacts at work.

It is a core hypothesis of this study that the quality of ethnic relationships changes according to type of ethnic environment and groups involved. In the context of intermarriage attitudes there is some evidence to this effect in the Arutiunian studies

Table 6.6 *Ethnic attitudes of Tatars and Russians as Related to Ethnic Composition of Village (in Percentages)*

| | Composition of village population | | | | | |
| | Primarily Tatar | | Primarily Russian | | Mixed | |
Attitude	Tatars	Russians	Tatars	Russians	Tatars	Russians
Favorable view of mixed marriages	68	59	73	73	89	89
Favorable view of interethnic contacts at work	82	81	87	82	87	94

Source: Iurii V. Arutiunian, *Sotsial'noe i natsional'noe, Opyt etnosotsiologicheskikh issledovanii po materialam Tatarskoi ASSR*, Moscow, Nauka, 1973, p. 283.

conducted in the Tatar ASSR. As can be seen from Table 6.6, Arutiunian subdivided his data both by nationality of respondents and by three types of villages. The most favorable attitudes toward mixed marriages were held in ethnically mixed villages, whereas predominantly Russian villages indicate a less "internationalist" outlook, and predominantly Tatar villages even less so. In the latter case it is also striking that the percentage of Russians holding favorable views of intermarriage drops significantly (by up to 30 percent) both as compared to the Russian rates for the other environments and also as compared to Tatar attitudes. It is rare that Soviet survey data reveal such negative interethnic attitudes among Russians and this finding implies that in their case increasingly negative attitudes are associated with environments in which a local nationality is numerically dominant. The same environment shows the most negative interethnic attitudes among locals, in our case the Tatars. This finding is, however, mitigated if one looks at differentials by occupational group. As Table 6.7 illustrates, the basic trend differs for professionals and white-collar workers who tend to retain similar or even increasingly nationalist attitudes when residing in ethnically mixed or Russian-dominated environments.[25]

Disregarding this exception for the moment, and looking at these same data from a more theoretical angle, one finds that Russians and Tatars show a similar increase in internationalist

Table 6.7 Relationship between Ethnic Attitudes and Contacts, Tatars Residing in Tatar ASSR (in Percentages)

Sociooccupational groups	Villages with primarily Russian or with mixed populations				Villages with primarily Tatar population			
	contacts		negative or vague attitude		contacts		negative or vague attitude	
	Have relatives married to persons of other nationality	Have spouse of other nationality	Toward ethnically mixed marriages	Toward job superiors of other nationality	Have relatives married to persons of other nationality	Have spouse of other nationality	Toward ethnically mixed marriages	Toward job superiors of other nationality
Professionals and paraprofessionals	41	15	11	10	30	1	11	10
White-collar workers	38	19	25	8	31	1	10	9
Machine operators and other skilled workers	22	3	4	2	8	0	10	10
Farmlaborers and other unskilled workers	9	4	9	6	—	0	14	15

Source: Iurii V. Arutiunian, "Konkretno-sotsiologicheskoe issledovanie natsional'nykh otnoshenii," *Voprosy filosofii,* 1969, no. 12, p. 139; in a subsequent publication the same table was reproduced without the data on primarily Tatar villages, cf. Iurii V. Arutiunian, *Sotsial'noe i natsional'noe, Opyt etnosotsiologicheskikh issledovanii po materialem Tatarskoi ASSR,* Moscow, Nauka, 1973, p. 295.

attitudes in mixed environments, but react differently in environments where the other group dominates. For Tatars the shift from native to Russian-dominated environment is associated with a slight increase in internationalist attitudes, whereas in the case of Russians a shift from their native (Russian) environment into one where Tatars dominate is associated with a major decrease of internationalist attitudes. Arutiunian fails to comment on this phenomenon, but it is likely that it is related to language problems (as in fact is stated by another source),[26] to the lower social prestige of Tatars as compared to Russians, or to a low Russian ability to adjust to a locally dominated environment.

While Soviet sources rarely comment on the ethnic attitudes of Russians, it is also rare that they provide comparative data for several nationalities living in the same region. This, however, is another important area of inquiry. Thus partial data from Moldavia suggest that the Ukrainians living there have the lowest ratio of people stating that nationality is insignificant in marriage, while the Moldavians and Gagauz fall in the middle, and the Russians rank on top.[27]

Returning to the analysis of the impact of ethnic contact on attitudes, one may note that while the differential ethnic composition of the place of residence provides one measure of ethnic contact, another measure is having family members of another nationality. The crosstabulation by both environment and occupational group provided in Table 6.7 suggests that—as is the case regarding Russian-language knowledge—diverging associations apply to different occupational groups. All occupational subgroups have more other ethnic relatives if they reside in villages with mixed or primarily Russian populations, but while some (skilled and unskilled farmworkers) exhibit a lower degree of negative or vague attitudes toward intermarriage, others show no change or even an increase of such attitudes (note especially the increasingly negative attitudes among white-collar personnel).

Although this type of general association cannot be taken as proof of a definite causal relationship, its implications in terms of social trends are of major importance. As Arutiunian noted in his seminal article in *Voprosy filosofii*,[28]

If this conclusion is true, it means that there can be no universally valid means of improving ethnic relationships. A given technique may lead to different and sometimes even directly opposite results in different social groups. The question of the role of the milieu is extremely urgent in this connection. The contact environment, the mixing of various ethnic groups in the population, is a powerful means for bringing about mutual adaptation of "ethnoses." It is presumed that living and working together necessarily facilitate mutual understanding among human beings, interpenetration of cultures, and improvement of ethnic relationships. If our conclusion about the two types of nationalism is true, it will be understood that the contact milieu must necessarily influence different population groups in different ways. For people engaged in physical labor (for whom it is only cultural differences that interfere with ethnic mutual understanding), such contacts must necessarily serve as a powerful stimulus to cultural integration, and thereby improvement in ethnic relations. However, contacts among professional and paraprofessional people, among whom competitive strivings exist in mixed environments, by no means necessarily result in similar consequences.

Such contrasting trends are said to complicate the "management of ethnic relations."[29] Or formulated in terms of developmental theory, the increasing mixing of ethnic environments brought about by modernization does not portend a unilinear change in ethnic attitudes. While there is reason to expect that skilled and unskilled workers will perceive ethnicity as being less significant, the opposite is true for white-collar personnel and professionals. The question then remains—which occupational strata are likely to have the greater influence on future social and political processes?

WESTERN SURVEYS

Sociological surveys with Soviet emigrants now in the West still are scarce and their findings must remain tentative in light of small samples and other methodological problems, but they are nevertheless useful for comparisons with Soviet surveys and as indicators of additional pertinent questions. Our survey with Soviet German emigrants included two questions about intermarriage attitudes, the first focusing on attitudes toward marriage between Germans and the respective republic nationality, and the second concerning marriage between Germans and Russians.[30] Two questions were asked because intermarriage attitudes may vary according to the ethnic group referred to. Since there are so many different nationalities in the Soviet

Table 6.8   *Soviet German Attitudes toward Intermarriage with Non-Russians (in Percentages)*

	Local nationality				
Attitude	Kazakhs, N = 69	Central Asians, N = 36	Balts, N = 35	Moldavians* and others, N = 21	Non-Russians in RSFSR, N = 30
Reject	94	92	74	67	60
No difference and no opinion	6	8	26	33	40

* All positive replies in this group relate to Moldavians (N = 14); the others included are Ukrainians (N = 5), one Belorussian, and one Georgian.

Union, the range of potentially differentiated attitudes is broad—in theory, it would have been best to present a lengthy list to explore the divergent "ranking" of nationalities as potential family members. This was not done for practical reasons, but a partial ranking can be derived indirectly since "local nationality" refers to different groups depending on region.

In all cases a majority of respondents stated that the marriage of family members to non-Germans would be undesirable, but the rejection of intermarriage with local nationalities differs in degree. As Table 6.8 illustrates, rejection of intermarriage with Kazakhs and Central Asians is high, but considerably lower in the case of Balts, Moldavians, or non-Russians living in the RSFSR. A comparison of the data in Table 6.8 with those in Table 6.9 furthermore shows that, depending on republic, the Soviet Germans see intermarriage with the local nationality as more or as less desirable than intermarriage with Russians. Thus

Table 6.9   *Soviet German Attitudes toward Intermarriage with Russians (in Percentages)*

	Last residence in USSR				
Attitude	Kazakhstan, N = 68	Central Asia, N = 36	Baltic, N = 35	Moldavia and other, N = 21	RSFSR, N = 33
Reject	79	81	80	76	58
No difference and no opinion	21	19	20	24	42

Russians are preferred to Kazakhs, but not to Moldavians or Balts. As this comparison and the data in Table 6.9 also illustrate, this difference relates mostly to nationalities and less to the republic of residence since attitudes toward marriage with Russians are strongly consistent no matter where the German respondents lived, but with one crucial exception. Those Germans who lived in the Russian Federal Republic reject intermarriage with Russians to a considerably lower degree than do Germans who lived in non-Russian areas. This suggests that within the RSFSR tendencies toward assimilation and integration are considerably heightened; or that an environment in which Russians dominate is the one in which the Soviet Germans have the highest incidence of "internationalist" attitudes.

The latter conclusion is strengthened if the data are tabulated by the ethnic composition of residential locales, since one finds that intermarriage with both Russians and local non-Russians is rejected least frequently in environments dominated by Russians, followed by those dominated by local non-Russians, mixed environments and, finally, those places where Soviet Germans formed a numerical majority of the population (see Table A.6, p. 235). This coincides with the findings of Soviet surveys, in that it associates a native environment with a higher level of intermarriage rejection; but it goes beyond Soviet research, in that it also shows differentials between types of non-native environments. Intermarriage attitudes are second most negative in an ethnically mixed environment, and less so in one dominated by local non-Russians.

As for the other factors cited in Soviet surveys, only some parallel associations emerge from our survey. Turning first to similarities, we too found that women reject intermarriage more often than men (by 5 to 8 percent), and so do highly religious individuals (by 14 percent in the case of marriages with Russians and 11 percent in the case of intermarriage with non-Russians). This association persists even if one controls for gender and age.

Age for its part is significantly associated with the extent to which intermarriage is rejected, the percentage differential being 20 percent in the case of intermarriage with Russians and 10 percent in the case of non-Russians (Table 6.10). How can one explain this drop in intermarriage rejection among younger Soviet Germans? One likely answer is that it is due to their closer ties to Russian culture since the younger generation typically has been educated only in Russian schools and has a much better knowledge of Russian than middle-aged or older people. But the

Table 6.10   *Attitudes toward Intermarriage with Russians, by Age Groups (in Percentages)*

	Age of Soviet German respondents		
Attitude	19–31 years-old, N = 72	32–43 years-old, N = 59	Older than 43 years, N = 62
Reject	64	81	84
No difference or no opinion	36	19	16

Chi-square—8·72 with two degrees of freedom; significance—0·0128.

data on language knowledge do not confirm this assumption and other explanations have to be looked for. In contrast to Soviet surveys, our data do not show an association between a better knowledge of Russian and more favorable attitudes toward intermarriage with Russians, but an association does exist between knowledge of a non-Russian local language and more favorable attitudes toward intermarriage with locals. Contrasting to this parallelism to the findings of Soviet surveys, no differential was found for blue or white collar personnel, although this may be explained by the generally low occupational level of the Soviet German respondent population which practically did not include any professionals or higher-rank white-collar workers.

In ethnic relations actual interaction is just as important as are attitudes. Therefore, respondents were asked whether any of their closest relatives, that is, a son or daughter, brother or sister, had married a non-German. In 34 percent of the cases this had happened, and among these, three-fourths were marriages of Germans to Russians. Among the non-Russians there were six Ukrainians, four Balts, three Kazakhs,[31] two Jews, one Moldavian, and one Buryat (who was listed as Russian in her passport). When asked about the non-German spouses' integration into their family, a majority (70 percent) called it normal, or positive. Of those giving negative evaluations many mentioned divorce or serious marital strife as the cause of the non-German spouses' rejection of the use of the German language in the family. In several cases a Russian wife had kept her own family name.

Similar to Soviet surveys, our survey touches on the relationship between attitudes and actual experience with intermarriage within the immediate family. Even though a majority of the

173

individuals who had a non-German family member had a good or normal relationship with them, basic attitudes toward intermarriage were hardly affected: while 76 percent of respondents with no Russian in-laws rejected intermarriage with Russians, rejection was 70 percent among those who had Russian in-laws. This decrease of negative attitudes by 6 percent is similar to the 7–8 percent decrease shown in Soviet surveys comparing respondents who do or do not have other-ethnic relatives.[32] If one compares the subsamples further, it is found that it matters whether the experience with the in-laws was negative or positive, but the overall difference is still relatively small. The same tendencies appear in regard to intermarriage with non-Russians, but our sample in this case is too small to allow meaningful evaluation.

Twenty-three of our respondents (11·5 percent of the total sample) had married non-Germans themselves, but rejection of intermarriage was considerable even in this group: 46 percent thought that marriages of Germans to Russians were undesirable, and 58 percent thought that marriages of Germans to local nationality members were undesirable. This variance is explained by four individuals who said that marriage to Russians was acceptable (having Russian spouses themselves), but that intermarriage with locals (in all cases Muslims) was undesirable. Our group includes a reverse case as well: one respondent with a Karelian spouse thought that intermarriage with Karelians was fine, but not desirable in the case of Russians.

In sum, one finds that in some cases positive experiences led to or reinforced acceptance of intermarriage—the same applying to negative experiences reinforcing negative attitudes—but there are also instances when experience has had no perceptible influence on attitudes. One may conclude that although the occurrence of intermarriage alters attitudes toward it to some degree, this tendency is by no means unidirectional or overwhelming.

Intermarriage with non-Germans was rejected by a majority of our Soviet German emigrant respondents: "Each nation should stay with its own people" being the most typical comment. Many thought that mixed marriages sooner or later encountered special difficulties. Others pointed to the rejection of intermarriage being reciprocal, especially so in the case of Soviet Muslims close to whom a majority of respondents had lived.

While the results of Western emigrant surveys generally do not diverge much from those of Soviet surveys (except, of course, for the marginals), there is one significant exception, in that Soviet surveys say little about differentials between, and in regard to, various nationalities. As our own survey as well as a study undertaken by Juozas Kazlas indicate, this constitutes one of the most important dimensions of the problem since nationalities not only differ in the degree to which they accept intermarriage *per se*, but also in the extent to which they accept it depending on the identity of the other group. While the differential intensity of exogamous rejection was already noted in regard to marriage behavior and in our data on attitudes of Soviet Germans who had lived in different republics, the differential "ranking" of Soviet nationalities as potential marriage partners emerges even more clearly from the Kazlas study.

Using both Soviet German and Lithuanian emigrant respondents, Kazlas established a typology of intraethnic relationships by the means of a social distance scale. Respondents were asked to choose a numerical score indicating acceptance or rejection of eighteen different Soviet nationalities as friends, marriage partners, coworkers, supervisors, or officials. The score ranged from +2 (total acceptance) to −2 (total rejection), with zero indicating neutrality. The results are very similar for both the German and Lithuanian respondents. Both samples have perfect acceptance scores for persons of their own nationality, and neutral or negative scores for all the other nationalities mentioned. The most negative scores ranging between −1·7 to −1·4 apply to all seven Muslim nationalities on the list (Kazakhs, Kirghiz, Uzbeks, Tadjiks, Turkmen, Azeri, and Tatars), as well as to Russians and Belorussians. Georgians and Armenians ranked −1·4 to −1·3. Slightly higher, but still strongly negative, scores were obtained for Ukrainians, Moldavians, and Jews (−1·4 to −1·1). The only groups ranked slightly positively were the Balts (+0·1 to +0·4).[33]

As noted, results to survey questions vary depending on the way a question is asked. Besides the general rating of individual nationalities, Kazlas also asked a forced-choice question where respondents had to express a preference between Russians and individual non-Russian nationalities. In this case the Lithuanians still exhibit a decided preference for fellow Balts as well as for Ukrainians, while the other nationalities are rated more or less the same as the Russians. In contrast, differentiations made by the Soviet German emigrant respondents are much wider in range. While they also prefer Balts over Russians, they strongly prefer Russians over the various Muslim nationalities as well as over Georgians and Armenians. Russians are rated approximately equally to Ukrainians, Belorussians, and Moldavians.[34]

What can we conclude from these data? Besides the general recognition of differential levels of acceptance of other nationalities, there is strong implication that in a "forced-choice" situation between Russians and the local inhabitants of Central Asia and the Caucasus, the Soviet Germans tend to choose the Russians, who are perceived as fellow Europeans. It is likely that a similar intra-European closeness applies to other groups as well, the most likely candidates being Soviet Jews, Ukrainians, Belorussians, and Moldavians.

Intermarriage Attitudes and Behavior: Conclusions

In their interpretations and conclusions about ethnic intermarriage both Western and Soviet authors contradict each other to a significant degree. Some of these contradictions are indirect and become apparent only with a reading of divergent sources, others have been openly expressed to the point of scholarly polemics. Why is there this amount of unclarity and controversy about a subject that appears to be relatively straightforward? For one, it is not *that* straightforward since basic data banks and measures of meaning are incomplete and underdeveloped. In addition, the controversy has arisen because ethnic intermarriage has been assigned a specific sociopolitical role in the official blueprint for the future of the multiethnic Soviet society.

Turning first to the problems of factual clarity, it bears reiterating that confusion arises due to the prevalence of contradictory types of situations and trends. There are ethnoenvironments—especially large urban centers and new intensive production zones—in which intermarriage occurs relatively frequently, but there are other environments in which intermarriage is rare. Smaller towns and rural areas in the non-Russian republics are the prime example for the latter case; also, individual nationalities differ in their general proclivity to intermarry and as regards the specific other nationalities they tend to intermarry with. Muslims are especially averse to intermarriage, much more so than the Slavs. Depending on the amount of information available to individual analysts, and depending on their overall outlook, they may emphasize groups and contexts where intermarriage is more or less prevalent.

There is also the problem of finding good data. While this was already noted in regard to behavioral statistics, it is also true for attitudinal data. Several difficulties apply. First, the best-known Soviet surveys were conducted in the Tatar ASSR, Northern Kazakhstan, and Western Siberia, areas which are more conducive to ethnic mixing and integration than the majority of union republic environments. Also Soviet sources typically do not cite data on the intermarriage attitudes of the indigenous populations of Central Asia and Kazakhstan. One must assume that this is due to the overwhelming rejection of intermarriage among these people, a rejection which has been attested to by qualitative studies as well as in one rare instance where a Soviet survey reference could be found, that is, a survey conducted in Western Siberia cites 65 percent of the local Kazakhs as favoring marriage to persons of their own nationality.[35] If this is true for Kazakhs living outside of Kazakhstan, what about those residing in their titular republic? The percentage favoring monoethnic marriages presumably is even higher, in the over-80 percent range.[36]

It matters which nationality is surveyed, and in what areas. The style of data presentation also matters and care has to be taken in the interpretation of Soviet survey results since their authors sometimes obfuscate politically uncomfortable findings. In the case of intermarriage attitudes this most often happens in reports which cite data for one of the answer categories only. A prime example of this is found in another rare instance where data on intermarriage attitudes of a Muslim people have been cited, in this case the Uzbeks. Thus a table in a major book by Drobizheva cites 24–30 percent of various occupational groups of Uzbeks as "feeling that interethnic marriages are undesirable."[37] Since no other data are given, the unwary reader could deduce that the rest of the respondents said that interethnic marriages were desirable. That this assumption is false becomes clear when one examines the data on Moldavians given in the same table and in the text. The Moldavians are said to have only a 0·8–4·4 percent rate of people "thinking that interethnic marriages are undesirable," and 63–76 percent "thought that nationality has no significance for marriage."[38] Since the two numbers do not add up to 100 percent, there clearly is a missing category of data. It appears that this category included a qualified rejection of intermarriage as was the case in the Tatar study (cf. p. 140), but the particulars remain unclear.

Another source of confusion is divergence in the interpretation of data and trends. The dominant recent Soviet interpretation has been that intermarriage constitutes a major progressive

177

development leading to a merging of nationalities into a new community, the "Soviet people." The notion that this is in fact happening, as well as the politics behind it, were attacked in at least one recent case by a Soviet analyst writing in a scholarly publication in Kazakhstan. She decidedly rejects the proposition that a "new non-ethnic unity" results from mixed marriages, arguing instead that "the new generation growing up in a mixed family, first of all acquires the traits of the one or the other nationality of both nations, among which one dominates. Secondly, it does not become de-ethnicized, but is certainly influenced by a definite nation."[39] The author furthermore argues that the integration of peoples through intermarriage not only does not occur in the contemporary period, but also represents a misconception for the stage of developed socialism:[40]

It would be an exaggeration to attribute to ethnically mixed marriages and families the main role in the process of integration between the socialist nations. These are expensive theoretical mistakes which can also entail practical mistakes. In China, for example, a group of Mao's soldiers and officers were directed to marry non-Chinese women to speed up sinification of the national minorities. Crude intervention in familial and marriage relationships with the goal of forced assimilation of the small peoples is a distortion of the theoretical position of Marxist–Leninist nationality policy.

While there is no sign of any such crude intervention in the Soviet Union, the author implicitly attacks the propagandistic encouragement of intermarriage as well as the indirect policies resulting in their encouragement such as interrepublic migration, the "exchange of cadre," investment policies, and similar.

In spite of the official intent of encouraging mixed marriages, it is doubtful, however, that significant changes will occur in the near future. Monoethnic marriages remain the overall norm, and in some cases have even begun to increase during the 1970s.[41] The trend away from mixed marriages is most likely—and politically most significant—in the case of primary ethnic groups. Thus one finds that in spite of a higher probability of Estonian–Russian marriages occurring in Tallinn due to the inmigration of Russians, the actual rate of such marriages decreased in the period between 1965 and 1975.[42]

To the degree that intermarriage does occur it typically does not lead to the erosion of nationality, but rather to the choice of one over the other. As was already noted in Chapter 1, the Soviet requirement that each citizen have an official passport nationality reinforces this social tendency. As to the choices made, it bears reemphasizing that a non-Russian nationality is frequently chosen by youngsters living in non-Russian republics. This tendency is especially pronounced among the Muslim nations,[43] which according to all our data are the ones least likely to be affected by exogamy and the sociocultural consequences it may entail.

The discussion of both intermarriage behavior and attitudes shows that similarly as in the case of work-related ethnic attitudes, different preferences are associated with a host of sociodemographic variables as well as language facility and the composition of microenvironments. The latter two associations are the most complex and also the most significant in their implications for future trends in ethnic relations in the USSR. While Soviet policy-makers base their policy of promoting Russian-language facility and more interethnic contact at work and in families on the assumption that this is correlated with warmer ethnic relations, empirical data suggest that at least for some social and ethnic groups the opposite correlation holds true and more negative attitudes appear. To repeat Arutiunian's words, "if this conclusion is true, it means that there can be no universally valid means of improving ethnic relationships."[44]

Notes: Chapter 6

1   A. P. Egurnev, "Mezhnatsional'nye braki i ikh rol' v sblizhenii natsii i norodnostei SSSR," *Nauchnyi kommunizm*, 1973, no. 4, p. 28.
2   O. R. Budina and M. N. Shmeleva, "Etnograficheskoe izuchenie goroda v SSSR," *Sovetskaia etnografiia*, 1977, no. 6, p. 28.
3   O. A. Gantskaia and L. N. Terent'eva, "Sem'ia—mikrosreda etnicheskikh protsesov," in *Sovremennye etnicheskie protsessy v SSSR* (Moscow: Nauka, 1975), p. 431.
4   Egurnev, "Mezhnatsional'nye braki," pp. 30–1.
5   Among Russians residing in the RSFSR 38 percent said yes, and so did 41 percent of Georgians and 61 percent of Moldavians surveyed: see Iu. V. Arutiunian, "O nekotorykh tendentsiiakh kul'turnogo sblizheniia narodov SSSR na etape razvitogo sotsializma," *Istoriia SSSR*, 1978, no. 4, p. 102.
6   L. M. Drobizheva, *Dukhovnaia obshchnost' narodov SSSR: istoriko-sotsiologicheskii ocherk mezhnatsional'nykh otnoshenii* (Moscow: Mysl', 1981), p. 174.
7   Iu. Arutiunian and Iu. Kakhk, *Sotsiologicheskie ocherki o Sovetskoi Estonii* (Tallinn: Periodika, 1979), p. 76.

8   V. P. Krivonogov, "Mezhetnicheskie braki u khakasov v sovremennyi period," *Sovetskaia etnografiia*, 1980, no. 3, p. 74; trans. in *Soviet Sociology*, vol. 19, no. 1 (Summer 1980), p. 64.

9   Gantskaia and Terent'eva, "Sem'ia," p. 465.

10 ibid., p. 473.

11 N. A. Tomilov, "Sovremennye etnicheskie protsessy v iuzhnoi i srednei polose Zapadnoi Sibiri;" trans. in *Soviet Sociology*, vol. 18, no. 2 (1979), p. 64.

12 cf. various writings by Alexandre Bennigsen.

13 yu. A. Evstigneev, "Mezhetnicheskie braki v nekotorykh gorodakh Severnogo Kazakhstana," *Vestnik Moskovskogo universiteta, Seriia istorii*, 1972, no. 2, pp. 73–82, trans. in *Soviet Sociology*, vol. 13, no. 3 (Winter 1974–5), pp. 3–15. The strength of intra-Slavic marriages may be illustrated by the data cited: ibid., p. 7, "Russians marrying outside their nationality chiefly wed Ukrainians (from 57% of the mixed marriages in Tselinograd to 75% in Kustanai) and Belorussians (from 12% in Kustani to 16% in Kokchetav). Likewise, among the Ukrainians and Belorussians, marriages with Russians predominate (on the average, 58% of the marriages entered by Ukrainians and 55% of those entered by Belorussians), followed by marriages between Ukrainians and Belorussians."

14 Gantskaia and Terent'eva, "Sem'ia," p. 467.

15 Alla E. Ter-Sarkisiants, "O natsional'nom aspekte brakov v Armianskoi SSR (po materialam zagsov)," *Sovetskaia etnografiia*, 1973, no. 4, pp. 94–5.

16 A reference should be made to a debate by two Western scholars about the linkage between intermarriage behavior and the ethnic consciousness of Soviet nationalities. The debate started after Wesley Fisher published a rather complex analysis of correlates of endogamy, concluding that ethnic consciousness had little to do with it. This conclusion was challenged in both a qualitative and quantitative critique by Brian Silver, who pointed out that religion (the focus being on Islam) and native language loyalty were the two factors most closely correlated with endogamous marital behavior. In a subsequent study published elsewhere Fisher implicitly agrees with Silver's statistical findings, but maintains his own interpretation that religion and native-language loyalty are not definitely linked to ethnic consciousness. Since Fisher fails to provide his definition of ethnic consciousness, apparently understanding it as a vague and purely emotional phenomenon, his analysis remains unclear and unconvincing, even more so since the general literature on ethnicity frequently has pinpointed the linkage between ethnicity, language, and religion. Wesley A. Fisher, "Ethnic consciousness and intermarriage correlates of endogamy among the major Soviet nationalities," *Soviet Studies*, vol. 29, no. 3 (July 1977), pp. 395–408; and Brian D. Silver, "Ethnic intermarriage and ethnic consciousness among Soviet nationalities," *Soviet Studies*, vol. 30, no. 1 (January 1978), pp. 107–16. In his later publication Fisher does not directly respond to Silver's critique, but adjusts his own analysis somewhat; see Wesley A. Fisher, *The Soviet Marriage Market: Mate-Selection in Russia and the USSR* (New York: Praeger, 1980), esp. pp. 222–40.

17 Iurii V. Arutiunian, "Konkretno-sotsiologicheskoe issledovanie natsional'nykh otnoshenii," *Voprosy filosofii*, 1969, no. 12, pp. 129–39; and L. M. Drobizheva, "Sotsial'no-kul'turnye osobennosti lichnosti i natsional'nye ustanovki (po materialam issledovanii v Tatarskoi ASSR)," *Sovetskaia etnografiia*, 1971, no. 3, pp. 3–15.

18 Iurii V. Arutiunian, *Sotsial'noe i natsional'noe, Opyt etnosotsiologicheskikh issledovanii po materialam Tatarskoi ASSR* (Moscow: Nauka, 1973), p. 283; cf. also Tables 6.5 and 6.6.

19 Arutiunian, "Konkretno-sotsiologicheskoe," p. 133; see English translation

of this article, in *Soviet Sociology*, vol. 11, no. 2–4 (Winter–Spring 1972–3), pp. 328–48.

20 See, for example, Arutiunian, *Sotsial'noe i natsional'noe*, p. 285; and Table 6.6.

21 Drobizheva, "Sotsial'no-kul'turnye," p. 7.

22 Arutiunian, "Konkretno", p. 132; see also Arutiunian and Kakhk, *Sotsiologicheskie ocherki*, p. 102.

23 cf. Table A.1, p. 230. For other references to age or gender see G. V. Starovoitova, "K issledovaniiu etnopsikhologii gorodskikh zhitelei," *Sovetskaia etnografiia*, 1976, no. 3, p. 63; Arutiunian, "Konkretno", p. 131; and Arutiunian and Kakhk, *Sotsiologicheskie ocherki*, p. 102.

24 Iu. V. Bromlei, "Etnos i endogamiia," *Sovetskaia etnografiia*, 1963, no. 6, pp. 85–7.

25 Arutiunian, "Konkretno," p. 138, cites data subdivided by village environment only; they show that the "intelligentsia" also has more negative attitudes in mixed or Russian villages.

26 "Some progress toward more positive attitudes toward persons of another nationality may also be observed among those Russian residents of the urban or rural areas of the Tatar ASSR who know the Tatar language to one degree or the other. Lack of knowledge of the Tatar language, on the other hand, worsens the attitudes of a part of the Russian population": M. N. Guboglo, "Vzaimodeistvie iazykov i mezhnatsional'nye otnosheniia v sovetskom obshchestve," *Istoriia SSSR*, 1970, no. 6, p. 39.

27 Drobizheva, *Dukhovnaia obshchnost'*, pp. 111, 174–5. The same source also suggests that level of education and rural v. urban residence are associated with differential views, but the data are too scattered to allow exact conclusions.

28 Arutiunian, "Konkretno;" trans. in *Soviet Sociology*, vol. 11, no. 3–4 (Spring–Winter 1972–3), p. 343.

29 ibid., p. 316.

30 The two questions were formulated in a parallel way, namely, "What do you think about marriages between Germans and [respective nationality], do you regard them as undesirable, or do you think that nationality doesn't make any difference?"

31 In all three cases Kazakh men had married German women; one of the Kazakhs involved had a German stepmother. Both Kazakh and German were used as the family languages.

32 Drobizheva, *Dukhovnaia obshchnost'*, p. 214.

33 Juozas A. Kazlas, "Social distance among ethnic groups," in Edward Allworth (ed.), *Nationality Group Survival in Multi-Ethnic States* (New York: Praeger, 1977), pp. 228–55.

34 ibid., pp. 270–1.

35 N. A. Tomilov, *Sovremennye etnicheskie protsessy sredi sibirskikh tatar* (Tomsk: University of Tomsk Press, 1978), p. 15; see also Table 5.11. For another instance where a high rate of endogamous preference (53 percent) is cited by a Soviet source see Tomilov, *Sibirskikh Tatar*, pp. 120–1; the specific nationality referred to is Tobolo-Irtysh Tatars.

36 This is supported by a rare newspaper reference that only 20 percent of urban Uzbeks indicate that they would not object if a close relative married someone of another nationality: see *Sovetskaia Latviia*, 20 July 1983, p. 3.

37 Drobizheva, *Dukhovnaia obshchnost'*, p. 124.

38 ibid., pp. 111, 174–5.

39 N. P. Skachkova, "Mezhnatsional'naia sem'ia kak faktor sblizheniia sotsialisticheskikh natsii," *Izvestiia Akademii nauk Kazakhskoi SSR, Seriia obshchestvennykh nauk*, 1975, no. 6, pp. 61–2.

40 ibid., p. 62; the reference to minority policies in China is to the polemical

book by T. Rakhimov, *Natsionalizm i shovinizmosnova politiki gruppy Mao Tse-duna* (Moscow: Mysl', 1968).

41   ibid., p. 62; it is stated that 86·5 percent of all Soviet marriages are monoethnic and another recent Soviet study of mixed marriages in Kishinev concludes that their number stabilized during the 1960s and decreased slightly in the 1970s: A. A. Susokolov and A. P. Novitskaia, "Etnicheskaia i sotsial'no-professional' naia gomogennost' brakov (po materialam otdela ZAGS Kishineva v poslevoennyi period)," *Sovetskaia etnografiia*, 1981, no. 6, p. 17.

42   A. Rooson, "Izmeneniia v sostave semei Estonskoi SSR," *Sotsiologicheskie issledovaniia*, 1984, no. 1, p. 96. On an increase of monoethnic Kazakh marriages see A. B. Kalyshev, "Mezhnatsional'nye braki v sel'skikh raionakh Kazakhstana (po materialam Pavlodarskoi oblasti. 1966–1979 gg.)," *Sovetskaia etnografiia*, 1984, no. 2, pp. 71–7.

43   In those instances where Muslims intermarry with non-Muslims nearly 90 percent involve men rather than women. Typically the non-Muslim wife is integrated into the Muslim family and community and the children nearly always take on the nationality of their father: cf. Table 1.2 and Chapter 7; see also S. M. Mirkhasilov, "Sotsial'no-kul'turnye izmeneniia i otrazhenie ikh v sovremennoi sem'e sel'skogo naseleniia Uzbekistana," *Sovetskaia etnografiia*, 1979, no. 1, p. 14, and A. B. Kalyshev, "K voprosu ob opredelenii natsional'noi prinadlezhnosti molodezhi v mezhnatsional'nykh sem'iakh," *Izvestiia Akademii nauk Kazakhskoi SSSR, Seriia obshchestvennykh nauk*, 1982, no. 3, p. 83.

44   See n. 28.

7

Communal Particularism

The social significance of ethnicity is closely linked to the extent to which communal particularism prevails, and this is a topic which deserves treatment in a separate chapter. Yet it is difficult to get a clear analytical and empirical handle on the notion of communalism. Conceptually the notion of *Gemeinschaft* as developed in traditional sociology comes closest to the definition used here. It refers to a bounded collectivity with intense feelings of solidarity based on either primordial ties or ties derived from common religious, or ideological commitment.[1] It is a community which perceives itself as having a special and valuable identity that is to be perpetuated and enhanced. While loyalty to the group's value system and its other members does not necessarily mean the rejection of other groups and values, it does mean that people feel tied to and stay with "their own."

Soviet scholars have begun to discuss this phenomenon as one of "ethnopsychology,"[2] but more than psychology is involved. We are dealing with a host of spiritual, cultural, religious, historical, and other bonds, which although elusive to the empirical eye can be identified in careful indepth study. Such study is yet to be undertaken. Although the existing literature on Soviet nations and nationalities tends to implicitly assume the persistence of ethnic communal *Gemeinschaften*, concrete explication is rare.

The lack of previous indepth studies is one of the reasons that a particular case is singled out for study here. Another reason is that communal particularism is expressed differently among each of the diverse peoples living in the USSR. It is beyond the scope of this study to cover all cases, and since we are most concerned with the communal phenomenon *per se*, the more detailed analysis of one case can be most helpful.

The case chosen is that of Islam which not only affects a large and dynamic part of the Soviet population, but also is more than just a religion, and comes closest to what we mean by *Gemeinschaft*. Islam in the Soviet Union has multiple identities and meanings: it is an ensemble of religous beliefs, social customs, familial and national traditions, a network of kinship ties, and a way of life. Our interviews with Soviet German emigrants presented a unique opportunity to learn more about it; many respondents had lived in Soviet Central Asia and Kazakhstan, usually in close contact with the native inhabitants. The study of communal particularism among the Muslim peoples of the USSR is also helped by the recent increase of Soviet writings on "modern Islam" and by the literature written for the use of propagandists of atheism.

Further illustrations for the persistence and content of Islamic communal identity can be found in the work of local poets and novelists. Thus the significance of historical memory, folk music and legends, and old customs is highlighted in Chingiz Aitmatov's most recent and well-received novel, *The Day Lasts More than a Hundred Years*.[3] The hero of the story is a Kazakh railway worker concerned about his best friend being buried "the right way" in an ancient tribal cemetery and with the traditional ritual. Its underlying message is that modern industrial development can coexist with respect for communal values and traditions. This perspective is close to the one developed during the 1970s by political scientists such as Samuel Huntington, who challenged the previously prevalent theory of modernization according to which tradition and modernity were perceived as mutually exclusive. In his words:[4]

Modern society is not simply modern; it is modern and traditional. The attitudes and behavior patterns may in some cases be fused; in others, they may comfortably coexist, one alongside the other, despite the apparent incongruity of it all. In addition, one can go further and argue not only that coexistence is possible but that modernization itself may strengthen tradition. It may give new life to important elements of the preexisting culture, such as religion.

It is the contention of this chapter that this theoretical perspective is crucial for the appreciation of the meaning of communal particularism in the contemporary USSR, especially as it applies to the traditionally Muslim peoples.

Islam as Communal Identity

In assessing the meaning and strength of Soviet Islam today we first of all rely on the experience of those of our Soviet German respondents who had spent twenty years and more living in Soviet Central Asia and Kazakhstan. When asked whether the indigenous people continue to observe their religion and traditions, the response was overwhelmingly affirmative. To quote a typical reply, "yes, very much so, they are in their country and hold on very strongly to everything of their own" (176, from Kazakhstan). Most respondents went on to add illustrative observations about praying or fasting, traditional burial, food taboos, and so on.

The recurrence of similar observations on the part of many respondents from different regions and walks of life are taken as the basic indicator of those aspects of Islam that are most relevant for Soviet Muslims today. Our interview question was open-ended, and as a result individual responses varied in detail, covering a broad range of traits perceived to characterize Islamic religion and traditions. This already is indicative for understanding Islam in the Soviet Union since specialists emphasize its broadness and variety of meaning. There is furthermore no "church" in Islam as there is no need for "middlemen," and a religious ritual or prayer can be performed by anyone who knows enough Arabic. Sunni-Islam which predominates in Soviet Central Asia, is even more a clergyless religion than that of the Baptists. The existing ecclesiastical establishment with its four mufti has been created by Soviet authorities after World War II in order to control Islam better.[5]

Since Islam cannot be defined easily, and since nowadays various facets of it are observed to a different degree, our discussion is divided into four major sections: (1) religious observance; (2) Islamic familial rites; (3) social customs associated to Islam; and (4) an assessment of the overall strength of Islam and the significance of communal particularism.

Religious Observance

Traditionally a believer has had to observe the five pillars of faith: fasting during the month of Ramadan, daily prayers, a pilgrimage to Mecca, the payment of alms, and the profession of faith. The

185

standard has been relaxed, however, and now none of the five obligations is in fact obligatory. Islam as an official doctrine is lax in the Soviet Union. As a Soviet commentator has remarked, "the objective of Islam's adaptation to Soviet life is to preserve the cult's influence on believers in a society where atheism is the predominant world view."[6] In this context the open observance of religious rites, such as fasting and praying, is even more notable.

FASTING

According to the mufti of the USSR, the fast during the month of Ramadan—which is not strictly observed in most of the Muslim World—may be replaced by a fast during the first ten days of Ramadan, or even three days. Yet respondents described it this way: "They also observe fasting, for one month they don't eat anything during the day, from the time of the fading of the morning star until the rise of the evening star, the entire day—not the young people, more the older ones, or the women" (126).

Fasting can hardly be prohibited, but it is regularly attacked by Soviet anti-religious propaganda, which accuses it of being anti-social. People who fast have difficulty working in factories or fields and this was noted by our respondents as well: "Sometimes they don't come to work during the fasting period, they grow too weak for working" (127, from Kaskelen, Kazakhstan). And a woman from Dushanbe gave this impression of the fast, "it lasts one month, then they don't have any weddings or anything. When the fast is over they have a big holiday, then they eat very much, so much that they get sick because of having fasted before. The hospitals already know about this, they prepare, because many people are taken to hospitals—some even die from overeating too suddenly" (181). Overall fasting during the month of Ramadan was noted by many of our respondents from various regions.

PRAYERS

A devout Muslim should perform five daily prayers (in the morning, at noon, at 5 p.m., and at sunset and midnight). It is also acceptable to say two daily prayers, or less. The prayers are silent, but should be performed kneeling on a carpet or a piece of cloth. Many respondents noted this demonstration of piety. Thus: "They are Muslims, they hold their prayers when it is their hour,

[they] throw everything down even at work, kneel down, on the streets as well, they put down a cloth and pray" (126, from Dushanbe); "Always at sundown, they spread a cloth on the field or on a sidewalk and pray" (139); and "A Muslim sits down and prays no matter whether there is a tractor coming, he doesn't move from his place" (80).

Others mentioned that people sometimes stop their cars in order to pray, or pray in train or bus stations. When asked about onlookers' reactions to such public praying, most respondents stated that it was accepted: "Nobody minds them, there is no ridiculing, nobody takes issue with the Kazakhs doing it" (91); or "no, it isn't ridiculed, you must know, it is like this with the Muslims, nobody ever laughs at an old person, the old ones are honored" (142, from Issyk, Kazakhstan). But occasionally pass-ers-by do react negatively: "some laugh, even Kazakhs, Chechen, Uzbeks, but these they [the others] already do not count as their own people" (179, from Vinsovkhoz, Kazakhstan); and "yes, they believe, they have their law and customs; for example at the specific time they knelt down and prayed, the Russians frequently kicked them in the streets, but they did it neverthe-less" (198, from Dzhambul, Kazakhstan). Such negative reactions are classified as wrong, perpetuated by people not to be taken seriously. Nevertheless, they have some effect, in that some young people are ashamed to pray openly in Russian-dominated environments.

There is also a religious tradition of collective prayers at a mosque on Fridays, but this was rarely commented upon. It appears that organized religious observance is less important—or visible—than individual praying or fasting. Nevertheless, mosques were mentioned occasionally, and so were unofficial mosques.

PILGRIMAGES, LEGAL ALMS, AND THE PROFESSION OF FAITH

In contrast to fasting and praying, the other three pillars of faith were hardly mentioned at all. Thus there was no comment on the once in a lifetime pilgrimage to Mecca, which in the Soviet Union is limited to thirty to sixty selected pilgrims per year, nor was there any mention of pilgrimages to local holy places. The obser-vance of the fourth pillar of faith, the payment of legal alms, is forbidden by Soviet law and has, in practice, been partly replaced by voluntary contributions by believers to the mosque. None of our respondents commented on this practice, maybe because it is less visible. The fifth pillar of faith eludes the observation of outsiders even more since the testimony of faith, the *shahada*, is a non-verbal profession of belief in Allah by the believer in his heart;[7] but one respondent did remark on this: "they say like this 'we younger people don't want to show our religion openly, in our hearts we are believers, but it is better not to show it'" (105).

OTHER RELIGIOUS RITES

The practice of Islam includes religious festivals, although again their observance is not obligatory, and they have become part of the national tradition. There are three main festivals: the Uraza-Bairam, which marks the end of fasting; the Birthday of the Prophet; and Kurban-Bairam, which is the most important occasion commemorating Abraham's sacrifice of his son. Quite a few respondents mentioned these festivals, frequently adding that people would not come to work on them and that bosses and officials were unable to prevent such absenteeism. To cite: "The Kazakhs hold themselves according to their law, in terms of their religion. They don't go to work when they have one of their holidays . . . yes, something is said about this, but they [the higher-ups] can't do anything about it, the Kazakhs say, I am in my country. I can live according to my own ways" (127). Soviet surveys confirm that a large segment of the Muslim population observes these holidays, especially in rural areas.[8]

Familial Rites

While Soviet Islam is lax in regard to obligatory religious observance, it is more persistent in the formal observation of the three main life-cycle rituals of circumcision, wedding, and burial. The tenacity of the traditional ceremonies can be largely explained by their not being regarded as purely religious in character, but rather as national traditions with a significant communal role. The elevation of basically religious rituals to national customs is often lamented by Soviet officials in charge of anti-religious propaganda since this greatly hampers their work.[9] Both their writings and the comments made by official Soviet Muslim religious leaders confirm our finding that the observance of traditional burial rites, as well as circumcision and traditional wedding ceremonies, is close to universal.[10] By implication even party members and people in higher positions participate in these rituals, and many of our respondents did in fact emphasize this point. Most mentioned it with notable surprise and awe because such a coexistence between religious ceremonies and party membership is hardly conceivable for non-Muslims.

BURIAL RITES

The first observation to make about burial is the existence of purely Muslim cemeteries, where believers and non-believers are buried in a traditional manner in a shroud and with prayers. There are even indications of clanic cemeteries, and certainly national ones, that is, separate cemeteries for various Muslim peoples. To quote: "There are separate cemeteries for Kazakhs, Chechens, and Turks. Each extended family has its own mound. There is a Korean cemetery too. The Germans, Russians, and Greeks are together . . . They bury in their own way even the sovkhoz director: first, in a coffin, then they take him out, the women wail at home. The burial is late in the afternoon" (99, from a village near Alma Ata).

Burial itself is performed in a traditional manner: "At funerals there are only men, [they] roll cloths around the dead and sit him in a niche . . . even the young and the party members are buried that way" (69, from Leninabad); and "Last year, in Alma Ata, the daughter of a school principal died, the funeral was first held according to Russian customs with a coffin, but afterwards, when all the schoolchildren had left, they quickly took the girl out of the coffin, rolled her into cloths and buried her—threw the coffin away—they stick very closely to their customs, and that was a party man" (179). One could add many similar quotations, varying slightly in detail but underlining that traditional burial is widely performed. In those instances where a non-Muslim custom is observed—such as laying the dead in a coffin—it is discarded in the final stage. This is typical of the Muslim approach: if necessary, they can be extremely flexible and accommodative, but they take care not to compromise the essence of their ways.

CIRCUMCISION

Circumcision usually takes place at the age of 7 or 8 because it supposedly is a free decision of the boy. It may be performed by anyone, a doctor or a mullah, or, as frequently is the case, a grandmother. There are some standard prayers in Arabic, which may be said by anybody. Circumcision is not obligatory for Muslims, and although it has certain religious elements associated with it, it has assumed the character of a national custom. Thus it is possible to be a Muslim without being circumcised but it is difficult to be a Kirghiz, Kazakh, or Uzbek without circumcision. Although Soviet propaganda denounces it as barbaric and unhygienic, the Muslims regard it as hygienic and significant as a national custom.[11] It is a joyous occasion, and as a rule there is a three-day celebration in which all members of the larger family participate. A circumcision celebration, *toi*, may be organized for several boys at once, and various forms of entertainment are provided. There is much food. Not surprisingly, it is rather expensive: "A Tadjik, a colleague at work, had three sons, he sold his car in order to be able to have a real celebration for them, that is very expensive, it is celebrated for three days and all the people from the village come" (126, from Dushanbe).

Again it is a custom observed by nearly everyone: "Circumcision is done by all—be they party members, or educated—no matter, in some cases they are even taken to hospitals. At a *toi* there usually are some 300 people" (69, from Leninabad); and "They come together mostly for a circumcision, then they erect a huge tent, the same is done for a wedding or a funeral" (141). Although circumcision is not illegal, it is officially attacked and, therefore, some persons of higher standing hide their participation. In such cases they call it a birthday celebration or hold it where they are unobserved. A respondent who worked for a high Kazakh party official gave the following account: "The sons are circumcised . . . the party members do that as well, not in their church, but somewhere in the open country, they call the militia in order that they form a cordon all around and then they begin . . . it is a huge celebration, sheep are slaughtered, everybody eats a lot and drinks . . . they are the ones in charge, the Kazakhs, that is their country and they live as they please" (127). In other words, ways are found to circumvent official political strictures.

WEDDINGS

Our respondents rarely mentioned the performance of the religious wedding ceremony, but the previously cited Soviet sources attest that it also continues to play a major role. Moreover, many national customs connected with wedding celebrations, such as men and women sitting separately, the holding of a prolonged and sumptuous feast, the payment of *kalym* (a bride price), and the like, persist as well. Since these practices are more appropriately called social customs, they are discussed in the next section.

Social Customs Associated with Islam

THE KALYM AND STEALING OF BRIDES

The *kalym*, the payment of a bridal price, or its avoidance by the means of abducting a girl, are unlawful and the two customs most violently attacked in the Soviet press. Nevertheless, both still occur on occasion. Thus a man who had lived in Dzetesai, Kazakhstan, related that there the *kalym* was very high, up to 20,000–30,000 roubles, and others mentioned valuable gifts being made to the family of the bride. Similarly, *Pravda* has reported the case of a collective farmer in Turkmenistan who received 10,000 roubles cash, 20 head of sheep, and 100 oriental robes.[12] In spite of such examples, it appears that the "stealing of brides" is more prevalent than payment of the *kalym*, maybe just because the latter is so expensive.

Our interviews revealed that the "stealing of the bride" rarely implies the actual forcible abduction of a girl and that it is typically done with the consent of the bride or her parents, or both. While an abduction that has been prearranged can hardly be called an abduction, respondents consistently talked of "stealing," suggesting that the local Muslims call it the same. They apparently wish to sustain the traditions associated with marriage and substitute a ritualistic equivalent, that is, the "stealing" of the bride instead of a highly impractical custom such as the *kalym*. Thus a concrete custom is superseded by a symbolic practice.

ATTITUDES TOWARD EXOGAMY WITH NON-MUSLIMS

Islam has traditionally been associated with a variety of exogamic and endogamic laws, but the ones most relevant today concern attitudes toward exogamy with non-Muslims. Comments overwhelmingly indicate a Muslim rejection of intermarriage. Some respondents emphasized that it is especially problematic for a Muslim woman, and others implied the same by unconsciously referring to mixed marriages in terms of non-Muslim women marrying Muslim men. This conforms with Islamic religious law, according to which a man may marry outside of his faith pro-

191

vided the woman belongs to one of the "people of the Book", that is, either Christian or Jewish, while a girl is not supposed to marry outside her community at all. The following case, although extreme, is indicative of basic attitudes: "[Intermarriage occurs] very rarely. A German wanted to marry a Kazakh woman, and the Kazakhs had a conference about that—just like a trial—and told him that he should disappear within twenty-four hours, otherwise he'll be killed. The families don't want such marriages" (98, from a village near Alma Ata).

If mixed marriages occur nevertheless, the non-Muslim wives usually have to adjust to the new community: "The family accepts [her] with difficulty, have her prepare the native dishes and speak their language," and "If a Russian woman marries a Tadjik, then she has to dress in their native dress, she is drawn into their traditions, Tadjik families don't like foreigners." These comments and other sources suggest that intermarriage typically leads to the integration of the non-Muslim spouse and her offspring into the Muslim community, a point already illustrated in Chapter 1 with reference to official nationality choice.

RELATIONS WITHIN THE FAMILY AND COMMUNITY

Traditional family structure and inequality between generations and sexes further inhibits intermarriage and the "merging" with other Soviet nations. The subordinate position of Muslim women was noted by some respondents, and others remarked on their not being allowed to work outside of the home,[13] or the emphasis on having many children. The high birth-rate among the Soviet Muslim population is well known, and one respondent suggested that it is related to religious strictures against abortion. Whatever its reason, it certainly acts as a safeguard of the biological continuity of the Muslim people.

While the status and role of women is consequential, this is also true for the older people holding a special position. Many respondents mentioned obedience toward parents and a pronounced respect for one's elders as a distinguishing trait of young Muslims: "All nations can take them as an example, they listen to every word their elders say. The students in Tashkent dress according to fashion, but when they return home they change their dress before they enter the house" (91). As this example suggests, reverence toward older people is not only significant in itself, but secures the survival of other traditions.

Due to the traditional respect for older people, especially those in one's own family, a young Muslim is less likely to marry a non-Muslim, or break specific customs. Even observance of religious practices is affected, as is evident from statements such as "the young people usually don't pray [openly], but they do so in the company of their elders." Or "They observe it [fasting]—do not eat or drink anything during daytime, the youth did the same, they had such reverence for the old ones, that they did it together with them" (141, 106, 109, 125).

Again the observations of our respondents are confirmed by Soviet ethnosociological sources. Both in general statements[14] and by referring to survey results Soviet scholars acknowledge that the special position of parents and other older people is consequential for the perpetuation of Islamic communal identity. The previously cited survey showing that 88 percent of Uzbek youth think that one should consult with one's parents before marriage is one case in point (see Chapter 6), another one is a survey conducted in Uzbekistan in which every one of over 2,000 young people interviewed acknowledged "the decisive significance of parents and family in the formation of their views."[15] This attests to the continuing influence of the family and communal grouping as well as barriers to Soviet attempts to socialize the youth according to their own blueprint.

RELATIONSHIP TO PORK AND ALCOHOL

In contrast to other traditions, the customary taboos against pork and alcohol appear to be weakening. They are rarely mentioned in Soviet sources and our own survey, although a few respondents said that young Muslims eat pork only secretly or if they have no alternative such as during military service or at the place of work. Respect for elders again plays a role, as can be seen from this account: "If Kazakh girls work in shops and an older Kazakh woman enters, they at once go to meet her and bow deeply . . . they revere their old ones very much, and if such a girl happened to be selling pork before, when an older Kazakh woman is in the store, the girl will not touch the pork, that is against their law (140, from Kaskelen, Kazakhstan).

As regards alcohol, it was the main thrust of the statements that it is now widely used among Muslims, but that they drink less than Russians and other non-Muslims. Several respondents said that there are few or no alcoholic beverages at family celebrations such as weddings.

The Overall Strength of Islam and the Significance of Communal Particularism

RANKING OF TRADITIONS

Among the various Islamic traditions and observances some clearly are more widely adhered to than others. As both Soviet sources and our interviews suggest, the most widely observed tradition is that of the burial rites, circumcision taking a close second place. In some intriguing cases respondents negated our question about the local population observing their religion and traditions, but shortly afterwards said, "but they do observe circumcision and their own way of burial" (163). There is also a consensus that the inhibition against intermarriage with non-Muslims is strong, especially for women.

If one asks about the implications of the near-universal observance of these three aspects of Islam, non-intermarriage is most easily understandable since the consequences are so concrete. It excludes ethnic integration from the familial and communal sphere in which particularism and "staying apart" are valued exceedingly highly. The emphasis on family and community is also evident from the importance attached to circumcision and traditional burial. Although classified as familial rites, both are highly significant for the larger community as well. Circumcision has become a symbol of belonging to the national community. And that ritual *per se* is important for inculcating the norms and values of a society has been underlined by the Soviet authorities who for the past fifteen years have made a concerted effort to introduce universal "new" traditions throughout the USSR. Their success in regard to the acceptance of new rituals associated with the life cycle has been especially low in the Islamic areas.[16] In the eloquent words of a Soviet ritual specialist "the struggle between the old and new does take place not only on the barricades, not only in the economic and political field, but also in the resting places of the dead."[17]

While non-intermarriage sets the Muslim community apart in practice, circumcision and burial rites do so symbolically. Symbolism also prevails in the observance of some other traditions, such as the *kalym*, which is frequently replaced by the symbolically equivalent ritual such as "stealing" the bride with her own or her parents' consent. In the case of the taboo against pork too, compromise is possible as illustrated by the shopgirls in Alma Ata who sell pork, and probably eat it too, but who refrain from doing so in the presence of their elders. Again the aim is to retain a symbolic gesture, even if a concrete social situation requires adjustment.

In sum, among the various Islamic observances in the USSR today the retention of social customs ranks lowest (especially in regard to attitudes toward alcohol and pork);[18] religious observance takes a middle place, with fasting and praying engaged in selectively, but in a manner impressive to the outside observer; and familial rites with a communal significance rank at the top. As one Soviet author writing about the difficulties of atheistic work among Muslims notes, Islamic burial rites and circumcision are widely observed by both believers and non-believers. In fact religious and national identity are inseparable for many Soviet Muslims, and "the repudiation of religion and the old traditions is interpreted as a repudiation of one's nationality."[19]

The retention of traditions is due both to the strength of religious and national identity and to inadequacies in the approach to introducing new rituals such as insensitivity to local attitudes. A Soviet author gives the example of the Russian custom of shouting "bitter!" at weddings and expecting the bridegroom to kiss the bride in response. Kissing a girl in public is regarded as the height of indecency in the Central Asian societies and, as a result, there are young people who reject the idea of a so-called "Komsomol wedding" simply out of fear that they will be forced to kiss each other in front of their parents, older relatives, and strangers.[20]

SOCIODEMOGRAPHIC AND REGIONAL VARIATION IN THE PERVASIVENESS OF ISLAM

Islamic observance appears to be less prevalent among the youth than among older people, especially as far as adherence to religious practices and various social customs is concerned. Certain considerations should be kept in mind, however, when evaluating this generational difference. First, the link to the Islamic community does not require the observance of all practices and customs some of which are more important than others. The most highly ranked traditions, namely, the life-cycle rituals, are nearly universally observed by young people as well.[21] Secondly, the youth is most affected by the patriarchal structure of the Muslim community and the respect for elders is a pervasive trait in many social interactions. For young people there are numerous concrete consequences of these primordial ties and communal traditions. The low level of ethnic intermarriage is

195

one example, since it leads to being shunned by the family and community and since nearly 90 percent of young Muslims think that it is mandatory to obtain their parents' consent for marriage.[22] Soviet ethnosociological research furthermore shows that multigenerational families are most dominant in the Muslim regions of the USSR and that traditional attitudes toward family life have other consequences such as a low inclination to migrate to cities. To cite:[23]

> The rural-to-urban migration rate for Russians is at least three to four times higher than the rate for Uzbeks. The Uzbeks' relatively stable attachment to rural life has to do in part with the circumstances of family life and with the national traditions of their culture. As a rule, Uzbeks have large families and complex family obligations that limit the possibility of their migration.

As the author notes, this behavior is in conflict with the needs of the Soviet economy, since the Uzbek countryside has a labor surplus, whereas there are labor shortages in other regions. This behavior is also in conflict with official ethnic policy which emphasizes the beneficial internationalizing role of migration, urbanization, and intermarriage.

Since nearly three-quarters of the indigenous population of Central Asia and Kazakhstan continues to reside in rural areas (cf. Table A.1, p. 230), which in most cases are monoethnic, the influence of communal traditions is strengthened. Thus Soviet sociological research confirms that in the USSR religious belief is higher among rural (approximately 30 percent) than among urban residents (approximately 15 percent) and that "the level of religiosity of the rural population is higher in the republics of Central Asia and Kazakhstan, in the Northern Caucasus, in Tataria and Bashkiria, and in Azerbaijan."[24] While the level of religiosity is relatively high, it should again be emphasized that the influence of Islam is by no means restricted to its religious aspects and that "in our days Islam not only unites the believers of a nation, but also integrates its believing and non-believing segments."[25]

The impact of Islam on the life of the indigenous population of Central Asia and Kazakhstan is more clearly felt in the countryside, but it is also evident among the urban population most of which migrated there recently and retain close ties to relatives remaining in the countryside. There are indications that indigenous urban workers put a premium on keeping familial and communal ties alive in the cities. Thus:[26]

> On the whole, the traditional ties to a family, relatives, and community are also preserved among the urban workers of the local nationalities. Among Uzbek workers the total volume of leisure time spent on various forms of togetherness within the home—on meetings with relatives, neighbors, acquaintances and other guests—is 2·5 times larger than among Russian workers.

While urban–rural differentials in the pervasiveness of Islam as a communal influence appear to be of minor significance, the same can be said for regional differentials. Both historical and currently available data suggest that Islam is strongest in Uzbekistan, followed by Turkmenistan, Tadjikistan, and Kirghizia, and finally by Kazakhstan. Northern Kazakhstan, which also has the strongest physical presence of non-locals, is the least "Islamic" area, but even here traditions such as non-intermarriage with non-Muslims remain strong both according to our interviews and available Soviet statistics.[27] On balance one may thus conclude that regional and sociodemographic variance in the influence of the Islamic way of life is of minor proportion.

THE ELUSIVENESS OF SOVIET ISLAM

Even though we have many indications of the continuing prevalence of the Islamic way of life, the summary evaluation of its strength and meaning is difficult due to its flexible nature as well as to the evaluative prism used by Western analysts. In any appraisal of a foreign culture and religion the appraiser's own cultural and religious background plays a role. For people with a Western tradition Islam in the Soviet Union poses a special problem because it is difficult to define, and also because it is highly flexible. This latter trait can be best illustrated by its relationship to the communist party. Islam in Soviet Central Asia is accommodative of the "powers that be," as was noted with a certain surprise by our German respondents. Coming as they do from a Christian tradition—mostly Lutheran, Baptist, and Mennonite—they perceive a strong tension between religious belief and communism and few join the Komsomol or the party. Muslim attitudes differ: "They are members of the communist party, but they believe nevertheless. In the case of the youth there is both, the party and faith" (102, from Tadjikistan).[28] Compromise is always possible in Islam, especially in regard to the open expression of religiosity. This "laxity" should not, however, be misinterpreted as a lack of conviction, but rather as an accommodative measure.

The dualistic nature of Soviet Muslim behavior can also be illustrated by the approach to the observance of life-cycle rituals, which are more obligatory than purely religious observance. As noted, it is by no means unusual for party members and declared atheists to participate in the traditional rituals related to birth, marriage, and death. Nor is it unusual, especially for individuals who are in the public eye, to observe both the traditional rituals and the appropriate new Soviet ritual. Soviet authors have complained about the formalistic approach taken to the new traditions such as when wedding ceremonies are called "new," but in fact retain the old ritual and customs. To cite: "Sometimes a mullah first pronounces the traditional wedding blessing and then the 'Komsomol' wedding begins."[29] Since similar examples were mentioned by our respondents, it appears that the formalistic going through the motions of a new ritual, while at the same time preserving the traditional custom, is relatively widespread. In a broader perspective this implies an intriguing reversal of the official Soviet approach, that is, the Muslim nationalities are pursuing a strategy of "socialist in form and national in content."

This point is important, since the Western observer visiting the metropolises of Central Asia and Kazakhstan is most likely to see that side of the indigenous population's behavior which is most in accordance with the Soviet way of life, easily interpreting this as a rejection of traditional ways.[30] This, however, is not the case since most Soviet Muslims do not perceive the situation as one of "either/or." They find ways to retain the most decisive aspects of their communal tradition, even if only symbolically, or side by side with the officially sanctioned way.

Conclusions

In order for a community to survive it requires both biological and normative continuity. In the case of the Muslim nations of the USSR both requirements are fulfilled. The dramatic demographic growth during the past few decades (cf. Table A.2, p. 231) leaves no doubt about biological continuity, which is reinforced by the reluctance to intermarry or migrate. Our data also show a high degree of continuity in communal practices and links. Islam as a religion remains strong, with some sources even suggesting the possibility of an Islamic revival.[31] But the strength of actual religious belief as well as observance of religious precepts is less important than the adherence to the communal norms and symbols of Islam, and this is nearly universal because it has come to mean the retention of an ethnic rather than purely religious identity. As an article in the *Komsomolskaia pravda* in early 1983 complained:[32]

The point is that the clergy has been quite successful in replacing the concept of "religious" with the concept of "national." And, while many Soviets' efforts to introduce modern civic ceremonies are merely pro forma or exist only on paper, the Moslem clergy is "modernizing" its activities in order to ensnare young people. Now a young person's graduation from [secondary] school, a technicum or a vocational–technical school, his first pay or a son's return from the Army can serve as an occasion for reading the Koran.

The same source also laments that young Tadjiks participate in religious customs in order not to offend their relatives or to appear as "non-Tadjiks."[33]

Granted that the Muslim peoples have retained their very own ethnic identity and that communal particularism exists, what is its meaning for general ethnic relations in the USSR as well as Soviet politics? For one, it is clear that the official notion of the emergence of a new community of people—the Soviet nation—hardly applies, and that *sblizhenie* [drawing together] is extremely limited.[34] In so far as the outward forms of the Soviet way of life and customs are accepted it is frequently in a superficial and formalistic manner. While contacts with other ethnic groups exist, they rarely extend into the familial and communal sphere; on the other hand, familial relationships are valued highly and are a major source of emotional and social sustenance. The special links to "one's own" people furthermore affect socioeconomic and political perceptions and behavior discussed in previous chapters. Be it just mentioned here that communal solidarity and the impulse to lend one's relatives a helping hand are one of the sources of the accelerating drive of the Central Asians and Kazakhs toward better and more influential socioeconomic and political positions within their own republics.

What about the other nationalities of the USSR, do they have comparable communal structures and normative ties? One may presume that this is the case, but since the communal identity of each nation differs and since relatively little previous work has been undertaken on this topic, it is beyond the scope of this study to attempt a detailed analysis. It must suffice to make some general points. Thus it appears that those nations which are characterized by a close congruence between religious and national identity are the ones who have been most able to retain a strong communal identity and particularism, with the Catholic Lithuanians being an important case in point.[35] Our interviews also indicated that the survival and strength of the Soviet German community in the USSR is closely linked to religious activities, particularly those of Lutherans, Baptists and Mennonites. Those respondents who had had close ties to a religious group typically were those who knew German best and had the most particularistic way of life within a circumscribed community of relatives and other believers.

While religious identity thus plays a major role in communal patterning, other factors such as common historical memories, a literary heritage, culture, and folklore do the same. Thus the literary heritage as personified by Taras Shevchenko is a major bond between Ukrainians, and the memory of the long history of the Armenian church as well as the more recent experience of genocide are of major significance to Armenian identity.[36] Folkloristic traditions, celebrations of midsummer night, and various forms of singing constitute communal unifiers in Latvia and Estonia. Thus Latvians and Estonians have since their national renaissance in the nineteenth century manifested their national cultural solidarity in song festivals in which hundreds of thousands participate.[37] Various aspects of folklore also are significant. Among these a recent emphasis on folkloristic elements in the wedding ritual have increased its popularity, especially among young people and the urban intelligentsia.[38] Soviet ethnographers go so far as to say that in Estonia and Latvia a national wedding ritual "has become one of the symbols in which ethnic consciousness finds an expression" and that this is "similar to the role played by the customs of national songs, in which they engage very widely."[39]

Since the symbols of ethnic consciousness and the forms of communal involvement differ from one people to another, it is difficult to compare their intensity crossculturally. If one takes a single indicator, such as ethnic preferences for traditional wed-

Table 7.1   *Preference of National Wedding Ritual, by Nationality (in Percentages)*

Location (within respective titular republics)	Uzbeks	Moldavians	Georgians	Estonians	Russians
Urban	78	55	45*	45	20
Rural	82	76	53	55	45*

Source: L. M. Drobizheva and L. A. Tul'tseva, "Svadebnaia obriadnost' v obshchestvennom mnenii (po materialam etnosotsiologicheskikh issledovanii u narodov SSSR)," *Sovetskaia etnografiia*, 1982, no. 5, pp. 35–8.

* The source only states that "nearly half" of the respondents fall in this group, 45 percent is chosen as the appropriate percentage figure since the same source cites it for the urban Estonians after also first referring to them as representing "nearly half."

ding ceremonies (Table 7.1), major gaps emerge between the nationalities, with the Russian ranking lowest in this context. It is entirely possible that other forms of communal involvement serve as substitutes, but data are extremely scarce. Table 7.1 confirms, however, that traditional weddings are a crucial ethnic custom for Moldavians,[40] as well as for the Muslim nations, in this case represented by the Uzbeks. The table also illustrates the relatively small rural–urban gap present in the Uzbek case. While it is wider within the other nations cited, this should not be taken as an indication that modernization—which is closely linked to urbanization—will necessarily lead to an erosion of such communal traditions as ethnic weddings since our source also states that compared to the 1930s and 1940s there has been a general renaissance in this ritual. The reason given is similar to Western explanations for a "post-modernist" ethnic revival in certain regions of Europe and America:[41]

> One cannot, however, exclude the possibility, that the interest in the national wedding ritual is related with the general tendency which manifested itself in the 60s and 70s to take the revival of ethnically particularistic forms of culture as a means to escape the excessive standardization of life resulting from the scientific–technical revolution. This was also linked to the striving to "aestheticize" life and most particularly to bring in color and playful elements into the emotionally intense moments of people's lives.

While this quotation emphasizes the aesthetic contribution of traditions and ethnic cultures, we shall conclude by restating the argument made in the introductory part of this chapter that people have a strong tendency to seek and to retain communal attachments and bonds, and while it is true that the *Gemeinschaft* providing such bonds can differ in identity, ethnicity constitutes one of its most tenacious forms.

Notes: Chapter 7

1　See especially Edward Shils, "Primordial, personal, sacred, and civil ties," *British Journal of Sociology*, vol. 8 (1957), pp. 130–45.

2　A. F. Dashdamirov, "K metodologii issledovaniia natsional'no-psikhologicheskikh problem," *Sovetskaia etnografiia*, 1983, no. 2, pp. 80–2; see also other authors in the same issue.

3　Chingiz Aitmatov, *The Day Lasts More than a Hundred Years*, trans. John French (Bloomington, Ind.: Indiana University Press, 1983).

4　Samuel P. Huntington, "The change to change: modernization, development, and politics," *Comparative Politics*, vol. 3 (April 1971), p. 295.

5　The Soviet authorities treat the mufti of Tashkent as a head of the church and he alone is allowed to elect mullahs who are officially entitled to perform religious rites. There are 300–500 official mosques in the USSR, but this clearly is insufficient for Islam to survive as a religion. Therefore, there has been a reversion to clergyless practices of the original Islam, to the establishment of underground mosques, clandestine schools for learning Arabic, and so on: Alexandre Bennigsen, "Muslim conservative opposition to the Soviet regime: the Sufi brotherhoods in the north Caucasus," in Jeremy R. Azrael (ed.), *Soviet Nationality Policies and Practices* (New York: Praeger, 1978), pp. 334–48.

6　N. Ashirov, "Musul'manskaia propoved'segodnia," *Nauka i religiia* (December 1978), p. 30.

7　For general comments about the acceptability of the non-observance of these three "pillars of faith" see ibid., p. 32; and Alexandre Bennigsen and Chantal Lemercier-Quelquejay, *Islam in the Soviet Union* (New York: Praeger, 1967), pp. 178–9.

8　T. S. Saidbaev, *Islam i obshchestvo* (Moscow: Nauka, 1978), p. 209.

9　See, for example, N. Bairamsakhatov, "Rozhdeno vremenem," *Nauka i religiia* (August 1979), p. 3; E. G. Filimonov, "Sotsiologicheskii issledovaniia protsessa preodoleniia religii v sel'skoi mestnosti itogi, problemy, perspektivy," *Voprosy nauchnogo ateizma*, vol. 16 (1974), p. 80; and Saidbaev, *Islam*, pp. 194–201.

10　ibid.; and Filimonov, "Issledovaniia," p. 81. In an interview with a Western correspondent, A. Abdoullah, the Soviet Union's second-ranking Muslim, similarly observed that "it is extremely rare for someone to get buried or get married here without a Muslim ceremony": interview by Robin Knight, *US News and World Report*, 14 May 1979, p. 36.

11　On this contrast of perceptions see also David C. Montgomery, "An American student in Tashkent with some notes on ethnic and racial harmony in Soviet Uzbekistan," *Asian Affairs*, vol. 59 (n.s., vol. 3), pt. 1 (February 1972), p. 37. One might also note that circumcision is a practice in regard to which the medical profession is divided according to the cultures they live in; while it is widespread in the USA, it is very rare in Western Europe and the western parts of the USSR.

12 *Pravda*, 14 March 1976, p. 3.

13 The custom of keeping women "at home" is waning, but persists to some extent as can be illustrated by enrollment data in higher educational institutions; while the rate of women among students of most nationalities in the USSR fluctuates between 40 and 55 percent, the ratio of female students among the Muslim groups fluctuates between 23 percent (Turkmen) and 45 percent (Kazakhs): *Narodnoe obrazovanie, nauka i kul'tura v SSSR* (Moscow: Statistika, 1971), p. 196. For a general appraisal of the status of Soviet Muslim women see Nancy Lubin, "Women in Soviet Central Asia: progress and contradictions," *Soviet Studies*, vol. 33, no. 2 (April 1981), pp. 182–203.

14 Filimonov, "Issledovaniia," pp. 79, 81.

15 A 1975 Tashkent dissertation cited in Lubin, "Women in Central Asia," p. 198.

16 Christel Lane, "Ritual and ceremony in contemporary Soviet society," *Sociological Review*, vol. 27, no. 2 (May 1979), pp. 266–70, and *The Rites of Rulers: Rituals in Industrial Society: The Soviet Case* (Cambridge: Cambridge University Press, 1981), pp. 80–6.

17 G. Gerodnik, *O parkakh dobrykh vospominanii* (Tallinn, 1970), p. 6, as cited in ibid., p. 258.

18 There are other aspects of the traditional way of life not covered here such as traditional dress, interior architecture, folklore, and so on. For an account of the continuing influence of these customs see G. P. Vasil'eva, "Nekotorye tendentsii razvitiia sovremennykh natsional'nykh traditsii v material'noi kul'ture narodov Srednei Azii i Kazakhstana," *Sovetskaia etnografiia*, 1979, no. 3, pp. 18–30.

19 Filimonov, "Issledovaniia," p. 80.

20 Bairamsakhatov, "Rozhdeno," p. 5.

21 Soviet Uzbek dissertation cited by Nancy Lubin, "Assimilation and retention of ethnic identity in Uzbekistan," *Asian Affairs*, no. 12, pt. 3 (1981), p. 281; cf. Table 7.1.

22 Iu. V. Arutiunian, "Natsional'no-regional'noe mnogoobrazie sovetskoi derevni," *Sotsiologicheskie issledovaniia*, 1980, no. 3, pp. 77–8.

23 ibid., p. 80.

24 Filimonov, "Issledovaniia," p. 73; see also Saidbaev, *Islam*, p. 184.

25 Saidbaev, *Islam*, pp. 194–5.

26 ibid., p. 207.

27 See Chapter 6 on intermarriage data.

28 In some recent instances party members have even performed leadership functions in religious associations; see article in *Sovetskaia Kirgizia*, 27 December 1981, p. 3, cited in *Current Digest of the Soviet Press*, vol. 34, no. 3 (February 1982), p. 3.

29 Bairamsakhatov, "Rozhdeno," p. 5. A similar case is described in *Pravda*, 14 March 1976, p. 3.

30 For other illustrations of the dualistic behavior of the native population see Lubin, "Retention," esp. pp. 278–81.

31 This was suggested by some of our respondents. See also Alexandre Bennigsen, "Islam in the Soviet Union," *Soviet Jewish Affairs*, vol. 9, no. 2 (1979), esp. p. 5.

32 *Komsomol'skaia pravda*, 20 January 1983, p. 4, cited in *CDSP*, vol. 35, no. 4 (1983), p. 7.

33 ibid.

34 On traditional rituals constituting a barrier to *sblizhenie* see also Iu. V. Bromlei, *Sovremennye etnicheskie protsessy v SSSR* (Moscow: Nauka, 1975), p. 346.

35   cf. Lithuanian samizdat sources such as *Chronicle of the Catholic Church in Lithuania*, and V. Stanley Vardys, *The Catholic Church, Dissent and Nationality in Soviet Lithuania* (Boulder, Colo.: East European Quarterly, 1978), *passim*.

36   Vahakn N. Dadrian, "Nationalism in Soviet Armenia: a case study of ethnocentrism," in George W. Simmonds (ed.), *Nationalism in the USSR and Eastern Europe in the Era of Brezhnev and Kosygin* (Detroit, Mich.: University of Detroit Press, 1977), pp. 202–58.

37   Romuald J. Misiunas and Rein Taagepera, *The Baltic States: Years of Dependence, 1940–1980* (Berkeley, Calif.: University of California Press, 1983), p. 170.

38   L. M. Drobizheva and L. A. Tul'tseva, "Svadebnaia obriadnost' v obshchestvennom mnenii (po materialam etnosotsiologicheskikh issledovanii u narodov SSSR)," *Sovetskaia etnografiia*, 1982, no. 5, pp. 37–8.

39   ibid., p. 38.

40   For another statement that traditional weddings are valued by more than 70 percent of Moldavians see Iu. V. Arutiunian, L. M. Drobizheva, and V. S. Zelenchuk, *Opyt etnosotsiologicheskogo issledovaniia obraza zhizni* (Moscow: Nauka, 1980), p. 163.

41   Drobizheva and Tul'tseva, "Svadebnaia obriadnost'," p. 39.

Conclusion

This study has had three main goals. First, it was to present a clear analytical framework for studying ethnic relations in the USSR, this framework being based on insights from comparative ethnic studies. Secondly, we wanted to contribute to filling the gap in the knowledge of the attitudinal, subjective side of ethnic relations in the Soviet Union. In other words, we have attempted to show and assess popular ethnic perceptions and the "perspective from below." Our third pivotal thought has been to bring out the content and forms of mass-based ethnic politics in the USSR. This last effort has been the most difficult one since sources are scarce, but some insights were nevertheless attained. This section will synthesize and highlight our main conclusions as well as outline prospective developments.

The Analytical Framework

Since Soviet multiethnicity involves a great number of nationalities and many types of interactions, it is important to set out with certain analytical clarifications. The ones used in this study relate to the distinction between primary and secondary ethnic groups, three levels of interaction, and diverse situational and structural contexts. In addition, we differentiated between various types of ethnic identification and hypothesized that the quality of ethnic relations is linked to both situational context and to the evaluations ethnic groups make about their standing on core issues of concern. The three issues emphasized in this study are ethnic intermingling, language use and dominance, and socioeconomic advancement.

The first crucial aspect of this analytical framework is that ethnic relations in the USSR are conceptualized as taking place on three distinctive levels of interaction. Members of ethnic groups interact with one another on the microlevel of individual and small group relations, and entire nationalities interact with one another both on the all-union level and within circumscribed

205

subterritories of which the union republics are the most important. While the differentiation between the individual and group levels of ethnic relations is analytically and empirically important in all societies, pinpointing the role of republic-level interactions is of special significance in the Soviet case. Territorially based group identity is at the core of the self-perception of the major nations as well as the practice of Soviet nationality policy. It is also the crucial criterion in some of the other analytical distinctions we have drawn, and also in the hypotheses linked to them. Thus the differentiation between primary and secondary ethnic groups is most of all a distinction between territorial and extraterritorial groups, and most of the political concerns of nationalities revolve around territorially linked issues. Moreover, the differentiation between types of ethnic environments, and the thesis about qualitatively different ethnic processes within each of them, makes sense only if a territorially differentiated settlement pattern exists.

Turning first to distinctions in official status and treatment under contemporary Soviet nationality policy, one notes that secondary ethnic groups—defined here as migrant and dispersed nationalities—have practically no cultural or other group rights or provisions.[1] As far as they have expressed ethnic group concerns these have primarily been aimed at securing or reclaiming a form of territorial status—the Crimean Tatars and Volga Germans being prime examples—or else seeking guarantees for individual non-discrimination of which the Soviet Jews are a major example. In contrast, the concerns and official status of primary ethnic groups are focused on intrarepublic processes and institutions.

Soviet federalism has provided the fourteen non-Russian republic nations with some administrative and cultural prerogatives as well as the promise of group equality. While the primary ethnic groups value this status, it is linked to the political tensions and dilemmas noted in Chapters 2–4 since Soviet nationality policy has pursued a two-pronged strategy of giving recognition to some group goals at the republic level and, at the same time, securing central priorities and a Russian preponderance unionwide. If one takes educational institutions and the armed forces as an example, the contrast in approach is evident both regarding language and cadre policy. Thus education at the republic level is available in native languages, whereas they are given no room in unionwide institutions. Similarly, ethnic stratification within the armed services embodies Russian dominance, whereas at the republic level ethnic proportionality of cadre representation has been the goal. In this instance another policy contradiction becomes evident, in that pivotal political positions are filled by cadre selected—and usually sent—from the center. More important, the Soviet authorities have relied not only on the support of a rotating security elite sent to the non-Russian republics, but also on the loyalty of the more permanent mass of Russian settlers.[2] But by giving these settlers the cultural and political status of a competing and sometimes superordinate primary ethnic group, their relations with the indigenous nations have taken on a volatile ethnopolitical quality.

Both politically and numerically, ethnic group relations between the titular non-Russian republic nations and local Russians constitute the most important type of ethnic interaction within the USSR. It is for this reason that our study began with an assessment of collective ethnic sentiments at the republic level. We argued that they revolve around a clash of interests and perceptions, three dimensions of which were singled out for analysis. The first concerns contrasting views about the reasons, justification, and consequences of the Russian presence; the second concerns differential interpretations of language priorities; and the third focuses on socioeconomic status.

The territorial rooting and history of the non-Russian republic nations sets the baseline for their perceptions and evaluations. They view their traditional homelands as their very own territory within which they have the right to cultural, communal, and political dominance. This is in contrast to the perceptions of the Russian population which perceives the borderlands as an extension of Russia and themselves as political and economic benefactors and *Kulturträger*. This view—anathema to most non-Russians—was epitomized in a speech given by General Secretary Andropov when marking the sixtieth anniversary of the formal creation of the USSR as a federal state:[3]

The peoples of our country offer special words of gratitude to the Russian people. Without their unselfish brotherly help, present-day achievements in any of the republics would have been impossible to attain. The one factor of exceptional importance in the economic, political, and cultural life of the country, in the rapprochement of all its nations and nationalities, in their introduction to the wealth of world civilization, has been the Russian language which has entered into the lives of millions of people of all nationalities in a natural way.

Whenever there is a clash of perceptions, values, and interests, politics comes into play. In the case of the ethnopolitical competition between the republic nations and the local Russians the latter have a much stronger position since their interests are usually safeguarded by the political center, but the republic nations do whatever they can to create a counterforce. This politics manifests itself in readiness to take advantage of contradictions in central policy, in occasional national communist policies of the native elites, in the stand of ethnic dissenters, in machinations of local administrative bodies such as college admissions offices, in cultural subtexts, and in anonymous expressions of popular ethnic disaffection. The latter emerge in unstructured daily encounters among individuals as well as in spontaneous flare-ups of group antagonism. This grassroots ethnopolitical will was described in Chapters 2–4, was referred to later when we noted the influence of political and cultural values on microlevel ethnic interactions.

The main difference between primary and secondary ethnic groups is that due to the lack of significant official status or cohesion in territorial settlement, the secondary ethnic groups have no ethnic relations at the intermediary, intrarepublic level of ethnic interaction. The secondary nationalities are "left out" of the main ethnopolitical action which takes place between the indigenous republic nationality and the local Russians. Members of secondary ethnic groups interact with others only on the microlevel of personal and small group relations and in unstructured relations with the central authorities. In contrast, primary ethnic groups interact on all three levels, namely, the microlevel, the intrarepublic level, and the all-union level.

In practice the boundary line between primary and secondary nationalities is not always as clear as suggested in this analytical summary. Besides the union republics, the USSR includes lower-level ethnic territorial units of which the twenty autonomous republics (ASSRs) are the most significant. Here some cultural provisions exist, and so do ethnic strivings about which more research is needed. Although territorially rooted, some of the ASSR nationalities such as the Karelians or Mordvinians have become passively dispersed through massive immigration. In light of the complexity and number of cases a thorough examination of these minorities has been beyond the scope of this study, but the few references that have been made suggest that the ASSR nationalities are closer to being secondary than primary ethnic groups.

Another argument in our analytical framework concerns the role of situational and structural contexts; the emphasis on context serves as the organizational basis for this study as well as the discussion within chapters. Situationally we focused on intermarriage, social–communal interaction, the workplace, educational institutions, the armed forces, and anonymous daily encounters. Each context is characterized by some specific determinants which influence the quality of ethnic relations, and this specificity cannot be extrapolated to other contexts. A summary of these findings follows below, together with a synthesis of conclusions about linkages between the various contexts the most important of which is the reappearance of the same issues, namely, language dominance, ethnic mixing, and ethnic stratification.

The political pertinency of these three core issues in various contexts is related to the formal and informal structuring of ethnic interaction. It matters whether individuals interact in work collectives, army units, classrooms, and residential areas in which their own nationality dominates; whether another ethnic group has the majority; or whether the composition is intensely mixed. It also matters who makes the decision about the type of structuring in force, and we have therefore asked about the decision-making process and the political values attached to it

The Quality of Ethnic Relations and its Determinants

Ethnic relations in each sphere of life are characterized by certain situational specifics. Thus the imperative to fulfill their primary functional task—be it production or education or military training—is of major importance in social institutions such as the workplace, the schools, and the armed forces. When asked about the role of ethnicity in such institutions, respondents tend to point to this primary role, and either add that ethnicity does not affect it much or else specify ways in which ease of cooperation is affected. Here the factors mentioned are mostly functional in nature, language facility being the primary case in point.

Some of the specific characteristics of contexts contribute to more positive ethnic relations, a prime example being the camaraderie soldiers develop during military service. By being thrown together during the trials and tribulations of military training, servicemen develop a common bond. But the new and alien environment also reinforces ethnic identity and the incli-

209

nation to seek out conationals, and thus two parallel and partly contradictory processes take place.

Next to context-specificity it is the main conclusion of this study that the quality of ethnic relations on both the individual and group level is linked to the evaluations people make about their standing in regard to major ethnic issues. Such evaluations depend on cultural, economic, and political values and perceptions of self-interest. Major changes in the distribution of values due to policy fluctuations, economic constraints, or demographic shifts lead to a reassessment of ethnic standings and are thus volatile in nature. In other words, changes in the status quo can lead to major jumps in the barometer of ethnic harmony.

In the following we summarize the status quo regarding the three major substantive issues covered in this study, and we also discuss the implications of our findings in regard to prospective change. We, first, deal with the topic of physical and social ethnic intermingling, then turn to language issues, and conclude by assessing questions linked to socioeconomic advancement and change.

ETHNIC MIXING IN THE USSR: INTERNATIONALIZATION OF ENVIRONMENTS, ATTITUDES, AND THE "SOVIET PEOPLE?"

It is a major point in the official Soviet argument about convergence that the nationalities in the USSR intermix more and more and that the resulting internationalization of macro- and microenvironments leads to an internationalization of attitudes as well. Both parts of this proposition can be questioned. One can also question the thesis that intermarriage is on the rise and that communal merging is leading to the appearance of a "new historical community—the Soviet people." While these processes have some impact on secondary ethnic groups, primary ethnic groups have remained largely unaffected.

ETHNIC ENVIRONMENTS, CONTACTS, AND ATTITUDES

As we have shown throughout this study, there are numerous ethnic environments in the USSR in which a non-Russian nationality dominates numerically. There is also a strong tendency for all ethnic groups to stay with members of their own nationality; and this is so both on the macro- and the microlevel. Adherents of the assimilationist school of ethnic theory argue that this type of ethnic structuring and lack of intense contact is a hindrance to ethnic harmony, whereas pluralists argue the opposite. What conclusions does our study allow for the Soviet case?

Turning first to macrolevel developments, one notes that the extent of physical intermingling of nationalities depends on migration and demographic growth rates. In most non-Russian union republics the trends in both cases have favored a growing "nativization" rather than "internationalization." The "nativization" of populations has been especially pronounced in the six republics named after Muslim peoples, that is, Uzbekistan, Tadjikistan, Turkmenistan, Kirghizia, Kazakhstan, and Azerbaijan. Between the censuses of 1959 and 1979 the proportion of the native population in these republics has increased by 6–10 percent. For Lithuania, Armenia, and Georgia there has been an increase of 1–5 percent. In contrast, the Ukraine, Belorussia, and Moldavia show slight proportional decreases in the indigenous population (2–3 percent), with the most dramatic proportional decreases applying to Latvia (−8 percent) and Estonia (−10 percent; cf. Table A.1, p. 230).

While these demographic changes are related to differential birth rates, migration flows also are important, and here various data indicate that the great majority of people prefer to stay in their indigenous republics. The inclination to leave their home territories is low among all primary non-Russian groups and is not overwhelming among the Russians either. In light of the official value placed on migration and physical mixing of the nationalities there is a likelihood that the authorities will try to take more regulatory steps, but their success is doubtful.

For one, recent Soviet migration policy has not been overly successful, and it is also at crosspurposes. While central ethnic policy promotes Russian migration to the borderlands, it is economically most desirable to have the Russian population stay within the RSFSR and to migrate to its eastern and northern parts which are suffering from an accelerating manpower shortage.[4] Thus the continued or even increased outmigration of Russians from the RSFSR, which in the past has been the primary means of "internationalizing" the environments of the non-Russian republics, appears doubtful. In fact a reverse process may even take place in the case of Central Asia and Kazakhstan, where the demographic expansion and assertiveness of the indigenous population has tended to push in the direction of Russian remigration to the RSFSR.

Moreover, the non-Russian rejection of the large-scale immigration of Russians to their republics is likely to have some impact. This rejection is political in nature and is due to notions that it implies a limitation of local territorial sovereignty as well as unwelcome consequences for local cultural and economic rights. While there have been several known instances where sudden inflows of migrants have led to high-level political conflicts between republic and central leaders, the rejection of immigration has also been evident on the popular level (see Chapter 3). Ethnic conflict on this score has been especially pronounced in those republics where the influx of "aliens" has been excessive and has either led to—or threatened to lead to—the indigenous nation turning into a numerical minority within its own republic. Kirghizia and especially Kazakhstan are the two republics which have experienced this fate in the past, while Latvia and Estonia increasingly move toward it in the current period (see Table A.1, p. 230), a change which has been accompanied by growing ethnic strife.

The controversy and disharmony resulting from large-scale immigration is one case in point that increased ethnic contact by no means necessarily leads to better relations. Some of our findings as well as Soviet surveys show a similar association. Thus Russians show higher rates of ethnic interaction rejection if they reside in predominantly non-Russian environments, and there are some instances where non-Russians have a higher preference rate for their own nationality if they have been exposed to a dominantly Russian environment. It is not always clear why this is the case—socioeconomic class apparently being one variable—and there are also contrary examples. Thus ethnic attitudes at the workplace indicate that some individuals who have worked in multiethnic collectives have a tendency to be more positive in evaluations of such collectives than people who have not had such an experience. But then this is not causal proof since people with a more "internationalist" outlook often are those who work in mixed collectives to begin with.

The latter touches on a significant point, namely, the differentiation between voluntary and involuntary ethnic intermingling. If the mixing is voluntary, it is much more likely to have positive attitudinal effects than if it is involuntary. As concerns the place of work, its choice is frequently voluntary in the USSR. But this is not the case where young men spend their time in the armed services, and thus ethnic contact within this institution is less likely to be associated with increases in attitudinal ethnic integration. As we noted, the recruits tend to seek out their conationals during offduty time, and references to the historical precedent of military units being formed for individual nationalities suggest a level of ethnic preference for such groupings.

In the educational sphere the nationally mixed general schools have hardly been a success, although this is due in part to language concerns to be discussed below. Overall language knowledge and preference play a major role in affecting the formal and informal structuring of ethnic contact. This link was shown both in the case of informal grouping in the armed services and at the workplace, but it is especially pronounced in the educational sphere. Ethnic groups in the USSR value native language education, and this limits ethnic mixing since interethnic contact in schools and universities is limited if instruction is carried out in varying languages.

In light of the official Soviet rhetoric and policy of promoting migration and ethnic mixing it is remarkable how members of particular nationalities in the USSR stick together to safeguard or create their own ethnic environment. The general reluctance of republic nationals to leave their own republic is just one indication of this. Another one is that migrants have frequently settled together, sometimes recreating homogeneous or nearly homogeneous ethnic neighborhoods or villages.[5] The reluctance of some nationalities, such as the Uzbeks, to move from the rural areas of their republic to the cities is similarly linked to the desire to reside in a native environment[6] rather than in the Russian dominated or "international" cities. All of this suggests that a great number of micro- and macroenvironments in the USSR will remain dominated by individual non-Russian nationalities for a considerable time to come, and that the special characteristics of ethnic relations within these environments will remain in force as well.

Familial and Communal Convergence

As one Soviet commentator has remarked, one can talk of "interethnic" relations only to the extent that distinct ethnic communities persist. With the emergence of the "new historical community—the Soviet people," relationships are said to attain a qualitatively new level of development best characterized by the term "international."[7] Can one indeed foresee the end of interethnic relations in the USSR? Is it accurate to speak of a trend toward a gradual fading of existing communal identities and ties?

213

Soviet ideologues see ethnic intermarriage as a key to ethnic convergence in the USSR, but in reality the Soviet nationalities differ widely in the extent that they intermarry. The non-Slavic primary nations, and especially the Muslim peoples, are least likely to do so. While members of Slavic primary ethnic groups tend to intermarry more, intermarriage is most frequent among secondary ethnic groups. Overall one can conclude that monoethnic marriages continue to constitute the norm for most people and that intermarriage has little effect on the group identities of the major nationalities in the USSR.[8]

Intermarriage is a good example that in a society as extensively multiethnic as the Soviet one it is misleading to speak of interethnic relations in general, without clearly specifying the groups one is talking about. It is vital always to keep in mind that "ethnic relations" refer to a relationship between at least two nationalities, and if the identity of one of the partners changes, so does the quality and intensity of interactions. Thus, for example, the relations Kazakhs have with Tatars differ from the ones they have with Russians since they are much more likely to intermarry with the former than with the latter. As a rule, culturally fraternal peoples intermarry most easily. It is just about meaningless to talk about intermarriage *per se*, or the consequences of intermarriage, since both are variable according to groups and contexts involved.

As to the latter point, the initial proposition of this study that the pattern and quality of ethnic relations in the USSR differ substantially according to ethnic environment has been confirmed. Ethnic intermarriage is most prevalent in highly mixed environments and relatively scarce in areas that are dominated by a specific non-Russian nationality, or the Russians. Also if a specific nationality predominates, children from mixed marriages tend to choose this nationality in the process of ethnic self-identification. While this comes as no surprise in the case of areas dominated by Russians, it is significant that the same process takes place in the non-Russian union republics (with the Ukraine and Belorussia constituting a partial exception).

The nationality choice of children from mixed marriages is one of the most poignant illustrations for the differential tenacity of the various ethnic identities in the Soviet Union. It shows that it is distinctly inappropriate to talk about all Soviet nationalities in the same breath since not only divergent, but even opposite, trends pertain to individual groups. As we found (cf. Table 1.2, p. 38), the cases are scattered over the entire range of numerical possibilities, including the extreme ends where in one case close to 100 percent of the youngsters choose the local nationality (Turkmen), and at the other end the proportion is close to 0 percent (Mordvinian). These rates can be taken as rough numerical measures of the value assigned to belonging to a specific nationality. As we have seen, some nationalities rank very low and thus are indeed good candidates for convergence or extinction. As indicated in some other places in this study and elsewhere,[9] dispersed nationalities as well as those whose official homelands in the USSR are below the union republic level are most vulnerable. In contrast, union republic nations in most instances hold their own ground, most overwhelmingly so in the case of Central Asia.

Our research suggests several explanations for the differential value assigned to belonging to one or the other nationality. First, the numerical ethnic composition of environments plays a role. A second element concerns the advantages to be gained by belonging to a republic nationality, especially in socioeconomic advancement. Republic nationals tend to be preferred in admissions to local institutions of higher education, and also for certain jobs, especially in Central Asia and Kazakhstan. A third point concerns the ethnic climate, which generally tends to emphasize the special historical and linguistic rights of the indigenous population, making it less attractive to be associated with the "alien" population segment. A non-Russian nationality is furthermore chosen if the respective nation has a strong communal identity, as is most clearly the case among Muslims, and also among the Caucasian nations and the Balts.

While the exceptional strength and attractiveness of the indigenous Muslim communal identities is evident in the choice of nationality by children from mixed families, it is also evident from intermarriage data, the observance of customs and religious traditions, and Muslim cultural pride and self-confidence. They are the nations most likely to remain distinct for a long time to come. None the less, their identity cannot be seen as static and inflexible. To the contrary, the data on the adherence to Islam suggest that outward adaptability combined with an unfaltering commitment to an essential core is a characteristic of the Muslim nations. Thus there may be some outward "convergence" toward the all-Soviet way of life without a real loss of ethnic identity, which brings us back to the problem of defining the relationship between "functional" and "attitudinal" integration. In this case it appears that some functional adaptation occurs in order to better preserve what is attitudinally the most important.

While discussing the likelihood of the various Soviet nations converging into a single new Soviet nation, one should also ask about the meaning of this process. The official convergence theory implicitly assumes that the various Soviet nationalities converge in one direction, but it is possible that convergence leads to several regional identities, or that republic nations assimilate smaller groupings within their republics. This has in fact been happening in some cases.[10]

As noted in Chapter 1, the Soviet practice of registering nationality in passports reinforces the persistence of personal and social ethnic identification. This consequence may be inadvertent since it contradicts the official goal of consolidating a unified Soviet people. The main purpose of the system of registration appears to be the creation of a tool of ethnic differentiation for purposes of state security and "ethnic management." It serves as a means of residential control, as a criterion for access to certain positions and to VUZy. There may be other purposes as well, yet to be explored. As noted, this practice and its political consequences have been paid little attention by Western analysts and it is greatly underreported in Soviet sources. At a minimum one may conclude, however, that this is a policy at crosspurposes.

The Politics of Language Use

In societies such as the Soviet Union where multiethnicity largely overlaps with multilinguality, the quality of ethnic relations is closely related to language commonality and policy. Numerous data indicate that if people have a common language, ethnic relations tend to improve. There are, however, also contradictory findings which show that increasing bilingualism can be associated with more negative ethnic attitudes. The crucial point in explaining this apparent contradiction is political, namely, whether commonality of language is achieved voluntarily and on the basis of equality of languages or not. The evaluation of which situation applies on its hand is closely linked to ethnic values and perceptions, and is thus highly subjective. Survey data and other material reflecting the popular outlook of ethnic groups are the most reliable sources for ascertaining the specifics; they indicate that there is a significant perceptual gap between non-Russian primary nations and both Russians and secondary ethnic groups.

While the latter two favor Russian as the dominant means of communication unionwide, the former emphasize the status of native languages within republics.

This gap in perceptions and values is closely related to the evaluation of the consequences of the current Soviet policy of prioritizing the knowledge and use of Russian as the "language of interethnic communication." The official assumption behind this policy is that increasing bilingualism among the non-Russian Soviet citizens will promote ease of cooperation and will lead to better and closer relations. The surveys noting an increase of "internationalist" views in cases where commonality of language is present in part support this view. But these sources also show a contrary association in the case of professionals and white-collar workers, and that commonality of language can refer to non-Russian languages as well. As Arutiunian and Drobizheva note in a summary of their findings in 1981, the language problem in the USSR should not solely be seen as a problem of increasing bilingualism among non-Russians, since[11]

the other "linguistic" problem is that of the Russians' and other non-local inhabitants of the republics knowing the languages of the indigenous nationalities. Those segments of the Russian population which know the languages of the ethnic majorities most easily feel at home and adapt to local conditions.

Not only do Russians feel more at home when they know the language of a non-Russian nationality they live side by side with, the non-Russians also feel more friendly both on an individual and on a group level. In the perception of a great number of republic nationals, especially in the Caucasus and in the Baltic region, equality of languages means reciprocity of language acquisition as well as broad support for the use of the local languages. If the indigenous nationality feels that this support is not forthcoming, both ethnic and political resentments rise. In the case of Estonia such resentment is reflected in the results of the 1979 Census which showed fewer Estonians admitting to knowing Russian than in 1970, in spite of increased contact with Russians and in spite of the new language programs.

As past experiences—such as the Georgian demonstrations of 1978—have shown, language policy constitutes one of the neuralgic points of the minority nations of the USSR and it is dangerous for the authorities to change the status quo. For the non-Russians more is at stake than just cultural or ethnic pride and preference. It is also a question of socioeconomic opportunity and interests as well as political images. As concerns the latter, it bears repeating that Lenin recognized that in the eyes of minority nationals a democratic approach to multilingualism plays a crucial role in neutralizing the unpopular image of a centralist and predominantly Russian Soviet government. If this image is effectively reversed, this does not bode well for attitudinal integration of these same people. Lenin's political insight found expression primarily in educational policy and it is here that one notes gradual changes toward a strengthening of the Russian language since 1958, with a major acceleration since 1978. If it should come to a direct challenge to native-language education in the non-Russian union republics, the political fallout could reach major proportions.

The official Soviet claim that the policy of increasing bilingualism among the non-Russian nations contributes to ethnic rapprochement is contradicted not only by numerous data from the USSR, but also by findings in comparable societies such as Quebec. There it has been shown that separatist leanings are highest in cities where bilingualism is most advanced, the explanation being that there the Quebecois feel most threatened by the advancing English culture.[12] While this type of development can apply to entire nations, it most easily emerges among those strata whose professional interests are linked to the cultural standing of the ethnic group they belong to. As found in Chapter 5, this is mostly true for workers in the arts and the humanities. It is a prime illustration for the link between language politics and competing economic interests.

Competition for Socioeconomic Access

Economic and social equalization is a further dimension affecting ethnic relations. Soviet sources argue that the gradual convergence of the social structures of the nationalities is progressing, that it is one of the characteristics of the new all-Soviet community,[13] and that this enhances good relations between nationalities. Without attempting a detailed statistical analysis, we have noted several complexities which should be summarized here.

Our first conclusion is that for the union republic nations the problem of ethnic stratification is most relevant within the context of their own republics. If they feel, as has increasingly been the case among Balts, that the Russians have too great a share of the leading positions, this undermines ethnic harmony. This is the classic case of indigenous nations resenting the superordinate position of an alien minority in their midst. As such, it is a political confrontation more than anything else. It is exacerbated by the not so distant memory of independent statehood and national self-determination.

The issue of ethnic stratification is also explosive in Central Asia and Kazakhstan, although for different reasons. Here the indigenous populations are gradually gaining educationally and in their share of desirable jobs. Here the disharmony in the ethnic climate is related to factors such as the aggravation felt by the Russians who perceive "affirmative action" as unjust and as a threat to their own socioeconomic status. As we noted in Chapter 5, a moving downward in economic status or social mobility tends to be transposed into more negative ethnic attitudes on the individual level, and the same is true for groups, in this case the Russians and other Europeans living in the region. On the other hand, the local population is discontented as well. It tends to see the gains as being too small and claims that it has a right to much more, especially in light of demographic pressures.[14] The phenomenon of increasing ethnic conflicts during transition periods when traditional stratification systems change has been noted in other societies as well,[15] and is not as surprising as it may appear.

It is also significant that the advancement possibilities of the indigenous republic nationalities are limited in scope. Educational enrollments suggest that the locals are overrepresented in fields such as pedagogy, agriculture, medicine, and the humanities, which in the Soviet case are both less prestigious and less sensitive politically. In contrast, Russians are overrepresented in technical professions, economics,[16] and in pivotal political positions. As the local elites develop their own strength they are more likely to discover the doors that are shut to them.

The limits to non-Russian advancement possibilities are more evident on the unionwide level, where the Russians are overrepresented in the CPSU,[17] in high-level governmental positions and the foreign service, in the military officer corps, and presumably also in the KGB. These are the most centralized and culturally Russified institutions of the Soviet Union which means that non-Russians interested in making a career in them have to adjust accordingly. This is one of the prime lessons the young draftees take home from their service in the armed forces. While some may accept it individually, it poses a problem on a group level since it raises the issue of group equality.

Perceptions of unequal access to socioeconomic and occupational status play a role not only on the macrolevel of group relations, but on the microlevel as well. As was noted in Chapter 5, several Soviet ethnosociological studies found unusually high rates of negative ethnic attitudes among 18–24 year-olds and related this to competition for access to higher education. Moreover, job dissatisfaction tends to be transposed into more negative ethnic views, which is bound to be even more pronounced when direct ethnic competition at work is involved. Several sources note that this is especially true for professionals and white-collar personnel, who in addition also tend to be the strata most concerned about the flourishing of native cultures.

There is every indication that the quality of ethnic relations in the USSR will continue to be affected by both individual and group perceptions about unjust ethnic stratification unionwide and within individual union republics. This is so not only because of the subjectivity of such perceptions, but even more important, because the Soviet policy-makers have raised expectations and tried to reconcile three fundamentally irreconcilable goals which imply different policies. Their most immediate goal has always been to secure central control over all crucial power positions, but they have at the same time declared that they aim for the political and socioeconomic equalization of all Soviet nationalities as groups. While these two goals already are at loggerheads since central control has in practice meant relying primarily on Russian cadre, the equal treatment of ethnic groups is also in contradiction to the normative vision of a unified Soviet society in which every citizen—as an individual—is treated the same, no matter what his ethnic identity.

As discussed in Chapter 3, there is an inherent tension between the equal treatment of individuals and groups, which means that numerous policy dilemmas arise with the likelihood that someone always remains dissatisfied in a decidedly ethnic manner. A policy aiming at the equality and proportional representation of groups implies an ethnically differentiated treatment, which is not in accord with the equality of individuals. Conversely, if individual merit alone decides, ethnic groups are unlikely to show a congruent stratification. This is a dilemma also faced in other multiethnic societies but the Soviet Union stands out, in that the issue is not debated openly or in the courts. Instead contrasting views and interests confront each other informally, which may be politically more dangerous in the long run.

The Soviet policy-makers face a further complication in that there is a link between language policy and policies of socioeconomic access. As the use of Russian is increasingly prioritized in higher education and other spheres individuals with non-Russian native languages are put at a competitive disadvantage. This strengthens the dilemma of the central decision-makers of having to choose between more emphasis on "affirmative action" which has the unwelcome effect of undermining the position of the local Russian population, or alternatively, giving up attempts at equalization at the risk of increased disaffection on the part of non-Russians.

Prospects

After summarizing our findings about competing ethnic perceptions and interests as well as political dilemmas faced by Soviet leaders, the final question to be posed is that of prospects for the next decades. Here the two decisive factors are the impact of general social developments on the one hand, and Soviet politics on the other. We shall shortly discuss each in turn.

As for general social developments, the comparative literature on ethnic relations includes divergent theories of change over time. Among these some propositions developed by Karl W. Deutsch are most helpful in their specificity. His first point refers to social communication which he conceptualizes as the main determinant of nationality. High intensity in all manner of social communication is the key characteristic of a people or nation. And since modern economic development and social mobilization bring about an immense intensification of social communication, the importance of the national factor increases with it.[18] The same thought has been expressed by other analysts noting that ethnic identity is formed or enhanced through interaction with "relevant others"[19] and as such becomes more pertinent through increasing contact.

In the case of the minority peoples of the USSR the basic question thus is whether in the process of mobilization the identification with their own nationality is intensified, or whether they increasingly identify with Russians and the "new historical community of people—the Soviet people." As our discussion has suggested, differential trends apply, and in those instances where an indigenous nationality dominates an ethnic environment the former will be the case, while in mixed or Russian-dominated environments a segment of the smaller nationalities will tend to choose the latter identity. Overall this segment is small.

Among the other factors associated with a growth of ethnic consciousness in the course of modernization one is psychological. Deutsch points out that newly urbanized people tend to undergo a torment of alienation which frequently leads to a new search for ethnic identity. More important, whenever two basic population groups are present, accelerated mobilization among only one of the population groups will lead to increased linguistic and cultural competition as well as economic conflict due to competition over jobs and advancement.[20] This pattern is close to the one found in the western and southeastern republics of the USSR, even though the identity of the increasingly dominant groups varies.

Although Soviet ideological sources have called the notion that Western social science theories linking modernization to an intensification of ethnic identity and assertiveness can be applied to the USSR a "bourgeois falsification,"[21] this is partly supported by the findings of Soviet ethnosociologists. Thus Arutiunian concludes a recent survey of his year-long work on ethnic processes by noting that while traditional ethnic identity is more prevalent in rural (and as Deutsch would say "non-mobilized") populations, a new type of ethnic identity and consciousness emerges with urbanization:[22]

In the course of urbanization, traditional ethnic forms are gradually being supplanted and the distinguishing features of nationalities are being erased, particularly in the workplace and in everyday life. At the same time, the role and significance of sociopsychological factors in the functioning of ethnic groups increase. As that which is traditionally ethnic "subsides," national selfconsciousness is growing stronger. Research data enable us to conclude that a high level of national selfconsciousness is most characteristic of major multinational population centers where the educational level is high. Moreover, the growth of national selfconsciousness is closely related to the individual's participation in multi-national culture and the formation of his attitudes within a cross-national context.

While Arutiunian speaks in general terms here, we previously referred to his detailed work where he pinpointed the professional people and white-collar workers as the groups most affected by this process. In a similar vein some Soviet ethnosociologists have noted that higher educational levels tend to go hand in hand with intensified ethnic consciousness.[23] Both phenomena were also found in Western surveys with emigrants from the USSR. Thus the "Harvard project" conducted in the early 1950s found that Ukrainians in white-collar jobs were more hostile to Russians than were peasants and workers, and related it to the more intimate contact between Ukrainian and Russian white-collar workers as well as to the higher degree of direct competition for more favored positions.[24] Similarly, the West German scholars Kussmann and Schäfer state that "the national identity of the younger Soviet German is promoted rather than impeded by access to education and training in a Russian-language environment,"[25] and that the younger and more highly educated Soviet Germans are the ones who evaluate Kazakh attitudes toward Russians to be most negative.[26]

Such findings support those scholars who have stipulated a link between education and the development of nationalism, especially as it relates to large national groups living in their traditional territory. Further support is found in a study conducted among young French Canadian managerial and professional people which noted a positive association between increasing education and nationalism. Some of the reasons cited are that these young elite members resent their professional advancement being hindered by the dominance of English Canadian culture and cadre in the higher levels, that they aspire to an all-encompassing Quebecois social environment (the "société globale"), and wish to be "maître chez nous,"[27] which is strikingly similar to the expression used by Central Asians demanding to be "the masters in their own republic."

In sum, professional and white-collar workers tend to become more ethnically concerned in the course of modernization, which also increases this group numerically. This process will continue to advance in the USSR. There is also a link between economic satisfaction and ethnic harmony which means that depending on the economic situation, ethnic tension could be further increased through the projection of general dissatisfaction on ethnic relations. A scarcity of resources also enhances competition, which as we found, frequently has ethnic connotations. Thus there is a considerable likelihood that ethnic relations in the USSR will deteriorate in the time to come.

This study has also shown, however, that ethnicity is variable according to context, and that the dynamics of ethnic relations has to be examined on various levels and in different situations, and case by case. Individuals have multiple roles each of which reflects a particular meaning of ethnicity in everyday life in the Soviet Union. While a certain individual may function smoothly in a multiethnic work collective, may know well the "language of interethnic communication," and may generally have a modern life style, this does not mean that he will not feel aggravated by ethnic competition for advancement or by a decreasing social role of his native language or strictures against engaging in certain forms of communal participation. Similarly, this individual may have friends among a variety of nationalities, especially if he has served in the armed forces or has attended a Russian-language VUZ, but could nevertheless participate in spontaneous confrontations with "whites" or "you Russians." In part this differential behavior is due to differences between individual and group-level identification and relationships, but the decisive aspect is the variability of the parameters determining each situation.[28] New situations bring forth new ethnic responses. Thus the group confrontation has strong political and historical connotations, whereas personal friendships are influenced by individual character and psychology.

Another way of formulating our main conclusion is that integration and conflict can exist side by side. In the words of Edward Shils,[29]

In some respects, various parts of the society might be well integrated, others less so; on other issues, the integratedness might have quite a different structure. Perhaps most important of all is the fact that within the spheres of authoritative and cultural integration, integration and conflict might exist simultaneously in the conduct of the same person.

Or in other words, man is not one-dimensional. The final question to ask, then, is which of the numerous dimensions outlined will emerge as the most prominent in the ethnic relations of the coming decade. This is primarily a political question and we thus come to our projections of Soviet politics.

In this study we have tried to show that politics is a two-way street even in a state as authoritarian as the USSR, and that it matters what large population subgroups such as nationalities think and want. The original Leninist political strategy toward the non-Russian nations has, on balance, been relatively successful, in that major escalations of conflict have been avoided. While the political control mechanism of the Soviet state has something to do with this, so has the "safety-valve" approach to ethnic politics.[30] This approach has meant that certain limited concessions—primarily in the cultural and territorial sphere—have been made in order to assuage ethnic claims and to increase long-term attitudinal integration. Whenever major inroads have been attempted on these concessions, as for example in the education reform of 1958–9 and more recently with the increasingly pro-Russian linguistic policy, the union republic populations and a considerable segment of their elites have reacted most negatively. From this we conclude that similar waves of ethnic protest and discord will rise whenever a more restrictive nationality policy is applied.

In this regard the trends evident since the late 1970s promise little good. The drive toward convergence and homogenization of nationalities has accelerated. The primary manifestation of this new policy has been a mass of new programs promoting the learning and use of Russian by non-Russians, but attention has also been paid to the need to encourage the physical mixing of nationalities and to promote "international work collectives."[31] There is also a renewed emphasis on the beneficial results to be obtained by an invigorated ideological campaign in the sense of both vigilance in the detection of "anti-socialist" ethnic tendencies and broad socialization efforts through the use of the mass media, lectures, and similar means.[32] The developing of closer ties among ethnic groups had high priority on the problem-solving agenda of General Secretary Andropov,[33] and it appears to hold the same place under the leaders who succeeded him. If, however, these leaders should continue to pursue a policy which equals ethnic harmony with homogenization, they are likely to get just the opposite.

225

Notes: Conclusion

1 It should be reiterated that the migrant segment of the union republic nations is also classified as secondary ethnic groups. There are signs that their cultural situation is improving, for example, in that it is becoming possible to subscribe to non-Russian periodicals outside of the titular republics: see Ann Sheehy, "Non-Russian periodical press to be available on subscription throughout the Soviet Union," *Radio Liberty Research Bulletin*, RL 335/82 (New York: Radio Liberty, 19 August 1982).

2 "The practice of sending settlers into a new area to establish and maintain political control is an old one," Tamotsu Shibutani and Kian M. Kwan, *Ethnic Stratification: A Comparative Approach*, (New York: Macmillan, 1965), p. 151.

3 *Pravda*, 22 December 1982, p. 2.

4 See, for example, G. I. Litvinova and B. Ts. Urlanis, "Demograficheskaia politika Sovetskogo Soiuza," *Sovetskoe gosudarstvo i pravo*, 1982, no. 3, pp. 42–4.

5 While this is noted in Iu. V. Bromlei (ed.), *Sovremennye etnicheskie protsessy v SSSR* (Moscow: Nauka, 1975), pp. 142–6, it is also evident in the case of the Soviet German community, which has retained surprisingly many residential centers.

6 Iu. V. Arutiunian, "Natsional'no-regional'noe mnogoobrazie sovetskoi derevni," *Sotsiologicheskie issledovaniia*, 1980, no. 3, p. 80.

7 M. I. Kulichenko (ed.), *Osnovnye napravleniia izucheniia natsional'nykh otnoshenii v SSSR* (Moscow: Nauka, 1979), p. 68.

8 Viktor Ivanovich Kozlov, *Natsional'nosti SSSR: Etnodemograficheskii obzor*, 2nd rev. ed. (Moscow: Finansy i statistika, 1982), p. 261, arrives at the same conclusion.

9 There are, of course, many different indices with which one can measure ethnic identity change in the USSR. For a study using Soviet census data on nationality sizes see Barbara A. Anderson and Brian D. Silver, "Estimating russification of ethnic identity among non-Russians in the USSR," *Demography*, vol. 20, no. 4 (November 1983), pp. 461–89.

10 Thus Poles have been partly assimilated by Ukrainians and Belorussians: see ibid., p. 28.

11 Iu. V. Arutiunian and L. M. Drobizheva, "Etnosotsiologicheskie issledovaniia v SSSR," *Sotsiologicheskie issledovaniia*, 1981, no. 1, pp. 68–9.

12 Susan Olzak, "Ethnic mobilization in Quebec," *Ethnic and Racial Studies*, vol. 5, no. 3 (July 1982), pp. 268–9. She also notes that those persons who had most contact with English Canadians at work were more separatist.

13 M. N. Rutkevich, "Sblizhenie natsional'nykh respublik i natsii SSSR po sotsial'no-klassovoi strukture," *Sotsiologicheskie issledovaniia*, 1981, no. 2, pp. 14–24.

14 See also Murray Feshbach, "The Soviet Union: population trends and dilemmas," *Population Bulletin*, vol. 37, no. 3 (August 1982), p. 20.

15 cf. Graham C. Kinloch, "Comparative race and ethnic relations," *International Journal of Comparative Sociology*, vol. 22, no. 3–4 (1981), pp. 260, 263; and Shibutani and Kwan, *Ethnic Stratification, passim*.

16 Thus at the Vilnius Institute of Engineering and Construction the ratio between Lithuanians and Russians is 4:1, while it is 72:1 at the Lithuanian Academy of Veterinary Medicine, calculation based on A. N. Baskakov and V. Iu. Mikhal'chenko (eds.), *Razvitie natsional'nykh iazykov v sviazi s ikh funktsionirovaniem v sfere vysshego obrazovaniia* (Moscow: Nauka, 1982), p. 77; see also ibid., pp. 34–9, 160, 225–6; Leonid Novikov, *Hochschulen in der*

Sowjetunion (Frankfurt-on-Main: Deutsches Institut für Internationale Pädagogische Forschung, 1981), p. 35; and M. Mobin Shorish, "Who shall be educated: selection and integration in Soviet Central Asia," in Edward Allworth (ed.), *The Nationality Question in Soviet Central Asia* (New York: Praeger, 1973), p. 95.

17 Russians constitute just 52·4 percent of the Soviet population, but make up 59·8 percent of the membership of the CPSU: *Narodnoe khoziaistvo SSSR 1962–1982*, p. 49. See also David Lane, *The End of Social Inequality?: Class, Status and Power under State Socialism* (Winchester, Mass.: Allen & Unwin, 1982), pp. 92–5.

18 Karl W. Deutsch, *Nationalism and Social Communication*, 2d ed. (Cambridge, Mass.: MIT Press, 1966) pp. 75, 110–11, 175–6, 188, 190.

19 Crawford Young, *The Politics of Cultural Pluralism* (Madison, Wis.: University of Wisconsin Press, 1976), p. 41; and I. A. Snezhkova, "K probleme izucheniia etnicheskovo samosoznaniia u detei i iunoshestva," *Sovetskaia etnografiia*, 1982, no. 1, pp. 80–8.

20 Deutsch, *Nationalism*, pp. 133, 144. On the search for identity see Karl W. Deutsch, *Nationalism and its Alternatives* (New York, Knopf, 1969), pp. 23–4.

21 Z. S. Chertina, "Burzhuaznaia teoriia 'modernizatsii' i real'noe razvitie narodov sovetskoi Srednei Azii," *Istoriia SSSR*, 1980, no. 2, pp. 204–8.

22 Arutiunian, "Natsional'no-regional'noe," p. 81.

23 A. A. Susokolov, "Vliianie razlichii v urovne obrazovaniia i chislennosti kontaktiruiushchikh etnicheskikh grupp na mezhetnicheskie otnosheniia (po materialam perepisei naseleniia SSSR 1959 i 1970 gg.)," *Sovetskaia etnografiia*, 1976, no. 1, p. 110.

24 Alex Inkeles and Raymond A. Bauer, *The Soviet Citizen, Daily Life in a Totalitarian Society* (Cambridge, Mass.: Harvard University Press, 1959), pp. 364–5.

25 Thomas Kussmann and Bernd Schäfer, *Nationale Identität: Selbstbild und Fremdbilder von deutschen Aussiedlern aus der Sowjetunion* (Cologne: Berichte des Bundesinstituts für ostwissenschaftliche und internationale Studien, 46, 1982), p. 175.

26 ibid., pp. 77–8.

27 Erwin C. Hargrove, "Nationality, values, and change: young elites in French Canada," *Comparative Politics*, vol. 2, no. 3 (April 1970), pp. 473–9.

28 cf. Shibutani and Kwan, *Ethnic Stratification*, p. 279; and the sources cited in the introduction.

29 Edward Shils, *Center and Periphery: Essays in Macrosociology* (Chicago: University of Chicago, 1975), p. 81; for a similar, although more vaguely formulated, conclusion see L. M. Drobizheva, "Ob izuchenii sotsial'no-psikhologicheskikh aspektov natsional'nykh otnoshenii (Nekotorye voprosy metodologii)," *Sovetskaia etnografiia*, 1974, no. 4, p. 25.

30 Terminology used by Seweryn Bialer, *Stalin's Successors: Leadership, Stability, and Change* (Cambridge: Cambridge University Press, 1980), p. 213.

31 During the past five years a great number of meetings and conferences have focused on these themes. On the recommendations of a unionwide "scholarly practical" conference on nationality problems held in Riga in June 1982 and attended primarily by party personnel see *Padomju Latvijas Komunists*, 1982, no. 8; and for a conference report of a more scholarly meeting of Soviet ethnosociologists see A. A. Susokolov, "Vsesoiuznaia nauchnaia sessiia XXVI s"ezd KPSS i zadachi izucheniia natsional'nykh otnoshenii v SSSR," *Sovetskaia etnografiia*, 1982, no. 2, pp. 111–15.

32 ibid., esp. pp. 26, 35; see also B. K. Mal'kova, "Nekotorye aspekty internatsional'nogo vospitaniia (po materialam respublikanskikh gazet)," *Sovetskaia*

etnografiia, 1980, no. 5, p. 101, where it is argued that republic newspapers should be urged to change their terminology and more frequently refer to the "Soviet people" and "the Soviet motherland" rather than make references to "our republic," and similar.

33 Nationality policy was in fact the first issue brought up at a meeting of the Presidium of the USSR Supreme Soviet on 12 January 1983: *Pravda*, 13 January 1983, pp. 1–2.

Appendix

Table A.1 Titular Nationality as Percentage of Republic Population and Subareas (in Percentages)

| | Republic population | | | Titular nationality as % of total | | | | |
| | | | | Rural population | Urban population | | Capital cities | |
Republic	1959	1970	1979	1970	1959	1970	1959	1970
RSFSR	83	83	83	76	87	87	89	89
Ukraine	77	75	74	89	62	63	60	65
Belorussia	81	81	79	90	67	69	64	66
Uzbekistan	61	65	69	80	37	41	34	37
Kazakhstan	30	33	36	48	17	17	9	12
Georgia	64	67	69	73	53	60	48	58
Azerbaijan	68	74	78	87	51	61	37	46
Lithuania	79	80	80	87	69	73	34	43
Moldavia	66	65	64	88	28	35	32	37
Latvia	62	57	54	73	52	47	45	41
Kirghizia	41	44	48	60	13	17	9	12
Tadjikistan	53	56	59	67	32	39	19	26
Armenia	88	89	90	82	92	93	93	95
Turkmenistan	61	66	68	86	35	43	29	38
Estonia	75	68	65	88	62	57	60	56

Sources: Narodnoe khoziaistvo SSSR 1922–82, Moscow, Finansy i Statistika, 1982, pp. 34–7; Itogi vsesoiuznoi perepisi naseleniia SSSR 1970 goda, Moscow, Statistika, 1973, Vol. 4, pp. 9–11, 178–320; Iu. V. Bromlei et al. (eds.), Sovremennye etnicheskie protsessy v SSSR, Moscow, Nauka, 1975, p. 155; Iu. V. Arutiunian, "Natsional'no-regional'noe mnogoobrazie sovetskoi derevni," Sotsiologicheskie issledovaniia, 1980, no. 3, p. 74.

Table A.2 *Major Soviet Ethnic Groups and their Growth Rates, 1959–79*

Ethnic group	Millions of people (1959)	(1979)	Percentage growth (1959–79)
Slavs			
Russians	114·11	137·40	20·4
Ukrainians	37·25	42·35	13·7
Belorussians	7·91	9·46	19·5
Irano-Turkic Muslims			
Uzbeks	6·02	12·46	107·1
Kazakhs	3·62	6·56	81·0
Tatars	4·97	6·32	27·2
Azeris	2·94	5·48	86·3
Tadjiks	1·40	2·90	107·4
Turkmen	1·00	2·03	102·5
Kirghiz	0·97	1·91	96·8
Balts			
Estonians	0·97	1·02	3·2
Latvians	1·40	1·44	2·8
Lithuanians	2·33	2·85	22·0
Others			
Armenians	2·79	4·15	48·9
Georgians	2·69	3·57	32·7
Moldavians	2·21	2·97	34·0
Germans	1·62	1·94	19·7
Jews	2·26	1·81	−19·9

Source: Modified from Viktor Ivanovich Kozlov, *Natsional'nosti SSSR: Etnodemograficheskii obzor*, 2nd rev. ed., Moscow, Finansy i statistika, 1982, p. 285.

Table A.3   *Settlement Pattern of Major Soviet Nationalities (in Percentages)*

Nationality	Reside in own republic (1970)	(1979)	Reside in contiguous region (1970)	(1979)	Reside elsewhere in the USSR (1970)	(1979)
Russians	82·5	82·6	—	—	16·5	17·4
Ukrainians	86·6	86·2	1·3	2·2	11·5	11·6
Uzbeks	84·1	84·8	15·0	14·4	0·9	0·8
Belorussians	80·5	79·9	6·0	6·5	13·5	13·6
Kazakhs	78·5	80·7	12·2	11·0	9·3	8·3
Azeris	86·2	85·9	8·3	9·4	5·7	4·7
Armenians	62·0	65·6	26·3	22·2	11·7	12·2
Georgians	96·5	96·1	—	—	3·5	3·9
Moldavians	85·4	85·1	9·8	9·9	4·8	5·0
Tadjiks	76·3	77·2	22·4	21·3	1·3	1·5
Lithuanians	94·1	95·1	1·5	1·3	4·4	3·6
Turkmen	92·9	93·2	4·6	5·2	2·5	1·6
Kirghiz	88·5	88·5	10·0	10·0	1·5	1·5
Latvians	93·2	93·4	—	—	6·8	6·6
Estonians	91·8	92·9	—	—	8·2	7·1

Sources: Itogi vsesoiuznoi perepisi naseleniia SSSR 1970 goda, Moscow, Statistika, 1973, Vol. 4, pp. 9–42; *Naselenie SSSR, Po dannym vsesoiuznoi perepisi naseleniia 1979 goda,* Moscow, Politizdat, 1980, pp. 23–30.

Table A.4   *Language Knowledge of Indigenous Nationalities and Russians Living in Non-Russian Republics, 1970–9 (in Percentages)*

Republic	Knowledge of Russian among republic nationality (1970)	(1979)	Knowledge of republic language among Russians (1970)	(1979)
Ukraine	44	63	27	31
Belorussia	62	79	22	31
Uzbekistan	13	53	4	6
Kazakhstan	43	52	1	1
Georgia	21	26	11	16
Azerbaijan	16	29	8	9
Lithuania	35	52	33	37
Moldavia	36	50	14	11
Latvia	47	61	18	20
Kirghizia	20	29	1	1
Tadjikistan	17	28	2	3
Armenia	24	35	22	27
Turkmenistan	16	25	2	2
Estonia	28	24	14	13

Sources: *Itogi vsesoiuznoi perepisi naceleniia СССР 1970 godu*, Moscow, Statistika, 1973, Vol. 4, pp. 152–320; *Vestnik Statistiki*, 1980, no. 7–12.

Table A.5 Dynamics of Negative Ethnic Sets, by Age Groups of Rural Population (in Percentages)

Ethnic attitude	Tatars, age						Russians, age					
	16–17, N= 75	18–27, N= 581	28–34, N= 595	35–49, N= 1065	50–59, N= 542	Over 60, N= 149	16–17, N= 43	18–27, N= 222	28–34, N= 296	35–49, N= 558	50–59, N= 202	Over 60, N= 95
Negative attitude to work contact	6·6	8·9	9·7	11·8	7·2	20·1	0	10·8	7·4	10·9	14·4	3·2
Negative attitude to mixed marriage	1·3	5·3	7·1	11·6	5·9	20·8	4·6	10·3	3·4	7·7	7·4	6·3

Source: Iu. V. Arutiunian, L. M. Drobizheva, and O. I. Shkaratan (eds.), Sotsial'noe i natsional'noe, Opyt etnosotsiologicheskikh issledovanii po materialam Tatarskoi ASSR, Moscow, Nauka, 1973, p. 285.

Table A.6 *Intermarriage Attitudes of Soviet Germans, by Ethnic Composition of Place of Residence (in Percentages)*

| Attitude | Dominant nationality in last place of residence | | | |
	Local non-Russians, N = 65	Germans, N = 28	Russians, N = 37	Ethnically mixed, N = 63
Rejection of intermarriage with Russians	74	89	63	79
Rejection of intermarriage with local non-Russians	77	97	69	89

235

Table A.7 Attitudes toward Intermarriage, by Religion and Age (in Percentages)

	19–31 year-olds			32–43 year-olds			Over 43 year-olds		
	not religious, N = 30	somewhat religious, N = 18	very religious, N = 24	not religious, N = 23	somewhat religious, N = 19	very religious, N = 17	not religious, N = 15	somewhat religious, N = 13	very religious, N = 34
Reject intermarriage with Russians	57	56	79	74	74	100	67	85	91
Reject intermarriage with local non-Russians	83	72	78	72	84	87	79	75	97

Table A.8 *Perceptions of Power Changes in Non-Russian Republics*

Republic*	Number of respondents seeing nationality power as			
	Increasing	Decreasing	Staying same	Don't know
Kazakhstan	44	1	10	11
Kirghizia	8	3	8	5
Tadjikistan	4	1	3	2
Turkmenistan	1	—	—	—
Uzbekistan	1	—	—	—
Estonia	0	3	2	1
Latvia	0	7	1	1
Lithuania	2	10	3	4
Moldavia	5	1	5	2
Ukraine	0	2	2	0
Belorussia	—	1	—	—
Georgia	1	—	—	—
RSFSR†	5	9	3	10
Totals	71	38	37	36

* See also companion Table 3.1, p. 81.

† Among the five respondents who noted increasing nationality power four were referring to Kazakhstan and one to all non-Russian republics; among those citing decreasing nationality power three were referring to the Komi, and one each to the Udmurts, Ossets, Yakuts, Karelians, Latvians, and Tadjiks.

Table A.9 Nationality of Students Enrolled in Soviet Higher Educational Institutions

Nationality	Students per thousand of total population of national group						Students per thousand of 16–19 year-olds in national group	
	1959*	Ranking	1970†	Ranking	1979‡	Ranking	1970†	Ranking
Russians	13·0	5	21·2	4	21·3	3	282	7
Ukrainians	9·2	12	15·2	11	15·7	11	242	10
Belorussians	8·1	15	14·4	13	16·4	10	226	12
Uzbeks	8·9	13	16·7	10	14·2	12	234	11
Kazakhs	11·2	7	18·9	6	18·9	6	275	8
Georgians	18·0	2	27·0	2	23·1	2	425	1
Azeris	9·7	10	19·6	5	16·6	9	291	6
Lithuanians	11·0	8	18·7	7	20·6	4	336	4
Moldavians	5·4	17	11·4	15	11·1	15	158	14
Latvians	11·8	6	15·2	11	16·8	8	339	3
Kirghiz	10·2	9	18·1	8	16·8	8	270	9
Tadjiks	8·5	14	13·2	14	12·0	14	200	13
Armenians	13·2	3	22·9	3	19·8	5	324	5
Turkmen	9·5	11	14·4	13	12·3	13	116	15
Estonians	13·1	4	17·8	9	18·9	6	373	2
Tatars	8·0	16	14·7	12	17·1	7	n.d.	n.d.
Jews	34·0	1	49·2	1	37·0	1	n.d.	n.d.

* Calculation based on 1959 Census data, and data on enrollments for 1960/1.
† Calculation based on 1970 Census data, and data on enrollments for 1970/1.
‡ Calculation based on 1979 Census data, and data on enrollments for 1976/7.

Sources: Vysshee obrazovanie v SSSR, Moscow, Gosstatizdat, 1961, p. 85; Narodnoe obrazovanie, nauka i kul'tura v SSSR, Moscow, Statistika, 1977, p. 196 ; Narodnoe khoziaistvo SSSR za 60 let, Moscow, 1977, p. 588; Itogi vsesoiuznoi perepisi naseleniia SSSR 1970 goda, Moscow, Statistika, 1973, Vol. 4, pp. 9–11, 360–4; Naselenie SSSR, Po dannym vsesoiuznoi perepisi naseleniia 1979 goda, Moscow, Politizdat, 1980, pp. 25–6.

Table A.10 Ratios of Indigenous and Russian Students within Union Republics (continued)

Republic	Nationality	Percentage of total population (1959)	(1970)	Percentage of total number of students (1960/1)	(1970/1)	Students per thousand conationals in republic (1960/1)	(1970/1)
RSFSR	Russians	83	83	83	83	12·7	20·7
Ukraine	Ukrainians	77	75	62	60	8·1	15·1
	Russians	16	19	30	33	17·6	29·3
Belorussia	Belorussians	81	81	67	64	6·1	12·2
	Russians	8	10	21	24	19·2	36·4
Uzbekistan	Uzbeks	61	65	47	57	9·5	17·2
	Russians	14	13	26	19	24·0	29·7
Kazakhstan	Kazakhs	30	32	41	40	11·2	18·9
	Russians	43	43	44	43	8·6	15·4
Georgia	Georgians	64	67	77	83	16·6	23·6
	Russians	10	9	10	7	13·2	14·6
Azerbaijan	Azeris	68	74	71	78	10·2	20·8
	Russians	14	10	15	12	10·6	23·7

(Table continues over)

(Table A.10 continues)

Table A.10 Ratios of Indigenous and Russian Students within Union Republics

Lithuania	Lithuanians	79	80	89	84	11·0	19·0
	Russians	9	9	6	10	6·8	21·9
Moldavia	Moldavians	65	65	50	59	5·1	10·1
	Russians	10	12	23	19	15·0	19·1
Latvia	Latvians	62	57	65	47	10·7	14·3
	Russians	27	30	24	40	9·4	22·6
Kirghizia	Kirghiz	41	44	47	47	9·8	17·8
	Russians	29	30	37	35	10·2	19·8
Tadjikistan	Tadjiks	53	56	47	50	9·0	13·6
	Russians	13	12	23	21	17·8	26·7
Armenia	Armenians	88	89	94	96	12·3	23·7
	Russians	3	3	3	3	11·4	21·7
Turkmenistan	Turkmen	61	66	55	65	7·9	13·4
	Russians	17	15	30	21	14·9	19·9
Estonia	Estonians	75	68	82	73	12·4	17·3
	Russians	20	25	14	22	8·0	14·5

Sources: Vysshee obrazovanie v SSSR. Statisticheskii sbornik, Moscow, Gosstatizdat, 1961, pp. 128–57; Narodnoe obrazovanie, nauka i kul'tura v SSSR, Moscow, Statistika, 1971, pp. 197–204; Narodnoe khoziaistvo SSSR za 60 let, Moscow, 1977, p. 588; Itogi vsesoiuznoi perepisi naseleniia SSSR 1970 goda, Moscow, Statistika, 1973, Vol. 4, pp. 13–15.

Selective Bibliography

Adekson, J. Bayo, "Military organization in multi-ethnically segmented societies," *Research in Race and Ethnic Relations*, vol. 1 (1979), pp. 109–25.

Aibazov, D. Kh., "Opyt sotsiologicheskogo issledovaniia internatsional'nogo vospitaniia trudiashchikhsia v mnogonatsional'nykh trudovykh kollektivakh," *Sotsiologicheskie issledovaniia*, 1980, no. 3, pp. 168–70.

Anderson, Barbara A. and Silver, Brian D., "Estimating russification of ethnic identity among non-Russians in the USSR," *Demography*, vol. 20, no. 4 (November 1983), pp. 461–89.

Arutiunian, Iurii V., "Etnosotsial'nye aspekty internatsionalizatsii obraza zhizni," *Sovetskaia etnografiia*, 1979, no. 2, pp. 3–18.

Arutiunian, Iurii V., "Izmenenie sotsial'noi struktury sovetskikh natsii," *Istoriia SSSR*, 1972, no. 4, pp. 3–20.

Arutiunian, Iurii V., "Konkretno-sotsiologicheskoe issledovanie natsional'nykh otnoshenii," *Voprosy filosofii*, 1969, no. 12, pp. 129–39.

Arutiunian, Iurii V., "Natsional'no-regional'noe mnogoobrazie sovetskoi derevni," *Sotsiologicheskie issledovaniia*, 1980, no. 3, pp. 73–81.

Arutiunian, Iurii V., "O nekotorykh tendentsiiakh kul'turnogo sblizheniia narodov SSSR na etape razvitogo sotsializma," *Istoriia SSSR*, 1978, no. 4, pp. 94–104.

Arutiunian, Iurii V., *Sotsial'noe i natsional'noe, Opyt etnosotsiologicheskikh issledovanii po materialam Tatarskoi ASSR* (Moscow: Nauka, 1973).

Arutiunian, Iurii V. and Kakhk, Iu., *Sotsiologicheskie ocherki o Sovetskoi Estonii* (Tallinn: Periodika, 1979).

Arutiunian, Iurii V. and Drobizheva, L. M., "Etnosotsiologicheskie issledovaniia v SSSR," *Sotsiologicheskie issledovaniia*, 1981, no. 1, pp. 64–70.

Arutiunian, Iurii V., Drobizheva, L. M., and Zelenchuk, V. S., *Opyt etnosotsiologicheskogo issledovaniia obraza zhizni* (Moscow: Nauka, 1980).

Ashirov, N., "Musul'manskaia propoved' segodnia," *Nauka i religiia* (December 1978), pp. 30–3.

Azrael, Jeremy R. (ed.), *Soviet Nationality Policies and Practices* (New York: Praeger, 1978).

Bahry, Donna, and Nechemias, Carol, "Half full or half empty?: the debate over Soviet regional equality" *Slavic Review*, vol. 40, no. 3 (Fall 1981), pp. 366–83.

Bairamsakhatov, N., "Rozhdeno vremenem," *Nauka i religiia* (August 1979), pp. 2–7.

Barkin, Florence, Brandt, Elizabeth A., and Ornstein-Galicia, Jacob (eds.), *Bilingualism and Language Contact: Spanish, English, and Native American Languages* (New York: Teachers College Press, 1982).

Baskakov, A. N., and Mikhal'chenko, V. Iu. (eds.), *Razvitie natsional'nykh iazykov v sviazi s ikh funktsionirovaniem v sfere vysshego obrazovaniia* (Moscow: Nauka, 1982).

Bennigsen, Alexandre, "Islam in the Soviet Union," *Soviet Jewish Affairs,* vol. 9, no. 2 (1979), pp. 3–14.

Bennigsen, Alexandre, and Lemercier-Quelquejay, Chantal, *Islam in the Soviet Union* (New York: Praeger, 1967).

Bennigsen, Alexandre, and Wimbush, S. Enders, *Muslim National Communism in the Soviet Union* (Chicago: University of Chicago Press, 1979).

van den Berghe, Pierre L., "Ethnic pluralism in industrial societies: a special case?" *Ethnicity*, vol. 3, no. 3 (September 1976), pp. 242–55.

Bilinsky, Yaroslav, "Education of the non-Russian peoples in the USSR, 1917–1967, an essay," *Slavic Review*, vol. 27, no. 3 (September 1968), pp. 411–37.

Bilinsky, Yaroslav, "Soviet education laws of 1958–9 and Soviet nationality policy," *Soviet Studies*, vol. 14, no. 2 (October 1962), pp. 138–57.

Birch, Anthony H., "Minority nationalist movements and theories of political integration," *World Politics*, vol. 30, no. 3 (April 1978), pp. 325–44.

Blalock, Hubert, Jr., *Toward a Theory of Minority-Group Relations* (New York: Wiley, 1967).

Bram, Joseph, "Change and choice in ethnic identification," *Transactions of the New York Academy of Sciences*, 2d series, vol. 28, no. 2 (December 1965), pp. 242–8.

Bromlei, Iu. V., *Sovremennye etnicheskie protsessy v SSSR* (Moscow: Nauka, 1975).

Bromlei, Iu. V., *Sovremennye problemy etnografii: ocherki teorii i istorii* (Moscow: Nauka, 1981).

Bruk, S. I., and Guboglo, M. N., "Faktory rasprostraneniia dvuiazychiia u narodov SSSR," *Sovetskaia etnografiia*, 1975, no. 5, pp. 17–30.

Carrère, d'Encausse, Hélène, *Decline of an Empire: The Soviet Socialist Republics in Revolt* (New York: Newsweek, 1979).

Chkhikvadze, V. M., "Pravovye osnovy sblizheniia sovetskikh natsii," *Sotsiologicheskie issledovaniia*, 1982, no. 3, pp. 3–11.

Chuiko, Liubov' V., *Braki i razvody* (Moscow: Statistika, 1975).

Connor, Walker, *The National Question in Marxist–Leninist Theory and Strategy* (Princeton, N.J.: Princeton University Press, 1984).

Dashdamirov, A. F., "Sotsial'no-psikhologicheskie problemy natsional'noi opredelennosti lichnosti," *Sovetskaia etnografiia*, 1977, no. 3, pp. 3–13.

Desheriev, Iu. D., and Tumanian, E. G. (eds.), *Vzaimootnoshenie razvitiia natsional'nykh iazykov i natsional'nykh kul'tur* (Moscow: Nauka, 1980).

Deutsch, Karl W., *Nationalism and Social Communication*, 2d ed. (Cambridge, Mass.: MIT Press, 1966).

Drobizheva, L. M., *Dukhovnaia obshchnost' narodov SSSR: istoriko-sot-siologicheskii ocherk mezhnatsional'nykh otnoshenii* (Moscow: Mysl', 1981).

Drobizheva, L. M., "Ob izuchenii sotsial'no-psikhologicheskikh aspektov natsional'nykh otnoshenii (Nekotorye voprosy metodologii)," *Sovetskaia etnografiia*, 1974, no. 4, pp. 15–25.

Drobizheva, L. M., "Sblizhenie kul'tur i mezhnatsional'nye otnosheniia v SSSR," *Sovetskaia etnografiia*, 1977, no. 6, pp. 11–20.

Drobizheva, L. M., "Sotsial'no-kul'turnye osobennosti lichnosti i natsional'nye ustanovki (po materialam issledovanii v Tatarskoi ASSR)," *Sovetskaia etnografiia*, 1971, no. 3, pp. 3–15.

Drobizheva, L. M., and Susokolov, A. A., "Mezhetnicheskie otnosheniia i etnokul'turnye protsessy (po materialam etnosotsiologicheskikh issledovanii v SSSR)," *Sovetskaia etnografiia*, 1981, no. 3, pp. 11–22.

Drobizheva, L. M., and Tul'tseva, L. A., "Svadebnaia obriadnost' v obshchestvennom mnenii (po materialam etnosotsiologicheskikh issledovanii u narodov SSSR)," *Sovetskaia etnografiia*, 1982, no. 5, pp. 33–40.

Dzhafarov, I. B., "Prevrashchenie russkogo iazyka vo vtoroi rodnoi iazyk narodov SSSR," *Sotsiologicheskie issledovaniia*, 1982, no. 3, pp. 11–16.

Dzharylgasinova, R. Sh., and Tolstova, L. S. (eds.), *Etnicheskie protsessy u natsional'nykh grupp Srednei Azii i Kazakhstana* (Moscow: Nauka, 1980).

Dzyuba, Ivan, *Internationalism or Russification? A Study in the Soviet Nationalities Problem* (London: Weidenfeld & Nicolson, 1968).

Egurnev, A. P., "Mezhnatsional'nye braki i ikh rol' v sblizhenii natsii i narodnostei SSSR," *Nauchnyi kommunizm*, 1973, no. 4, pp. 28–34.

Ekkel', B. M., "Opredelenie Indeksa mozaichnosti natsional'nogo sostava respublik, kraev i oblastei SSSR," *Sovetskaia etnografiia*, 1976, no. 2, pp. 33–42.

Enloe, Cynthia, *Ethnic Conflict and Political Development* (Boston, Mass.: Little, Brown, 1973).

Enloe, Cynthia, *Ethnic Soldiers: State Security in Divided Societies* (Athens, Ga.: University of Georgia Press, 1980).

Etzioni, Amitai, *Complex Organizations: A Sociological Reader* (New York: Holt, Rinehart & Winston, 1962).

Evstigneev, Iu. A., "Mezhetnicheskie braki v nekotorykh gorodakh Severnogo Kazakhstana," *Vestnik Moskovskogo universiteta, Seriia istorii*, 1972, no. 2, pp. 73–82.

Farago, Uri, "The ethnic identity of Russian immigrant students in Israel," *The Jewish Journal of Sociology*, vol. 20, no. 2 (December 1978), pp. 115–27.

Fierman, Bill, "Uzbek feelings of ethnicity: a study of attitudes expressed in recent Uzbek literature," *Cahiers du Monde Russe et Sovietique*, vol. 22, no. 2–3 (1981), pp. 187–229.

Fierman, Bill, "The view from Uzbekistan," special issue on 'The changing status of Russian in the Soviet Union', *International Journal of the Sociology of Language* (1982), no. 33, pp. 71–8.

Filimonov, E. G., "Sotsiologicheskie issledovaniia protsessa preodoleniia religii v sel'skoi mestnosti: itogi, problemy, perspektivy," *Voprosy nauchnogo ateizma*, vol. 16 (1974), pp. 71–88.

Fishman, Joshua A. (ed.), *Readings in the Sociology of Language* (The Hague: Mouton, 1968).

Foster, Charles R., "Political culture and regional ethnic minorities," *Journal of Politics*, vol. 44, no. 2 (May 1982), pp. 560–8.

Francis, E. K., *Interethnic Relations: An Essay in Sociological Theory* (New York: Elsevier, 1976).

Gantskaia, O. A., and Terent'eva, L. N., "Etnograficheskie issledovaniia natsional'nykh protsessov v Pribaltike," *Sovetskaia etnografiia*, 1965, no. 5, pp. 3–19.

Gantskaia, O. A., and Terent'eva, L. N., "Sem'ia—mikrosreda etnicheskikh protsesov," in *Sovremennye etnicheskie protsessy v SSSR* (Moscow: Nauka, 1975), pp. 430–80.

Garinov, Ia. Z., and Argunova, K. D., "Analiz faktorov rasprostraneniia dvuiazychiia v SSSR," *Sotsiologicheskie issledovaniia*, 1980, no. 3, pp. 52–61.

Giglioli, Pier Paolo (ed.), *Language and Social Context* (London: Penguin Modern Sociology Readings, 1972).

Gitelman, Zvi, "Are nations merging in the USSR?" *Problems of Communism*, vol. 32 (September–October 1983), pp. 35–47.

Glaser, Daniel, "Dynamics of ethnic identification," *American Sociological Review*, vol. 23 (February 1958), pp. 31–40.

Glazer, Nathan, and Moynihan, Daniel P. (eds.), *Ethnicity: Theory and Experience* (Cambridge, Mass.: Harvard University Press, 1975).

Goldhagen, Erich (ed.), *Ethnic Minorities in the Soviet Union* (New York: Praeger, 1968).

Guboglo, M. N., *Razvitie dvuiazychiia v Moldavskoi SSR* (Kishinev: Shtiintsa Press, 1979).

Guboglo, M. N., "Vzaimodeistvie iazykov i mezhnatsional'nye otnosheniia v sovetskom obshchestve," *Istoriia SSSR*, 1970, no. 6, pp. 22–41.

Gurr, Ted R. (ed.), *Handbook of Political Conflict: Theory and Research* (New York: The Free Press, 1980).

Gurvich, I. S., "Etnokul'turnoe sblizhenie narodov SSSR," *Sovetskaia etnografiia*, 1977, no. 5, pp. 23–35.

Gurvich, I. S., "Nekotorye problemy etnicheskogo razvitiia narodov SSSR," *Sovetskaia etnografiia*, 1967, no. 5, pp. 62–77.

Hargrove, Erwin C., "Nationality, values, and change: young elites in French Canada," *Comparative Politics*, vol. 2, no. 3 (April 1970), pp. 473–99.

Hechter, Michael, *Internal Colonialism* (Berkeley, Calif.: University of California Press, 1975).

Hodnett, Grey, *Leadership in the Soviet National Republics* (Oakville: Mosaic Press, 1978).

Inglehart, R. F., and Woodward, M., "Language conflicts and political community," in Pier Paolo Giglioli (ed.), *Language and Social Context* (London: Penguin Modern Sociology Readings, 1972), pp. 358–75.

Inkeles, Alex, and Bauer, Raymond A., *The Soviet Citizen, Daily Life in a Totalitarian Society* (Cambridge, Mass.: Harvard University Press, 1959).

Jones, Ellen, and Grupp, Fred W., "Measuring nationality trends in the Soviet Union: a research note," *Slavic Review*, vol. 41, no. 1 (Spring 1982), pp. 112–22.

Jones, Ellen, and Grupp, Fred W., "Modernisation and ethnic equalisation in the USSR," *Soviet Studies*, vol. 36, no. 2 (April 1984), pp. 159–84.

Kakhk, Iukhan, *Cherty skhodstva* (Tallinn: Eesti Raamat, 1974).

Kalyshev, A. B., "K voprosu ob opredelenii natsional'noi prinadlezhnosti molodezhi v mezhnatsional'nykh sem'iakh," *Izvestiia Akademii nauk Kazakhskoi SSR, Seriia obshchestvennykh nauk*, 1982, no. 3, pp. 81–4.

Karklins, Rasma, "Ethnic interaction in the Baltic republics: interviews with recent emigrants," *Journal of Baltic Studies*, vol. 12, no. 1 (Spring 1981), pp. 16–34.

Karklins, Rasma, "Ethnic politics and access to higher education: the Soviet case," *Comparative Politics*, vol. 16, no. 3 (April 1984), pp. 277–94.

Karklins, Rasma, "The interrelationship of Soviet foreign and nationality policies: the case of the foreign minorities of the USSR," Ph.D. dissertation, University of Chicago, 1975.

Karklins, Rasma, "The nationality factor in Soviet foreign policy," in Roger Kanet (ed.), *Soviet Foreign Policy in the 1980s* (New York: Praeger, 1982), pp. 58–76.

Karklins, Rasma, "Nationality power in Soviet republics: attitudes and perceptions," *Studies in Comparative Communism*, vol. 14, no. 1 (Spring 1981), pp. 70–93.

Katz, Zev, Rogers, Rosemarie, and Harned, Frederic (eds.), *Handbook of Major Soviet Nationalities* (New York: The Free Press, 1975).

Katznelson, Ira, "Comparative studies of race and ethnicity," *Comparative Politics*, vol. 5, no. 1 (October 1972), pp. 135–54.

Kazlas, Juozas A., "Social distance among ethnic groups," in Edward Allworth (ed.), *Nationality Group Survival in Multi-Ethnic States* (New York: Praeger, 1977), pp. 228–55.

Keech, William R., "Linguistic diversity and political conflict," *Comparative Politics*, vol. 4, no. 3 (April 1972), pp. 387–404.

Kholmogorov, A. I., *Internatsional'nye cherty sovetskikh natsii. (Na materialakh konkretno-sotsiologicheskikh issledovanii v Pribaltike)* (Moscow: Mysl', 1970).

Kinloch, Graham C., "Comparative race and ethnic relations," *International Journal of Comparative Sociology*, vol. 22, no. 3–4 (1981), pp. 257–71.

Klement'ev, E. I., "Natsional'no-kul'turnye orientatsii karel'skogo gorodskogo naseleniia," *Sovetskaia etnografiia*, 1976, no. 3, pp. 57–68.

Kohn, M. L., and R. M. Williams, "Situational patterning in intergroup relations," *American Sociological Review*, vol. 21 (April 1956), pp. 164–74.

Kozenko, A. V., "O standartizatsii metodik izucheniia natsional'no-smeshannoi brachnosti," *Sovetskaia etnografiia*, 1978, no. 1, pp. 72–6.

Kozlov, Viktor Ivanovich, *Natsional'nosti SSSR: Etnodemograficheskii obzor*, 2d rev. ed. (Moscow: Finansy i statistika, 1982).

Kozlov, Viktor Ivanovich, "O nekotorykh metodologicheskikh problemakh izucheniia etnicheskoi psikhologii," *Sovetskaia etnografiia*, 1983, no. 2, pp. 74–9.

Kreindler, Isabelle, "Lenin, Russian, and Soviet language policy," *International Journal of the Sociology of Language*, 1982, no. 33, pp. 129–35.

Kulichenko, M. I., "Obrazovanie i razvitie sovetskogo naroda kak novoi istoricheskoi obshchnosti," *Voprosy istorii*, 1979, no. 4, pp. 3–23.

Kulichenko, M. I. (ed.), "Osnovnye napravleniia izucheniia natsional'nykh otnoshenii v SSSR (Moscow: Nauka, 1979).

Kussmann, Thomas, and Schäfer, Bernd, *Nationale Identität: Selbstbild und Fremdbilder von deutschen Aussiedlern aus der Sowjetunion* (Cologne: Berichte des Bundesinstituts für ostwissenschaftliche und internationale Studien, 46, 1982).

Lane, Christel, "Ritual and ceremony in contemporary Soviet society," *Sociological Review*, vol. 27, no. 2 (May 1979), pp. 253–78.

Lenin, V. I., "K voprosu o natsional'nostiakh ili ob 'avtonomizatsii'," *Kommunist*, 1956, no. 9, pp. 22–6.

Lewis, E. Glyn, *Bilingualism and Bilingual Education* (Albuquerque, N. Mex.: University of New Mexico Press, 1980).

Lewis, Robert A., Rowland, Richard H., and Clem, Ralph S., "Modernization, population change and nationality in Soviet Central Asia and Kazakhstan," *Canadian Slavonic Papers*, vol. 17, no. 2–3 (Summer and Fall 1975), pp. 286–301.

Lieberson, Stanley, *Language and Ethnic Relations in Canada* (New York: Wiley, 1970).

Lieberson, Stanley, *Language Diversity and Language Contact* (Stanford, Calif.: Stanford University Press, 1981).

Lieberson, Stanley, "A societal theory of race and ethnic relations," *American Sociological Review*, vol. 26, no. 6 (December 1961), pp. 902–10.

Litvinova, G. I., and Urlanis, B. Ts., "Demograficheskaia politika Sovetskogo Soiuza," *Sovetskoe gosudarstvo i pravo*, 1982, no. 3, pp. 38–46.

Lorwin, Val R., "Belgium: religion, class, and language in national politics," in Robert Dahl (ed.), *Political Oppositions in Western Democracies* (New Haven, Conn.: Yale University Press, 1966), pp. 147–87.

Lubin, Nancy, "Assimilation and retention of ethnic identity in Uzbekistan," *Asian Affairs*, vol. 12, pt. 3 (1981), pp. 277–85.

Lubin, Nancy, "Women in Soviet Central Asia: progress and contradictions," *Soviet Studies*, vol. 33, no. 2 (April 1981), pp. 182–203.

Mal'kova, V. K., "Primenenie kontent-analiza dlia izucheniia sotrudnichestva sovetskikh narodov (po materialam respublikanskikh gazet)," *Sovetskaia etnografiia*, 1977, no. 5, pp. 71–80.

McAuley, Mary, "Party recruitment and the nationalities in the USSR: a study in centre–republican relationships," *British Journal of Political Science*, vol. 10, no. 4 (1980), pp. 461–87.

McRae, Kenneth (ed.), *Consociational Democracy: Political Accommodation in Segmented Societies* (Toronto: McClelland & Stewart, 1974).

McRoberts, Kenneth, and Posgate, Dale, *Quebec: Social Change and Political Crisis* (Toronto: McClelland & Stewart, 1976).

Meissner, Boris, *Die Sowjetunion, die Baltischen Staaten und das Völkerrecht* (Cologne: Politik und Wirtschaft, 1956).

Miller, John H., "Cadres policy in nationality areas. Recruitment of CPSU first and second secretaries in non-Russian republics of the USSR," *Soviet Studies*, vol. 29, no. 1 (January 1977), pp. 3–36.

Mirkhasilov, S. M., "O nekotorykh tendentsiiakh razvitiia sovremennoi sem'i v Uzbekistane," *Sotsiologicheskie issledovaniia*, 1979, no. 1, pp. 121–3.

Misiunas, Romuald, J., and Taagepera, Rein, *The Baltic States: Years of Dependence 1940–1980* (Berkeley, Calif.: University of California Press, 1983).

Montgomery, David C., "An American student in Tashkent with some notes on ethnic and racial harmony in Soviet Uzbekistan," *Asian Affairs*, vol. 59 (n.s. vol. 3), pt. 1 (February 1972), pp. 28–40.

Myl'nikov, A. S., "Narodnaia kul'tura i genezis natsional'nogo samosoznaniia," *Sovetskaia etnografiia*, 1981, no. 6, pp. 3–13.

Nelson, Daniel N., "Leninists and political inequalities: the non-revolutionary politics of communist states," *Comparative Politics*, vol. 14, no. 3 (April 1982), pp. 307–28.

Novikov, Leonid, *Hochschulen in der Sowjetunion* (Frankfurt-on-Main: Deutsches Institut für Internationale Pädagogische Forschung, 1981).

Okamura, Jonathan Y., "Situational ethnicity," *Ethnic and Racial Studies*, vol. 4, no. 4 (October 1981), pp. 452–65.

Olzak, Susan, "Ethnic mobilization in Quebec," *Ethnic and Racial Studies*, vol. 5, no. 3 (July 1982), pp. 253–75.

Pankhurst, Jerry G., and Sacks, Michael Paul, *Contemporary Soviet Society* (New York: Praeger, 1980).

Pennar, Jaan, "The nationality of the children of mixed marriages in Tallin," *Radio Liberty Research Bulletin*, RL 120/83 (New York: Radio Liberty, 16 March 1983).

Pennar, Jaan, Bakalo, Ivan I. and Bereday, George, *Modernization and Diversity in Soviet Education* (New York: Praeger, 1971).

Pipes, Richard, *The Formation of the Soviet Union: Communism and Nationalism 1917–1923* (Cambridge, Mass.: Harvard University Press, 1970).

Pokshishevskii, V. V., "Metody izucheniia etnicheskoi smeshannosti gorodskogo naseleniia," *Sovetskaia etnografiia*, 1983, no. 1, pp. 16–23.

Popovsky, Mark, *Manipulated Science* (New York: Doubleday, 1979).

Prokof'ev, M. A., "V protsesse sblizheniia natsii," *Russkii iazyk v natsional'noi shkole*, 1979, no. 4, pp. 11–22.

Ragin, Charles, "Class, status, and 'reactive ethnic cleavages'," *American Sociological Review*, vol. 42, no. 3 (1977), pp. 438–50.

Rakowska-Harmstone, Teresa, "The nationalities question," in Robert Wesson (ed.), *The Soviet Union: Looking to the 1980s* (Stanford, Calif.: Hoover Institution, 1980), pp. 129–153.

Rakowska-Harmstone, Teresa, *Russia and Nationalism in Central Asia: The case of Tadzhikistan* (Baltimore, Md.: Johns Hopkins University Press, 1970).

Rakowska-Harmstone, Teresa, "The study of ethnic politics in the USSR," in George W. Simmonds (ed.), *Nationalism in the USSR and Eastern Europe in the Era of Brezhnev and Kosygin* (Detroit, Mich.: University of Detroit Press, 1977), pp. 20–36.

Rakowska-Harmstone, Teresa, "The Soviet army as the instrument of national integration," in John Erickson and E. J. Feuchtwanger (eds.), *Soviet Military Power and Performance* (London: Macmillan, 1979), pp. 129–54.

Rothschild, Joseph, *Ethnopolitics, a Conceptual Framework* (New York: Columbia University Press, 1981).

Rutkevich, M. N., "Sblizhenie natsional'nykh respublik i natsii SSSR po sotsial'no-klassovoi strukture," *Sotsiologicheskie issledovaniia*, 1981, no. 2, pp. 14–24.

Rybakovskii, L. L., "O migratsii naseleniia v SSSR," *Sotsiologicheskie issledovaniia*, 1981, no. 4, pp. 7–14.

Rywkin, Michael, "Central Asia and Soviet manpower," *Problems of Communism*, vol. 28, no. 1 (January–February 1979), pp. 1–13.

Saidbaev, T. S., *Islam i obshchestvo* (Moscow: Nauka, 1978).

Saunders, George (ed.), *Samizdat: Voices of the Soviet Opposition* (New York: Monad Press, 1974).

Schermerhorn, R. A., *Comparative Ethnic Relations* (New York: Random House, 1970).

Shalin, Dmitri N., "The development of Soviet sociology, 1956–76," *Annual Review of Sociology*, vol. 4 (1978), pp. 171–91.

Shapovalova, G. G., "Konferentsiia 'Voprosy razvitiia sotsialisticheskikh prazdnikov i obriadov'," *Sovetskaia etnografiia*, 1983, no. 1, pp. 140–2.

Sheehy, Ann, *The Crimean Tatars, Volga Germans and Meskhetians: Soviet Treatment of Some National Minorities*, Report No. 6, new ed. (London: Minority Rights Group, 1973).

Shibutani, Tamotsu, and Kwan, Kian M., *Ethnic Stratification: A Comparative Approach* (New York: Macmillan, 1965).

Shils, Edward, *Center and Periphery: Essays in Macrosociology* (Chicago: University of Chicago Press, 1975).

Shils, Edward, "Primordial, personal, sacred, and civil ties," *British Journal of Sociology*, vol. 8 (1957), pp. 130–45.

Shorish, M. Mobin, "Dissent of the Muslims: Soviet Central Asia in the 1980s," *Nationalities Papers*, vol. 9, no. 2 (Fall 1981), pp. 185–94.

Shpiliuk, V. A., *Mezhrespublikanskaia migratsiia i sblizhenie natsii v SSSR* (L'vov: Vishcha shkola, 1975).

Shtromas, A., "The legal position of Soviet nationalities and their territorial units according to the 1977 Constitution of the USSR," *Russian Review*, vol. 37 (July 1978), pp. 265–72.

Silver, Brian D., "Ethnic intermarriage and ethnic consciousness among Soviet nationalities," *Soviet Studies*, vol. 30, no. 1 (January 1978), pp. 107–16.

Silver, Brian, "Levels of sociocultural development among Soviet nationalities: a partial test of the equalization hypothesis," *American Political Science Review*, vol. 68, no. 4 (December 1974), pp. 1618–37.

Silver, Brian D., "Soviet nationality problems: analytic approaches," *Problems of Communism*, vol. 28, no. 4 (1979), pp. 71–6.

Silver, Brian D., "The status of national minority languages in Soviet education: an assessment of recent changes," *Soviet Studies*, vol. 26, no. 1 (January 1974), pp. 28–40.

Simmonds, George W. (ed.), *Nationalism in the USSR and Eastern Europe in the Era of Brezhnev and Kosygin* (Detroit, Mich.: University of Detroit Press, 1977).

Skachkova, N. P., "Mezhnatsional'naia sem'ia kak faktor sblizheniia sotsialisticheskikh natsii," *Izvestiia Akademii nauk Kazakhskoi SSR, Seriia obshchestvennykh nauk*, 1975, no. 6, pp. 55–63.

Smith, Anthony D., *The Ethnic Revival* (Cambridge: Cambridge University Press, 1981).

Solchanyk, Roman, "Russian language and Soviet politics," *Soviet Studies*, vol. 34, no. 1 (January 1982), pp. 23–42.

Starovoitova, G. V., "K issledovaniiu etnopsikhologii gorodskikh zhitelei," *Sovetskaia etnografiia*, 1976, no. 3, pp. 45–56.

Suny, Ronald, "Georgia and Soviet nationality policy," in Stephen F. Cohen, Alexander Rabinowitch, and Robert Sharlet (eds.), *The Soviet Union since Stalin* (Bloomington, Ind.: Indiana University Press, 1980), pp. 200–26.

Susokolov, A. A., "Neposredstvennoe mezhetnicheskoe obshchenie i ustanovki na mezhlichnostnye kontakty," *Sovetskaia etnografiia*, 1973, no. 5, pp. 73–8.

Susokolov, A. A., "Vliianie razlichii v urovne obrazovaniia i chislennosti kontaktiruiushchikh etnicheskikh grupp na mezhetnicheskie otnosheniia (po materialam perepisei naseleniia SSSR 1959 i 1970 gg.)," *Sovetskaia etnografiia*, 1976, no. 1, pp. 101–11.

Susokolov, A. A., and Novitskaia, A. P., "Etnicheskaia i sotsial'no-professional'naia gomogennost' brakov (po materialam otdela ZAGS Kishineva v poslevoennyi period)," *Sovetskaia etnografiia* 1981, no. 6, pp. 14–26.

Sutherland, Margaret B., "Comparative perspective on the education of cultural minorities," in Anthony E. Alcock, Brian K. Taylor, and John M. Welton (eds.), *The Future of Cultural Minorities* (New York: St. Martin's Press, 1978), pp. 44–62.

Taagepera, Rein, "Size and ethnicity of Estonian towns and rural districts, 1922–1979," *Journal of Baltic Studies*, vol. 13, no. 2 (Summer 1982), pp. 105–27.

Terent'eva, L. N., "Etnicheskaia situatsiia i etnokul'turnye protsessy v sovetskoi Pribaltike," *Rasy i narody*, vol. 9 (1979), pp. 136–60.

Terent'eva, L. N., "Opredelenie svoei natsional'noi prinadlezhnosti podrostkami v natsional'no-smeshannykh sem'iakh," *Sovetskaia etnografiia* 1969, no. 3, pp. 20–30.

Terent'eva, L. N., "Forming of ethnic self-consciousness in nationally mixed families in the USSR," in *Sociological Studies: Ethnic Aspects*

(Moscow: Papers presented at the Eighth World Congress of Sociology, Toronto, Canada, 1974).

Ter-Sarkisiants, Alla E., "O natsional'nom aspekte brakov v Armianskoi SSR (po materialam zagsov)," *Sovetskaia etnografiia* 1973, no. 4, pp. 89–95.

Theriault, George F., "Separatism in Quebec," in Raymond L. Hall (ed.), *Ethnic Autonomy—Comparative Dynamics* (New York: Pergamon, 1979), pp. 102–36.

Tomilov, N. A., "Sovremennye etnicheskie protsessy u tatar gorodov Zapadnoi Sibiri," *Sovetskaia etnografiia* 1972, no. 6, pp. 87–97.

Tomilov, N. A., "Sovremennye etnicheskie protsessy v iuzhnoi i srednei polose Zapadnoi Sibiri," *Sovetskaia etnografiia* 1978, no. 4, pp. 9–20.

Tomilov, N. A., *Sovremennye etnicheskie protsessy sredi sibirskikh tatar* (Tomsk: University of Tomsk Press, 1978).

Van Dyke, Vernon, "Collective entities and moral rights: problems in liberal-democratic thought," *Journal of Politics*, vol. 44, no. 1 (February 1982), pp. 21–40.

Van Dyke, Vernon, "The individual, the state, and ethnic communities in political theory," *World Politics*, vol. 29, no. 3 (April 1977), pp. 343–69.

Vardys, V. Stanley, *The Catholic Church, Dissent and Nationality in Soviet Lithuania* (Boulder, Colo.: East European Quarterly, 1978).

Vardys, V. Stanley, "Language, Lenin and politics," *International Journal of the Sociology of Language*, 1982, no. 33, pp. 119–27.

Vincent, Joan, "The structuring of ethnicity," *Human Organization*, vol. 33, no. 4 (Winter 1974), pp. 375–9.

Warburton, T. Rennie, "Nationalism and language in Switzerland and Canada," in Anthony D. Smith (ed.), *Nationalist Movements* (New York: St. Martin's Press, 1976), pp. 88–109.

Weber, Cynthia and Goodman, Ann, "The demographic policy debate in the USSR," *Population and Development Review*, vol. 7, no. 2 (June 1981), pp. 279–95.

Welsh, William A. (ed.), *Survey Research and Public Attitudes in Eastern Europe and the Soviet Union* (Des Moines, Iowa: University of Iowa, 1980).

Wheeler, Geoffrey, "The Russian presence in Central Asia," *Canadian Slavonic Papers*, vol. 17, no. 2–3 (Summer and Fall 1975), pp. 189–201.

Wimbush, S. Enders, and Alexiev, Alex, *The Ethnic Factor in the Soviet Armed Forces* (Santa Monica, Calif.: Rand Corporation, 1982).

Yanov, Alexander, *The Russian New Right: Right-Wing Ideologies in the Contemporary USSR*, research series, No. 35 (Berkeley, Calif.: Institute of International Studies, 1978).

Young, Crawford, *The Politics of Cultural Pluralism* (Madison, Wis.: University of Wisconsin Press, 1976).

Zaslavsky, Victor, "The ethnic question in the USSR," *Telos*, vol. 45 (Fall 1980), pp. 45–76.

Zaslavsky, Victor, *The Neo-Stalinist State: Class, Ethnicity and Consensus in Soviet Society* (Armonk, N.Y.: Sharpe, 1982).

Zaslavsky, Victor, and Brym, Robert J., *Soviet–Jewish Emigration and*

Soviet Nationality Policy (New York: St. Martin's Press, 1983).

Zaslavsky, Victor, and Luryi, Yuri, "The passport system in the USSR and changes in Soviet Society," *Soviet Union/Union Sovietique*, vol. 6, no. 2 (1979), pp. 137–53.

Zaslavsky, Victor, "Sociology in the contemporary Soviet Union," *Social Research*, vol. 44, no. 2 (Summer 1977), pp. 330–53.

Index

Note page numbers in italic type refer to tabulated information